Loading RCMP vehicles used during Princess Elizabeth's 1950 Tour onto a Dakota. (Courtesy of 412 (T) Squadron).

The first Dash 8 and crew, AC# 142801, in Ottawa April 10, 1987 Enroute to LAHR. Left to right: MCPL M. Theaker, Cpl J. Butler-Smythe, MCPL J. Arseneau, Capt. G. Harrison, MAJ. T. Baker, LCOL R. Gage, MAJ. J. Reid, W.O. D. Lawrence, MCPL J. Soulard, MCPL C. Krueger, and J. Ritchot. (Courtesy of the 412 (T) Squadron.

Dash 8 (CC-142) over West Germany

1936 – 1995

TURNER PUBLISHING COMPANY
Paducah, Kentucky, U.S.A.

TURNER PUBLISHING COMPANY
412 Broadway, P.O. Box 3101
Paducah, Kentucky, U.S.A. 42002-3101
Phone (502) 443-0121

Turner Publishing Company Staff:
    Pamela Reynolds-Wood, Project Coordinator

412 Transport Squadron Staff:
    Capt. M. E. Waterberg
    Capt. Dale Hackett
    Christine McCarthy
    Capt. Tony Jones
    Mrs. Joyce Peppard
    Maureen Kay

Copyright © 1995 Turner Publishing Company.
All rights reserved.

This book or any part thereof may not be reproduced without the written consent of the publisher. This publication was compiled using available information. The publisher regrets it cannot assume liability for errors or omissions.

Library of Congress Catalog No. 90-71721
ISBN 978-1-63026-954-8
Printed in the U.S.A. Limited Edition.

Additional books may be purchased directly from:
412 SQUADRON
Pilot Officer John Gillespie Magee Annex
58 Service Road
Gloucester, Ontario CANADA
K1V 9B2

DeHaviland Comet Mk 1
(Courtesy of Major A.L. Auld)

Challenger (600 Series)
(Courtesy of 412 (T) Squadron)

TABLE OF CONTENTS

Foreword 6

Publisher's Message 7

The Legacy of No. 412 Squadron 9

412 Fighter Squadron in World War II 18

412 Transport Squadron – A New Career 43

Squadron Stories 49

Investiture of Honorary Colonel 79

Personnel Biographies 84

Foreword

Lt. Col. Wayne Thompson
CO 412 (T) Sqn. 1993/94

As the current Commanding Officer of such a proud and distinguished Squadron, it is my honour and privilege to dedicate this book to all 412 Squadron members, past and present, and in particular to those who gave their lives in the service of their country.

The compilation and publication of this book has taken much time. Without the perseverance of the History Book Committee, this humble attempt to pay tribute to such an important part of Canadian aviation heritage would not have been possible. While acknowledging the splendid work of all committee members and contributors, special thanks must go to: Mrs. Joyce-Margaret Peppard, my secretary, who worked overtime supporting the History Book Committee, including typing minutes of meetings and coordinating correspondence; Mrs. Pamela Wood of Turner Publishing Company, who provided historical details, autobiographies and photos expanding upon the Committee's research and helping to establish a degree of chronological order; and Mr. Terry Martin, a civilian author and friend of 412 Squadron, who volunteered to undertake the "consistency of terms" editing of this book.

On your behalf, I thank everyone who participated in this project for their initiative and determination in carrying it through for the last three years. If this book contains particular errors or oversights, I challenge those who follow to live up to our honourable motto, "*Swift to Avenge.*" Above all, it is my hope that this work proves to be only the first step towards producing a richer and deeper record of a Squadron whose accomplishments and continuous record of conspicuous service are unmatched in the annals of Canadian airforce history.

Sic itur ad astra.

EDITORS NOTE:
Lt. Col. Wayne Thompson was promoted to Full Colonel in 1994 and is currently base commander at CFB Namao, Alberta. Lt. Col. Frank Burke is the current commanding officer of 412 (T) Sqn.

Publisher's Message

Dave Turner
President

From battles in the skies over Europe to transporting dignitaries on world tours, the 412 (T) Squadron represents the best of Canadian aviators.

It was indeed a pleasure to produce this book for our neighboring Canadians as a tribute to their dedication to their country and to the cause of freedom worldwide. Contained within these pages is a detailed historical record outlining the outstanding service of 412 aviators. The course of the 412 may have changed over the years but their loyalty and auspicious service remained faithful and swift.

Many people within the 412 deserve our heartfelt thanks and appreciation but we particularly wish to thank Glen Parslow and Gary Scott for persevering when it got down to the wire to publish this historic keepsake. We also especially thank those individuals who comprise the 412 (T) Squadron for sending in their personal autobiographies and special remembrances of their time with the squadron – this book is your history told in your words.

This historic book represents our second publication for the armed services of Canada, hopefully the second of many to come. If you are interested in having your history recorded for future generations please contact us. We must preserve our past in printed word so that future generations will know of our sacrifices and the 412 (T) Squadron now has a lasting legacy to their service to hand down to children and grandchildren.

412 Transport Squadron

The Legacy

The Legacy of No. 412 Squadron
Beginings of Canadian Aviation

The first controlled flight of an airplane by a British subject within the British Commonwealth occurred on 23 February 1909, over the frozen Bras d'Or Lakes at Baddeck, Nova Scotia. It was in a Silver Dart aircraft piloted by John A.D. McCurdy.

Canadian aviation was thus launched, and since then has soared to increasingly greater heights. The Canadian Aviation Corps was formed in 1914, consisting of two officers and one Burgess-Dunne biplane. In World War I many Canadians flew with the Royal Flying Corps (RFC).

There were many fine RFC pilots who came out of those humble first years. They included Major W.A. (Billy) Bishop, Major Raymond Collishaw and Captain Roy Brown; in fact, of the 27 RFC aces, 10 were Canadian and all were credited with 30 or more victories.

The Canadian Air Force began in 1920 as a non-permanent operation to provide refresher courses for RFC pilots and to assist with the air defence of Canada. In 1924, "Royal" was added to the title; thus the Royal Canadian Air Force came into being, with primary tasks involving communications, transport, forest fire patrol, aerial photography, and anti-smuggling patrols.

In 1936, the Canadian government formed the Department of Transport, and the RCAF was released from its civil aviation duties.

World War II saw an expansion program for the RCAF, resulting in the formation of eleven permanent and twelve auxiliary squadrons. One of those squadrons - No. 412 - would build one of the most distinguished legacies as a fighter unit in World War II and later as a VIP transport unit.

412 Squadron RCAF

The present-day 412 (Transport) Squadron possesses a proud heritage. The squadron traces its history to the formation of No. 7 General Purpose (GP) Squadron at Rockcliffe on 29 January 1936, later to No. 12 Communications Squadron formed at Rockcliffe on 30 August, 1940 and subsequently to 412 (Fighter) Squadron in Britain on 30 June 1941. On 1 April 1947, No. 12 Communications Squadron was redesignated 412 (Composite) Squadron to perpetuate the name of No. 412 Squadron. Two years later on 1 April 1949 the unit assumed its present identity of 412 (Transport) Squadron when it became a unit of Air Transport Command. At that time 412 (Transport) Squadron was based at Canadian Forces Base (CFB) Ottawa (Uplands) and was responsible for transporting both foreign and Canadian dignitaries, and for conducting global aero-medical evacuation operations.

The Beginning- 1935
7 General Purpose (GP) Squadron

No. 7 (GP) Squadron was formed at RCAF Station Ottawa in the autumn of 1935 by an amalgamation of the Test Flight, General Purpose Flight and two Mobile Photographic Detachments (nos 6 and 7) which previously had been based at that Station. In the following year (1936-37), the two photographic detachments were amalgamated with other detachments and personnel of No. 8 (GP) Squadron from Winnipeg to form a re-organized No. 8 Squadron at Ottawa. This left No. 7 with only its two flights, "A" for test and "B" for communications work. The squadron remained at Ottawa (Rockcliffe) from the time of its formation in 1935 until its disbandment four years later after

Hawker Tomtit, 12 (Comm) Squadron and 12 Comm Flight.

Northrop Delta Mk II, 12 (Comm) Squadron and 12 Comm Flight.

the outbreak of war in September 1939. The General Purpose Flight became the Air Force Headquarters Communications Flight on 10 September 1939, and subsequently the nucleus of No. 12, later 412 Communications Squadron.

No detailed record of the operations of No. 7 Squadron exists before 1 May 1937, at which time S/L GR Howsam, MC, was in command. It is known that S/L EG Fullerton commanded the Squadron from 29 January 1936 to 14 August 1936. In August, 1937, S/L Howsam was succeeded by F/L (later S/L) DA Harding, AFC. F/L LE Wray, who had been in command of "A" Flight for some time, took over from S/L Harding on 5 December 1938 and F/L GG Truscott replaced him as commander of the test flight. It is worth noting that eight years later, LE Wray, now an Air Commodore, commanded 9 Transport Group at Rockcliffe (the forerunner of Air Transport Command). In the spring of 1939, F/L RC Davis appears as the Squadron OC, retaining that position until the unit's record closes in September 1939.

Through these years, the work of No. 7 Squadron consisted of practice flying, communications flights for service personnel, test and acceptance of new or reconditioned aircraft and a great variety of test flying for aircraft and equipment. One of the constant factors in the test program was periodic drop-testing of parachutes used in the service. Other projects during 1937 were testing of an RAF Hawker Hart, the Northrop Delta, Avro Tutor and the Fleet Trainer Model 21; and in the equipment field, a cockpit hood for the Wapiti, brakes for the Fleet, air heater for the Fleet, skis and de-icer for the Hart, and skis for the Delta, as well as radio equipment. Late in the year, the Squadron took delivery of a number of new Deltas from Montreal for test and acceptance flights prior to ferrying the aircraft to units.

In June 1937, three Walrus aircraft from two cruisers of the Royal Navy, HMS APOLLO and YORK, which were visiting Canada, flew into Rockcliffe and, the Squadron diary notes, one of the amphibians was the first aircraft to taxi up the slipway at the station. On 25 July 1937, two of the Squadron's Fairchilds, piloted by F/L Harding and FS Fleming, set out on a long distance flight to Aklavik, carrying the Governor-General; they returned on 22 August.

Early in 1938, the test work was chiefly concerned with skis for various tests of aircraft - the Delta, Shark and Avro 626. Drop-testing of parachutes continued, as well as testing of de-icer and oil cooler equipment for the Hart. For communications work and practice flying, the squadron had a Fleet, three Fairchilds and a pair of Tomtits; when seaplane operations began late in May a Vedette was also brought into use. In August, a Grumman amphibian was added to the squadron's equipment and extensively used through the next year for communications and transport of distinguished personages. The squadron also had several Bellancas in use during the latter part of the year.

Some testing was done of a Fairchild Super-71, and the Noorduyn Norseman (now being introduced into the service); an air cooler for the Blackburn Shark was also tested, and flights were made to check on carbon monoxide in the Avro Tutor. On 24 June 1938, F/O HGM Colpitts began a series of flights on a Fairchild for cathode ray tests, the flights continuing as late as November. On 9 November, the first Stranraer delivered to the RCAF by Canadian Vickers arrived at Rockcliffe for test and acceptance by No. 7 Squadron; a second flying-boat was delivered at the end of the month.

In addition to the normal communications flights, the squadron made several special flights during the year to search for missing people. Late in May, F/O Truscott flew to Fitzroy Harbour to search for the bodies of some men who were missing on the Ottawa River, and again in July he went to Lake Deschenes to look for a drowned man; in both searches the results appear to have been negative. The squadron served as a practice flight for staff officers at Air Force Headquarters.

There is a gap in the squadron's record through the first three months of 1939. When the record resumes, No. 7, now under F/L RC Davis, was continuing its usual routine - testing parachutes and aircraft, chiefly the Atlas, and carrying out carbon monoxide tests on the Delta, the latter tests continuing for several months. The RAF Hawker Hart was still being tested. The Grumman amphibian was still busy flying VIPs about the country, one of the most frequent passengers being A/M WA Bishop. Between 23 May and 12 June, F/L Wray flew the Minister of National Defence to Vancouver and return; while on the west coast the Grumman visited Victoria, Prince Rupert, Bella Bella, Alliford Bay, Swindle Island and Coal Bay to examine sites where the RCAF was preparing air bases. A few weeks later, between 27 July and 7 August, F/L Wray again took the Grumman to the west coast and back with the Honourable Ian Mackenzie and A/M Bishop as passengers.

In June, the squadron accepted a group of nine Avro 626s from the Ottawa Car Company, the deliveries being made at Uplands airfield for test flights prior to ferrying to Auxiliary squadrons. A new Airspeed Oxford was also accepted by the squadron at Montreal in June, and another Stranraer in July. Through the summer months, squadron pilots ferried a number of Tiger Moths to flying clubs across the Dominion for use in the new elementary training scheme. Armament tests were carried out on the Delta, an aircraft that was originally acquired for photographic work and was now being modified for operational use.

The threat of war did not make any great impression on the squadron's work - apart from the armament tests perhaps - but there was much more practice flying by AFHQ officers, it would appear. On 27 August, six Deltas of No. 8 Squadron at Rockcliffe left for Sydney, NS. Three days later, seven Wapitis of No. 3 Squadron landed at Rockcliffe en route from Calgary to Halifax; they were refuelled, serviced and "bedded down" for the night. On 2 September, two Hurricanes of No. 1 Squadron arrived at Rockcliffe on their way from Calgary to Dartmouth. War was drawing near, and No. 7 Squadron quietly vanished from the scene 10 September 1939. Not being an operational unit, its continuance as a squadron was presumably no longer necessary.

7 General Purpose Squadron
Officers Commanding and Commanding Officers

Squadron Leader E.G. Fullerton	24 Jan 1936 - 14 Aug 1936
Squadron Leader G.R. Howsam, MC	15 Aug 1936 - 7 Aug 1937
Squadron Leader D.A. Harding	8 Aug 1937 - 4 Dec 1938
Flight Lieutenant L.E. Wray	5 Dec 1938 - 31 Jan 1939
Flight Lieutenant R.C. Davis	1 Feb 1939 - 10 Sep 1939

Aircraft Types
Dates indicate when first taken on RCAF strength to the date the aircraft left active service.

29 Jan 1936 - 10 Sep 1939

Fairchild 71	Jan 1936 - Sep 1939
Bellanca Pacemaker	Jan 1936 - Sep 1939
Hawker Tomtit	Dates unknown
Vedette	Dates unknown
Grumman Amphibian	Dates unknown

Queen Juliana and Prince Bernhardt at Mont Tremblant beside a 12 Communications Squadron norseman, 1 January 1945.

Fairchild 51, 12 (Comm) Squadron and 12 Comm Flight.

Grumman Goose Mk II, 12 (Comm), 412 (Comp), and 412 (T) Squadrons and 12 Comm Flight.

Aircraft Tested by 7 Squadron

Hawker Hart	Northrop Delta
Avro Tutor	Wapiti
Fleet Trainer Model 21	Avro 626
Blackburn Shark	Noorduyn Norseman
Stranraer	Airspeed Oxford
Atlas	

12 (COMMUNICATIONS) SQUADRON

The General Purpose Flight of No. 7 Squadron was transformed into Number 12 Communications Flight on 10 September 1939, the day Canada entered the Second World War. Commanded by F/L R.C. Davis, its original strength was two officer pilots, three NCO pilots and 26 ground crew personnel. Its aircraft establishment included four Fairchilds, two Hawker Tomtits, a Grumman Amphibian and a Fleet Fawn. Within the next 12 months such aircraft as the Hudson, Delta, Digby, Goose, Norseman, Yale and famed Harvard were added to the inventory.

On 30 August 1940, coincident with the renaming of Station Ottawa to Station Rockcliffe, the flight was redesignated No. 12 Communications Squadron. At that time the Squadron consisted of Squadron Headquarters, Communications Flight and Practice Flight, the latter being operated for the benefit of AFHQ officers who wanted to keep their hand in as pilots, navigators or wireless operators during their headquarters tour. In 1941, the squadron added the twin-engine Boeing 247D, a Bolingbroke and a Stinson 105.

The Squadron carried out many tasks during World War II, including the testing of pilots recruited in the United States for service in the RCAF, and the operation of float-equipped

Fleet Fawn Mk II, 12 (Comm) Squadron and 12 Comm Flight.

Norsemen aircraft in northern Alberta, British Columbia, and the Yukon Territory during the construction of the North West Staging Route. In its VIP role, Number 12 Communications Squadron flew many missions between Ottawa, Washington, D.C., and to Quebec City during the Quebec Conference in 1943. Even during this early period the squadron was transporting VIPs across Canada and the United States, namely the Prime Minister of Canada, top-ranking officers of the three services and countless military and government dignitaries from other countries.

In 1942 Number 12 Communications Squadron added a Lockheed Lodestar and an Avro Anson to its establishment. Then in March 1943 the Squadron received its first Douglas DC-3, or Dakota. Many more DAKS were used by the Squadron over the years with Dakota No. 1000 probably being the most famous.

Dakota 1000 came to the Squadron in January 1947 and carried numerous international dignitaries until its retirement from service in March 1968. During that 21-year period with the Squadron it had flown a total of 11,496 hours.

New aircraft acquired by the Squadron between April 1944 and April 1946 were the Hawker Hurricane, undoubtedly the most famous single-engine aircraft ever flown by the unit; the Beechcraft Expeditor and finally, the Squadron's first four-engine aircraft, the Liberator.

12 COMMUNICATIONS FLIGHT
10 Sep 1939 - 30 Aug 1940

Fairchild 51	Jul 1939 - Oct 1946
Fairchild 71B	1 Sep 1939 - Oct 1941
Hawker Tomtit	Sep 1939 - Jul 1947
Grumman Goose	Jul 1938 - Mar 1946
Fleet Fawn	Sep 1939 - Mar 1946

MEMORIES
by Air Vice Marshall John L Plant (Deceased)
Pilot 12 (Comm) Sqn 1940-41

For the first ten months of war, those in authority gave little attention to 12 Comm Flight which had been established from the remains of the disbanded #7 GP Squadron. In early June 1940, disaster struck. The Minister of National Defence was killed in the crash of a Hudson which was based at Rockcliffe.

The formation of 12 Squadron on 30 August 1940 represented far more than a cosmetic change of name and upgrading of the commander's rank to Squadron Leader. About half a dozen pilots were posted in, all of whom had at least a modicum of experience in instrument flying. Very importantly, Trans-Canada Air Lines was asked for help. On the outbreak of hostilities, an Order-in-Council was passed which prevented the RCAF from calling up for air force duty any reserve officers who were employed by the airline. The company responded to the Air Force request by releasing Flight Lieutenant HM (Marlowe) Kennedy. Marlowe, as well as being a highly capable airline captain, had an innate weather sense and an ability to explain weather conditions to other people. He trained us all - on the Link trainer, under the hood and on the airways under actual instrument conditions.

The squadron which Marlowe helped to build and then commanded became the model for Air Transport Command. I met him first on the morning of 16th September 1940 when we each reported for duty to the Squadron and became close friends. He crossed the "GREAT DIVIDE" from Vancouver on June 10, 1989. May all his landings be safe and smooth.

There are a couple of personal anecdotes concerning my service with 12 Squadron from mid September, 1940.

On joining the Squadron 17 Sep 1940, the first task was to meet the officers and airmen and to study the qualifications of

DC-3 Aircraft towed to Ottawa Central Canada Exhibition: Front row: unidentified, Lac Pritchard, unidentified, Lac C. Patafie, Lac Hammell, Lac R. Godarre, Lac J. Molter, unidentified. Second Row: F/S J. Stoker, unidentified, unidentified, Cpl. T. Sheridan, Cpl. J. Beale, unidentified, F/L O'Kelly, unidentified, unidentified, unidentified, unidentified. (Courtesy of C. Patafie)

the pilots. Following this, the job was to become familiar with, and qualify on aircraft of the station which the Squadron might be required to fly. This was to be followed by a most strenuous effort to bring the capability of all pilots to existing airline standards.

For some time, there had been operating in the United States a British-Canadian group called the Clayton-Knight Committee which was paving the way for Americans to get into the RCAF for flying training and subsequent active service without jeopardizing their citizenship. The increasing ferrying to and within the United Kingdom set up a need for civilian pilots so qualified as not to require much flying training. The story goes, that of the first contingent of these pilots sent to England, all were returned home as unqualified except for one who had been killed in a flying accident. In any event, with no warning, Station Rockcliffe was instructed to be prepared to flight-test future applicants to ascertain that there was some credibility to the logbook entries that had been submitted in support of their applications.

At that time, I was the only officer on the station with a valid instructor's rating. Between Sep 26 and Oct 4, using a Harvard aircraft, I tested sixteen applicants. They varied in competence. The best one flew better than I, the tester, and the worst gave no evidence that he had ever handled the controls of an aircraft in flight. Later, some of those tested were being returned from Prestwick to Montreal in connection with their ferry duties when the Liberator in which they were passengers crashed on takeoff. All aboard were killed.

The next extraneous job of the Squadron was to test a secret US bombsight which had been installed in a Digby aircraft. Many sorties were flown on which both practice and live bombs were dropped in the target area. The need for extremely accurate flying to produce meaningful results meant that the pilots gained valuable practice while doing this job.

G/C GEORGE BROADLEY'S MEMORIES
of 12 (Communications) Squadron and 412 (Composite) Squadron

Following an operational accident while flying Catalina aircraft out of Shelburne, NS, I was posted to RCAF Station Rockcliffe so that a medical review board could assess my suitability for further flying duties. While the medical review board pondered (their decision was expected to be precedent-setting), I was "usefully employed" in various capacities around Station Rockcliffe.

At that time, 12 Comm had a hodge-podge of responsibilities. The Squadron's prime task was, of course, the transport of

Oliver, Smiley, Brown, Thompson and Magladry at Rockcliffe, Ontario, in front of a Dakota # 650. 1943.

VIPs, government officials and military personnel. In addition, however, the Squadron provided practice-flight facilities for AFHQ and conducted an instrument flying training section for repatriated aircrew returning from combat duties. It was the latter tasks that afforded me an opportunity to get back to active flying duties, albeit on an ad hoc basis.

Because I had demonstrated that I was able to fly single and twin-engined aircraft in the course of the medical board proceedings, the CO of 12 Comm Sqn. at the time, (W/C Marlowe Kennedy) decided that I could be "usefully employed" as a "look-out" and second pilot on training and practice flights despite the fact that I had yet to receive my official re-instatement as qualified aircrew. Finally, on 30 December, 1943, I was restored to aircrew status.

Ironically, my first official flight with 12 Comm, on 7 January, 1944, proved to be an interesting one. W/C Gordie Diamond (Who had taken over as CO from W/C Kennedy), F/L Leech, F/O Reid and myself were scheduled to take Lockheed 10 number 7648 to #6 Repair Depot, Trenton, for major overhaul. F/O Reid and I were to bring another aircraft back to Rockcliffe.

Weather conditions were good, although a recent snowstorm had produced substantial snow banks along the runway, but not of such a size as to present a hazard to normal take-off. In fact, both Gordie Diamond and Cec Leech agreed that a "hooded" take-off was possible.

With Gordie under the hood, and Cec in the right hand seat,

*Maintenance Crew of Communications work on a Lodestar's engine. **L to R:** Cpl. Al Gordon, LAC Joe Wiseman, LAC Al Lachappelle and LAC Earl Magladery.*

the take-off started quite well. However, on becoming airborne, the aircraft started to drift to starboard. About halfway down the runway, the right wheel struck a protruding hillock of snow with sufficient impact to snap the worm-gear strut that retracted the wheel. After an exploratory circuit around the tower and confirmation that the right wheel could not be retracted, but the left wheel could, we headed off to Trenton.

At Trenton, Gordie made a beautifully executed belly landing, with no injury to the occupants and apparently little damage to the aircraft. However, later examination at the Depot revealed that the broken worm-gear strut had been driven through the main spar of the starboard wing, effectively precluding a safe or economical rebuild of the aircraft.

For me, the next few months formed a period of adjustment while I attained "qualified status" on the Squadron's various aircraft. By September, I was sufficiently "broken-in" as to allow my inclusion as part of the Squadron detachment assigned to Ancienne Lorette in support of the Quebec Conference of 1944. The detachment provided courier service and personnel transport for officials involved in the conference.

Besides the exhilaration of being involved in an historical event (however remotely), my stay at Quebec was highlighted by a couple of amusing events. In the first instance, I happened to be the duty operations officer on the second or third night of our stay at Ancienne Lorette when a call came through from Dorval tower that an RAF Liberator was being diverted to Ancienne Lorette because of weather conditions at Dorval. No indication was given that there was anything special about the flight or that it was carrying passengers.

Having dutifully alerted the Motor Pool that we might need transport, I waited on the ramp for the Liberator to roll in. As the props came to a stop a single figure in civilian clothes dropped out of the rear escape hatch, carrying an umbrella in one hand while putting on a familiar-looking blue homburg hat with the other. It was Mr Anthony Eden! With typical 12 Comm efficiency, Mr Eden was made comfortable, officials at Chateau Frontenac were alerted, motor transport was laid on and Mr Eden was on his way. Phew!

As a footnote, it appears that information concerning Mr Eden's movements had been deliberately kept very restricted, so much so that the unexpected diversion had left some gaps in the proper flow of information.

The second event involved a trip that I made from Ancienne Lorette to Toronto and back. On the morning of 15 September, 1944, I reported to Operations as usual, whereupon I was handed a sealed envelope marked SECRET and instructed to fly to Toronto Island Airport where I would be met by a driver with a staff car. The driver was to take me to an address on University Avenue, where I would be given further instructions. Armed with the SECRET document and convinced that we were about to be involved in some momentous aspect of the conference, I took off in Expeditor 1390 with F/O Hood as first officer, and headed for Toronto.

On arrival at Toronto Island airport, I was duly met by the driver and staff car and whisked off to the address on University Avenue which, I noted, bore a sign saying "Liquor Board of Ontario." Dismissing any thought of a connection with my mission, I was ushered into a pretentious-looking office where I was greeted by an equally pretentious-looking gentleman, to whom I immediately surrendered my SECRET document.

I must admit I experienced considerable deflation when the pretentious-looking gentleman informed me that I was being en-

trusted with the delivery of a case of very special scotch whiskey for Mr. Winston Churchill!

They also serve who only help sustain the HIGH and MIGHTY!!

After the Quebec Conference, and with the war moving to its ultimate climax, 12 Comm Sqn. was kept so busy performing its basic role that events that might otherwise have merited special attention seemed to merge into the every-day picture of routine operations. Such operations as a quick trip to take Gracie Fields to Toronto for a special concert on VE Day and a hastily arranged flight to get the Russian military attache to Edmonton so that he could greet Mr Molotov on his way to the first meeting of the fledgling United Nations, were typical of these almost forgotten events.It was not until the period of semi-suspended animation that followed the end of the war had passed,that noteworthy operations began to appear.

Just such an operation occurred in late April of 1947, just after 12 Comm Sqn. had been re-designated 412 Composite Squadron on 1 April.

The RCAF had negotiated a deal to acquire a number of Mustangs from the USAF with which to equip the auxiliary. As part of the deal the RCAF was to pick up some twenty odd aircraft at Olmstead Air Force Base at Middleton, Pennsylvania, and ferry them to Gimli, Manitoba.

Planning for the ferry operation was conducted by AFHQ. 412 Composite Sqn. was charged with providing a Dakota to carry the servicing crews. S/L Fowler, an RAF exchange officer, was named to lead the ferry operation.

S/L Fowler's first task was to find enough pilots with single-engine fighter experience and current flying status to man the operation. Among the "suitables" was (then F/L and later W/C) Gordie Miller of 412 Sqn. After a hectic search and some brief refresher training, S/L Fowler was able to assemble a group of about eight or nine "suitable" pilots. With Dakota 350 and F/O Chaster as my first officer, we joined the operation at Olmstead on 28 April, 1947, where the "squad" was being given a quick qualifying check on the Mustang.

Assembled in two flights of four planes each, with S/L Fowler leading one and Gordie Miller the other, the "squad" headed west on 29 April with Fort Baer, near Fort Wayne, Indiana, as the destination. Their orders were to remain VFR and keep in touch by reporting to the civilian airways stations enroute. However, as we got into Ohio, the weather started to deteriorate. S/L Fowler elected to take his flight into the civilian airport north of Columbus while Gordie Miller made the more logical choice of going into Lockbourne AFB south of the city. Dakota 350 followed into Lockbourne.

To our surprise, the Base turned out to be an "all-black" Base with a most hospitable black Commanding Officer. The weather forced a one-day layover during which we enjoyed the company of a most friendly group of servicemen.

Having re-established contact with the Fowler flight, the two flights left Columbus on 1 May, headed for Orchard Place near Chicago where the USAF had a large repair and maintenance base. On arriving at Orchard Place, we were greeted with the news that one of the Fowler group, had become lost and, running low on fuel, had landed at a small civilian airport at Muskegon on the east side of Lake Michigan. Assured that plane and pilot were safe, S/L Fowler instructed the pilot to remain there and he would be picked up on the return trip to Olmstead. The remainder of the "squad" continued on to Gimli with stops at Minneapolis, Grand Forks, North Dakota, and Winnipeg. Seven planes were delivered safely at Gimli on 3 May, 1947.

On the return trip to Olmstead, we dropped into Muskegon on 5 May to pick up the "stray," where we learned the details of his exploit.

It seems that back in Olmstead, The "stray," whom I will call F/O "X" because I cannot recall his name, had sent his uniform to be cleaned before the first departure. For some reason, the uniform was not available before take-off and F/O "X" was obliged to leave in civilian clothes and with very little money. None of this would have been a problem as long as he remained with the group. However, the manager of the civilian airport at Muskegon was not about to provide fuel and servicing, or waive landing fees, for a stranger in civilian clothes, without much money and flying a military aircraft!

But F/O "X" was not without imagination and somehow managed to persuade the nearest USAF base to deliver fuel, after which he took off and flew back to Rockcliffe. I am not sure if he ever settled his account with the airport manager.

To bring this anecdote to a conclusion, the operation was completed with two more round trips and without the "loss" of any more planes or pilots.

One more story may serve to illustrate the diversity implicit in the designation "Composite." On 5 June 1947, F/L Johnson and I took off in on floats in Norseman 371, carrying three gentlemen from the Dept. of Transport on a ten-day mission into Quebec, the purpose of which was to examine a number of sites being considered for the location of stations on the Pine Tree Line.

Our first stop was at Senneterre, which at that time was a busy jumping-off spot for prospectors seeking their fortunes in the area north of Val d'Or. Senneterre was to be our operational base for the next few days while we made reconnaissance flights over the surrounding country. During our stay, we ate and slept at the Senneterre Hotel which offered basic (read primitive) accommodation.

However, it did provide evening entertainment in the person of the local alcoholic who broke beer bottles over his bare head for a nominal charge of 25 cents per viewer (minimum of four spectators per smash). To keep ourselves in shape during this period of high living, we "wobble-pumped" our fuel into the aircraft from 45 gallon drums.

To extend the area of coverage, we flew over to Oskelaneo River for a three-day stay. While there, we "boarded" with a local family and enjoyed French Canadien cuisine a L'Oskelaneo - a very interesting culinary experience. Mission accomplished, we returned to Rockcliffe on 16 May.

Although I moved on to less exotic things before the Squadron was finally designated 412 (Transport) Squadron, I did acquire another 700-odd hours of memorable flying. During that time, there were innumerable unique and amusing incidents but, as the passage of time and failing memory are prone to do, I cannot be sufficiently sure of detail to risk the publishing of erroneous or perhaps embarrassing information.

A SPECIAL STORY
by Patrick B. Ivey

In August, 1942, F/L Carl Crossley and I, accompanied by four crewmen, flew two float-equipped Norsemen aircraft from Rockcliffe to Whitehorse to begin the construction of the three most northerly emergency strips on the Northwest Staging Route. F/O H.M. (Hank) Rideout joined us at Whitehorse, flying an ancient Norseman from Patricia Bay. Our crewmen were Corporal R.V.T. Williams, LAC David A. White, LAC Joseph Dixon, Sergeant Jerry Brooks and Corporal Frank MacMillan. In the Norsemen we carried tents, sleeping bags, food, spare parts and anything else we might conceivably need because we would be living on the riverbanks until freeze-up.

From my point of view this beginning of the Northwest Staging Route gave me an opportunity to do some of the most enjoyable flying of my life. Everything was new and exciting. The Yukon still had the flavour of the Klondike. The air route to Russia was in its infancy. The Alcan Highway was a tote road. The Snag, Aishihik and Toobally Lake (later moved to Smith River) sites were totally isolated, and everything needed to build even temporary strips had to be flown by seaplane into nearby lakes.

That summer every effort of the RCAF was focused on the Empire Air Training Plan, and it had few qualified float pilots that it could divert to the Arctic. It settled for Crossley, a long-time Ontario Provincial Forestry pilot; Rideout, who had flown boats for Catalina Airways in California; and me, an ex-California private pilot; lately from #12 Communications Flight at Rockcliffe.

Eskimo family at Frobisher Bay. Centre right: Cpl. Harvey Canual, next behind F/Sgt. Gerry O'Connell. (Courtesy of Robert Cameron.)

The equipment to build Snag was brought down the Yukon to use at Coffee Creek by stern wheelers pushing enormous barges. There we loaded it into the Norsemen and ferried it 60 miles across a low range of mountains to a small lake adjacent to the construction site. I spent most of my time flying off the river at Coffee Creek, hauling hardware, fuel and imperishable food to the sites. We flew in some terrible weather but, thanks to good maintenance and a little bit of luck, we always managed to bring the airplanes home.

Of course, I like to think that our maintenance was outstanding. My two mechanics, Dave White and Joe Dixon, may have been short on experience, but they were long on dedication. Dave pulled off creative engine repairs by flashlight on the river that would have done credit to a mechanic twice his age. And I watched Little Joe change the Norseman to skis at Whitehorse with his bare hands at thirty below zero, because the camp at Snag was running out of food.

These exceptional young men, along with Corporal Vic Williams, Sergeant Jerry Brooks and Corporal Frank MacMillan, were a credit to the RCAF. To them, in large part, we owed the success of the operation, and our ability to finish the job on time.

12 COMMUNICATIONS SQUADRON
Commanding Officers

Squadron Leader J.L. Plant	30 Aug 1940 - 2 Feb 1941
Squadron Leader H.M. Kennedy, AFC	3 Feb 1941 - 22 Oct 1943
Wing Commander G.G. Diamond, AFC	23 Oct 1943 - 1 Jul 1945
Wing Commander A. Tilley	2 Jul 1945 - 7 Nov 1945
Wing Commander E.B. Hale, DFC	8 Nov 1945 - 31 Jul 1946
Wing Commander G.G. Diamond, AFC	1 Aug 1946 - 21 Mar 1947
Wing Commander W.H. Swetman, DSO	22 Mar 1947 - 31 Mar 1949

Squadron Aircraft

Lockheed 10A	Oct 1939 - May 1946
Lockheed Hudson	Sep 1939 - Feb 1948
Northrop Delta	Sep 1936 - Feb 1945
Douglas Digby	Dec 1939 - Nov 1946
Noorduyn Norseman	Feb 1940 - May 1946
North American Harvard	Jun 1940 - Oct 1960
Lockheed 12A	Jun 1940 - May 1945
Lockheed 212*	Jun 1940 - Feb 1946
Barkley Grow*	Sep 1939 - Oct 1941
Boeing 247D	Jun 1940 - Dec 1942
Stinson 105	Jul 1940 - Jan 1946
Lockheed Lodestar	Jan 1943 - Feb 1948
Avro Anson	Sep 1941 - Aug 1946
Hawker Hurricane	Jun 1942 - Jun 1946
Boeing Flying Fortress	Dec 1943 - Dec 1946
Consolidated Liberator	Sep 1943 - Nov 1947

Indicates only one of type in service.

412 (COMPOSITE) SQUADRON - 1947

The post-war reorganization of the RCAF on 1 April 1947 resulted in No. 12 Communications Squadron being redesignated Number 412 Composite Squadron, reflecting its dual role of providing air transport and training. The training role was deleted on 1 April 1949 and the Squadron assumed its present identity, 412 (Transport) Squadron.

Squadron Aircraft
1 Apr 1947 - 1 Apr 1949

Douglas Dakota	Mar 1943 - Feb 1968
Beechcraft Expeditor	Apr 1947 - Apr 1969

412 Squadron History World War II

Airpower was the deciding factor in the outcome of the war in Europe. Control of the air was absolutely necessary for the successful completion of any military operation. Germany had air superiority in the early days of the war, but her leaders never fully realized the strategic importance of airpower. As a result, the build-up of Allied air strength turned the tide of battle against Germany. Ever-increasing air attacks prepared the way for the invasion of Europe and Germany's final defeat. Canadian forces would play a prominent role in this defeat as part of the Allied armies. And as part of the Allied air strength, 412 Sqn. RCAF was to establish an unsurpassed list of achievements.

On 1 September 1939, Germany invaded Poland, initiating World War II with Hitler's grandiose scheme of world conquest. The German blitzkrieg was led by Luftwaffe bombers sweeping ahead of ground troops to strike at Polish airfields, railroads, bridges and other lines of communication. On 3 September, Britain, Australia, New Zealand and France declared war on Germany. Britain's first blow against Germany was from the air. On 4 September, the Royal Air Force struck by bombing German warships in the North Sea bases of Schillig Roads and Wilhelmshaven. Canada entered the war on 10 September 1939.

With the defeat of Poland on 3 October 1939, there was a deceptive calm called the sitzkrieg, which lasted through the close of 1939. The year 1940 began with Hitler pressing his generals to attack in the West, with airpower playing a major role in the German conquest. Luftwaffe bombers, fighters and paratroops led the sweep through northern and central Europe, pushing British and French troops across the English Channel to Great Britain.

On 22 June 1940, France signed an armistice with Germany, ending what was called the Battle of France. Britain and her Empire were left alone to face the onslaught of the Axis powers. Britain prepared for an assault. On 8 August 1940, the Luftwaffe began the assault in an attempt to gain permanent air control over Britain and the English Channel, thus beginning the Battle of Britain.

The battle ended 30 September, having been won by the Royal Air force. However, the Luftwaffe continued night raids, beginning what was termed the "Blitz". These raids ended in May 1941.

412 (Fighter) Squadron
Swift to Avenge

412 (Fighter) Squadron was created on 30 June 1941 at Digby, Lincolnshire, England. Equipped with the famous Spitfire, the Squadron was thrust into an accelerated training program. By August it was operationally ready and began four years of unceasing action against the enemy. From bases in England, operations over Europe included combat air patrol, ground interdiction and bombing escort.

Squadron Leader C.W. Trevena became the first Commanding Officer of 412 Sqn. He had joined 120 (Bomber) Squadron in the Auxiliary back in 1936 as an AC2 and had been commissioned soon thereafter, receiving his private pilot's license the next year. Leaving the accounting department of the Regina Leader-Post for active service when war broke out, he had transferred to fighters soon after arriving in England. By the time he assumed command of the fledgling Falcons, he had already made his mark in the Battle of Britain.

The Squadron received its first two aircraft, Supermarine Spitfire Mk 1's, about a week after its creation on paper. In early August the Mk 1's were exchanged for Spitfire Mk II aircraft. Throughout its long and successful tour overseas, 412 Squadron flew all the best-known marks of R.J. Mitchell's famous Spitfire. The pilots began training with the IIA, and it was with this mark that the unit became operational on 30 August 1941. A couple of months later, they adopted the 5B modification. The Mark V was used in many raids over France, the Low Countries, and Northwest Germany. The Squadron flew the 5B until the 9E replaced it in November 1943. After the end of the war, the Falcons were equipped with Spitfire XVIs and later, as occupation forces, with Spitfire XIVEs. Through the war the Spitfire changed minimally in external appearance, but the introduction of new power plants and refinements modified the plane admirably to serve in a variety of combat missions, as 412 Squadron could attest.

The Squadron's first major action in Europe was participation in the famous Dieppe raid on 19 August 1942, with 412 Sqn pilots providing cover for shipping in the morning and escorting two long-range Hurricane Bomber raids to the Dieppe area in the afternoon. 412 Sqn also took an active part in the Allied invasion of the European mainland, D-Day, 6 June 1944, by successfully patrolling the beaches without reporting a single Squadron casualty.

Ten days later, on 16 June 1944, the Squadron performed another memorable mission when pilots escorted a convoy of one cruiser and two destroyers carrying the King of England on his visit to France. This marked the one and only time 412 (Fighter) Squadron was involved with VIP operations.

On 18 June 1944, after moving its base 17 times within England, the Squadron transferred its 18 Mk IX Spitfire aircraft from Tangmere, England to Beny-Sur-Mer, France. A highly memorable two-day action occurred 26-27 September 1944 when the Squadron destroyed 31 enemy aircraft and damaged another seven. By 14 December 1944, the Squadron had tallied 65 enemy aircraft destroyed, two "probables" and 23 damaged, ranking it first in the entire 2nd Tactical Air Force for aircraft destroyed since D-Day. 412 Sqn was also the leading squadron in 126 Wing at that time, making it appropriate that the King of England during this month approved the Squadron's badge, the flying falcon, and the Squadron's motto, "Swift to Avenge".

Before the war ended, the Squadron moved 13 additional times to operate from ever-changing airfields as the battle line progressed eastward and deeper into enemy territory: the final station was at Utersen, Germany. In April 1945, a Squadron move occurred which few could have foreseen three years earlier, when 412 Sqn transferred its base forward into German territory. From a former Luftwaffe air station, its role of close air support for the Army continued unrelentingly until operations were halted in May 1945 with the cessation of hostilities. At that time the Squadron was equipped with the Spitfire Mk XVI.

Following VE Day, the Squadron formed part of the British Air Force of Occupation until March 1946 when it was disbanded and its members repatriated to Canada.

Upon disbandment, the combat record of 412 (Fighter) Squadron was one of the longest and most victorious of Canada's famous fighter squadrons. The Squadron's contribution to the war effort was second to none, earning a total of eight battle honours according to its standard and statistics: Sorties — 12,761; Operational flying hours — 16,995; Non-operational flying hours — 14,359. Squadron pilots claimed 106 enemy aircraft destroyed, recorded 11 "probables" and damaged 46 while making sure that the enemy surface transport suffered no less severely. From 1944 to May 1945, the Squadron destroyed 250 mechanized transports (METs), damaged another 575 and destroyed 20 locomotives and their carriages.

Victory, however, was not without its price. Twenty-five

members of the Squadron lost their lives in combat operations. Also lost was John Gillespie Magee, Jr., who composed the famous sonnet "*High Flight*" in September 1941, three months before he died in a flying accident. The poem, which heralds the exultant freedom of soaring at 30,000 feet, has been an inspiration to aviators worldwide.

During these dark and uncertain days mobilization was enacted throughout the British Empire. Men and machines were gathered together for the defence against and ultimate destruction of the Axis powers.

In June of 1941 there were five Canadian squadrons overseas, all stationed at Digby, Lincolnshire. Three were formed in Britain, No. 412 Squadron being one of them. It was the third Spitfire squadron overseas. 412 Squadron was formed 30 June 1941 in 12 Group, RAF Fighter Command, and immediately entered into an accelerated training program.

On 7 July 1941, Sergeant L.W. Powell, a peacetime butcher in Edmonton, logged four local flying hours and became the first Falcon to soar. The following day, five more Spitfires arrived and all available pilots were practising circuits and bumps. The Squadron's first flight was rapidly taking shape, albeit one of the spanking new planes was badly bent the next morning by a sergeant pilot who overshot the runway and tried to enter an air raid shelter with it.

When intermittent rain and persistent ground mists in Lincolnshire caused the cancellation of flights, the pilots gathered for instruction in the handling of the dinghy and the tommy gun, for aircraft recognition exercises, or for films on intelligence and aerial combat techniques. Those previously with Hurricane squadrons were especially anxious, however, to "get checked out

Magee's plane "Czar".

Pilot officer John Magee, best known for his poem "High Flight" poses next to his aircraft "Czar".

Wreckage from Magee's collision with an Oxford on December 11, 1941.

412 members give their last respects during a memorial service.

on the Spitfires, and on 30 August Squadron Leader Trevena's unit was signed out as "Operational State 1."

The Squadron immediately commenced operational patrols. Three days after being declared operational, the Squadron flew three scrambles without sighting any enemy aircraft.

The men of 412 Squadron were to go on and write their history: "In rhubarbs, rodeos and ramrods, in sea sweeps and armed reconnaissance, in dive bombing and army cooperation, in tedious patrols and fierce dogfights in the skies of France, these men wrote with bullets and bombs. They won honours in the defence of Britain, over the Channel and the North Sea, over the heart of Hitler's "impregnable" Festung Europa. They were there at Dieppe, over the beaches at Normandy, over Arnhem and over the Rhine."

They Won Honours in the Defence of Britain

During the next four years of enemy action, 412 Fighter Squadron had one of the longest and most successful records in Canadian history. The Squadron proudly bore the badge of the flying falcon, accumulating sixteen D.F.C.s, seven bars to that decoration and four Mentions in Dispatches (MIDs), testifying to this unit's outstanding record. Its Spitfires accounted for 106 Luftwaffe aircraft destroyed, 11 more possibly destroyed and 46 damaged in combat.

It was with the Spitfire that the aces of the Falcon Squadron wrote their names large in the annals of Canada's fighting airmen. There were famous names like Flight Lieutenant Don Laubman, D.F.C. and Bar, who destroyed 14 enemy aircraft and shared two more kills; Flt. Lt. W.J. Banks, D.F.C. and Bar, who scored 9-3-1; and Flying Officer D.R.C. Jamieson, D.F.C. and Bar.

The story of 412 Squadron is one of sustained courage and devotion throughout its ranks. It is also one of remarkable personal triumph over danger and adversity displayed on a daily basis as the war in Europe rolled on.

In Tedious Patrols And Fierce Dogfights...

After the Squadron was activated on 30 August 1941, its operations were uneventful for the first few months during which time convoy patrols and sector reconnaissances formed the bulk of the Squadron's activity. The first offensive mission did not occur until 21 September when an uneventful sweep by 12 fighters was conducted over the French coast.

412 Squadron crew on their way to England. (Courtesy of William Carlton)

During the month of September the Squadron maintained aircraft readiness, flew several scrambles and began flying convoy patrols, all of which were uneventful. On 21 September a dozen aircraft flew to Manston, Kent, and from there, in company with 411 and 266 Squadrons, flew an offensive sweep over the French coast. The Squadron encountered flak, but no enemy aircraft. A similar sweep, also uneventful, was flown six days later.

Early in October, following a brief period spent on army manoeuvres, the Falcons received several Spitfire LF Mk VBs, and were completely re-equipped by mid-month with this variant. The MK VB had an armament of two 20-mm cannon and four .303 machine guns.

It was not until 13 October that the Falcons chalked up their first aerial victory. Wing Commander Jamieson led 266, 411 and 412 Squadrons in a patrol from Boulogne to points south of Hardelot. About one dozen Squadron pilots proceeded to West Malling, Kent, and from there to the French coast. It was the Fal-

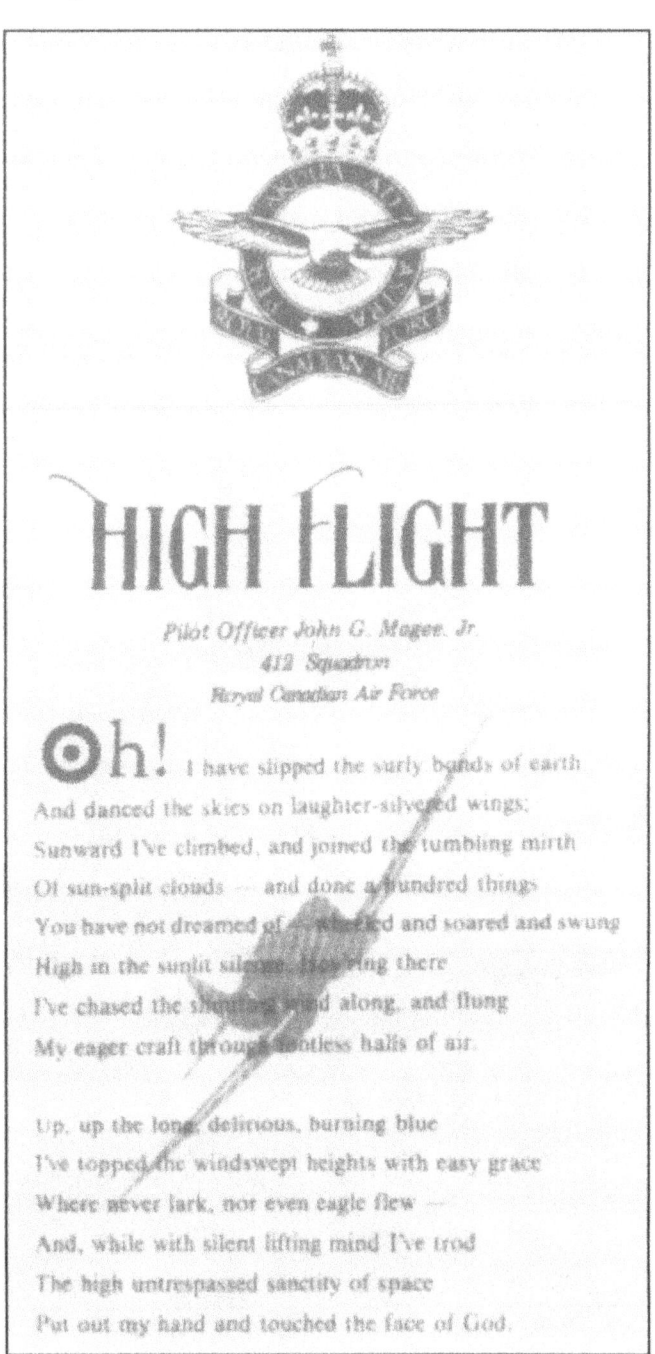

cons' job to patrol the French coast between Boulogne and Hardelot to cover the bombers' withdrawals.

Flying Red 2, Sgt. Edward N. Macdonell became detached from the main force on the return journey. As he neared the English coast, he observed two Me-109s below him. Attacking out of the sun at 20,000 feet, his first burst spattered the cockpit of one of the Messerschmitts. Sgt. Macdonell followed it down in a dive, streaking after the smoking German fighter at nearly 600 miles per hour. He blacked out completely as he pulled out of his screaming dive and regained consciousness to find himself flying straight and level at 400 feet above the water. Jerry was nowhere to be seen, but Wing Cdr. Jamieson passed over the spot a short time later and reported a large oil slick on the sea. This was regarded as confirmation.

No aircraft were yet equipped with cine-guns (motion picture camera operated simultaneously with machine-gun and/or cannon) to record their victories; however the Falcons marked up their first score high on the board, leaving room for many more. From then until 30 April 1945, when 412 added the last five victims to its scoreboard, the Germans knew the Falcons as a force to be reckoned with.

On 20 October 1941, the Squadron made the first of nearly 30 moves that were to carry them all the way from Digby, England, to Utersen, Germany. This move was short, just a few miles to Digby's satellite field at Wellingore, Lincolnshire. There the Squadron operated for the winter with its new Spitfire 5Bs.

On 25 October there was great excitement in the Squadron over Sgt. O.F. Pickell's return from the Rolls-Royce works at Hucknall. One of the Spit 5Bs had been fitted out with a novel negative "G" carburator and, as well as flying it back for them, Pickell was able to explain its mysteries to the Squadron: the device prevented the engine from cutting out when the control column was jerked sharply forward. There had been difficulty with the Spitfires in manoeuvring against the German planes, which already had injection carburation. 412 was the first squadron in Britain to be fitted with this new carburator.

Throughout the autumn and into the winter the Squadron continued to operate under 12 Group, operationally engaging in readiness states, scrambles, and convoy and standing patrols. These were interspersed with the occasional circus (combined bomber-fighter operations) and, beginning in early November, the rhubarb (low-level attacks on ground targets usually by pilots working in pairs).

In November 1941, patrols of the French coast became common. It was on one of these patrols that the Squadron experienced its first loss. Flt. Lt. C. Bushell, acting as Squadron Commander, Pilot Officer K.R.E. Denkman and Sgt. Pickell were all lost in action. Pickell's last report was, "Have used up all my ammunition. Am going home. Have got one." He was never heard from again.

On 11 December, Pilot Officer John Gillespie Magee Jr., was killed when he collided in cloud with an Oxford from Cranwell. Magee arrived from 53 O.T.U. to join 412 at Digby on 23 September. An American citizen, he was born of missionary parents in Shanghai, was educated at Rugby and brought to the United States in 1939. The next year, at the age of 18, he turned down a scholarship from Yale University to come to Canada and join the RCAF.

Pilot Officer Magee had recently returned from a high-level flying course at Farnborough. There he received the inspiration for his poem and scribbled it on the back of a letter to his mother. The poem, "High Flight," expressing the feelings that must have

412 Squadron members in Wellingore, England, 1941. **Standing:** *Sgt. Ken Robb and Sgt. Joe Richards;* **seated on wing:** *Sgt. Tommy Thompson and P/O Rod Smith;* **Seated on nose:** *Sgt. Pearce and F/Sgt. Lloyd "Pipsqueak" Powell. (Courtesy of R.I.A. Smith)*

Democratic Goosestep. On a visit to a Canadian Squadron in England, H.M. The King was much amused by the unexpected appearance of the Squadron's Christmas dinner. November 1941. (Courtesy of W. Needham)

been felt by so many of Magee's comrades, has become one of the most highly quoted poems.

Unfortunately, more accidents dogged the Squadron the next month. In the middle of January the first powdering of snow heralded the beginning of some difficult flying weather. Two Spitfires were no longer operational due to heavy landings and in February another shuddered to an abrupt halt in a snowbank.

While the Squadron was grappling with its accident problems, the Unit's hockey team provided a much-needed outlet of entertainment. Led by Flying Officer Howe (with Leading Aircraftman Blas, Corporal Leclaire and Aircraftman Clark in the forward line and Cpl McQuestion joining Howe on defence) the team distinguished itself that winter. After an unbroken string of victories with other squadrons, it met its match in 400 Squadron at the championship game in London. However, it proudly retained Group Captain Campbell's trophy for the leading team in 12 Group.

Over the Channel and the North Sea...

Operational time in February 1942 was the highest to date; the Squadron's 18 Spitfires and the Miles Magister flew a total of 209 hours on convoy patrols and 301 hours in training. None of the patrols, however, spotted the enemy as the weather factor continued to play a major role.

On 12 February 1942 the Squadron was called to readiness at 1315 hours, and its nine serviceable aircraft took off for Biggin Hill, Kent. After refuelling, they took off from Biggin Hill at about 1500 hours with 609 Squadron, giving close escort to a Beaufort torpedo squadron detailed to attack the Scharnhorst on its Channel dash. The ceiling was below 1,000 feet, and at times dropping right down to the water. The fighters were unable to accompany the Beauforts to the target off the Dutch coast. They waited, however, to escort them back after the torpedo attack and landed at Biggin Hill one hour and 40 minutes after take-off. No enemy aircraft were encountered during the operation.

With the coming of better weather in March, the Squadron increased its operational activity, and in addition to maintaining readiness states and flying combat patrols, it took part in several circuses and flew a rhubarb.

On 15 March, ten Falcon pilots, operating from Coltishall, Norfolk, took off in the late morning to search for a presumably captured E-boat escorted by Royal Navy Motor Torpedo Boats. Five vessels identified as E-boats were located and attacked with cannon and machine gun fire. Hits were observed to all the vessels and one appeared to be seriously damaged.

On 24 March, eleven Squadron aircraft did an early afternoon sweep over the Abbeville marshalling yards as part of a circus in which six Bostons bombed the yards. The operation cost 412 Sqn plenty when FW 190s attacked the bombers and their cover force; Squadron Leader Morrison, the OC, was killed in action while leading the Squadron, and Pilot Officer A.T.A.

Pictured: Dave McKay, Pat Davis, Mary McNickle, Spit Hart, Maj. Deane, Lucky, George Koelhoffer, Maj. Taying and General Gunn.

Young fell prisoner of war in the same engagement and spent three years in the notorious confines of Stalag Luft III. This Stalag was made famous by the movie The Great Escape. The movie relates one of the most ambitious escape enterprises undertaken by P.O.W.s. Elaborate and painstaking plans were made by "X Organization," formed by personnel of the prison camp, and three tunnels were started. One was finally completed and, on the night of 24 March 1944, seventy-six air force officers made their escape. Three escapees eventually made their way to freedom, but the others were all recaptured and fifty of them were murdered by the Gestapo. Many R.C.A.F. officers in the Stalag had been active in "X Organization." A number were included among the escapees while six lost their lives in the execution of the fifty prisoners.

On the first day of April 1942, 412 Squadron, now commanded by Squadron Leader R.C. Weston, left 12 Group and moved south to the more active 11 Group zone. They moved from Martlesham, Heath, Suffolk and were joined by 3048 Echelon for servicing. The Squadron continued to take part in an increasing number of circuses which brought steady losses without further enemy aircraft claims. By the end of April 1942, the Falcons had lost twelve pilots for only one enemy aircraft shot down.

May was spent mostly on a busy round of convoy patrols with some readiness states and scrambles; good weather enabled the Falcons to log 632 operational hours. Early in June 1942 the Squadron moved to North Weald, Essex, and later to Merston, Sussex.

For the next eight months it continued to operate from southern England, still under 11 Group, flying standing and convoy patrols and also taking part in many circuses and rodeos (squadrons or wings operating en masse at varying heights and blanketing the sky) and carrying out rhubarbs over occupied France. But the Squadron's apprenticeship was over, and it was finding itself frequently being "moved up" to where the real action was. By the time the Falcons' first anniversary rolled around in June, 412 Squadron was full-grown.

In Rhubarbs, Rodeos and Ramrods...

The Squadron had begun flying rhubarbs in November 1941 and on 15 July 1942 it took part in its first mass operation of this type. Fifteen squadrons swept low over the channel and shot up gun positions, wireless/telephone (W/T) stations, observation posts, troop emplacements and rail targets in the St. Valery, Dieppe, Etaples area. With 129 Squadron, the Falcons were detailed to provide cover by flying just off the French coast without taking part in the actual strafing attack.

26 July 1942 was another exciting day when 412 Sqn recorded its most successful encounter with the Luftwaffe up to that time. With two other fighter squadrons, 412 flew a rodeo over the Abbeville area, and after crossing the Channel at zero feet, climbed as fast as possible to reach 10,000 feet over the Abbeville airfield where intense light and heavy flak was encountered. One section of 412's six-man patrol was detailed to dive on enemy aircraft below. They attacked six FW 190s near ground level, as well as others which were just taking off. F/L F.E. Green destroyed one and damaged a second (on 29 July, Green would claim another FW 190 shot down). Flying Officer G.C. Davidson scored a probable kill, and F/O K.I. Robb damaged still another.

In the same combat action, one of the pilots, Lt. Col. A.P. Clark, failed to return from the operation. He was one of three American pilots then attached to the Squadron to gain operational experience.

On 1 August 1942 a section of two Squadron pilots flying a standing patrol off Shoreham intercepted two bomb-carrying FW 190s on a tip-and-run raid. They shot one down into the sea and damaged the other, pieces being seen to break away under cannon and machine gun hits. Later in the day two more bomb-carrying FW 190s were damaged by a 412 Sqn section that was scrambled to intercept the raiders.

August saw F/L Green and S/L Fee, who had very recently taken over command of the Squadron, become the first pilots to receive the DFC. These two illustrate something of the international character of the Squadron. Frederick Ernest Green, a product of the British Commonwealth Air Training Plan and by now a veteran with three kills to his credit, was a native of Petersburg, Virginia; Clark John Fee was a native of Calgary, Alberta, and was cited as "a fine pilot and skilful leader" whose outstanding ability was mainly responsible for the high standard of fighting efficiency of the Squadron.

During the summer of 1942, the Squadron began taking part in circuses with bombing carried out by USAAF B-17s. One of the first missions fell on 17 August 1943.

At Dieppe...

On the night of 18 August, the pilots of many RCAF, as well as RAF, squadrons were briefed for the great combined opera-

F/L A.C. "Pappy" Crimmins of Westmount, Quebec, was nicknamed because he was one of the oldest pilots with the 2nd Tactical Air Force.

Members of the 412 Squadron relax in front of their dispersal hut. (Courtesy of Kenneth Robb)

tion which was set to take place the following morning. The Battle of Dieppe was about to begin.

The action at Dieppe marked the largest-scale operation to date by co-ordinated forces of the Navy, Army and Air Force against defences of enemy-occupied Europe. It provided the first test of the importance of airpower to such an undertaking, and of the extent to which aircraft might be utilized in any projected cross-Channel assault upon the Continent.

The objective of the operation was two-fold: firstly, to test German defences, and secondly, to lure as many German aircraft as possible into the air. At dawn on the 19th, the pilots were standing at readiness. Shortly afterwards the first fighter patrols were airborne to cover the landings.

412 Squadron had a busy day, flying 56 sorties in conjunction with the Dieppe raid. Eleven aircraft, previously positioned at Merston, Sussex, took off for the day's first patrol at 0620 hours and flew shipping cover off the beach. They engaged half a dozen FW 190s with neither claims nor casualties. The pilots were up again at 0945 hours to escort Hurribombers attacking an unspecified target. No enemy aircraft were encountered, but two 412 Spitfires were hit by flak and one, its tail assembly blown off, crashed in France, killing its pilot. Listed as one of the Canadian pilots lost that day was Pilot Officer J.N. Brookhouse. Flight Sergeant W.F. Aldcorn was more "fortunate." After being forced to bail out near Beachy Head, he survived a forty-minute swim in the Channel and was rescued by a naval launch.

At 1345 hours, the Squadron took off to escort Hurribombers again and engaged one dozen FW 190s in a "terrific dogfight" which ended without casualties to either side. Later in the day the Falcons flew a series of scrambles, presumably to provide cover for the returning naval forces. The Squadron recorded no victories that day: total enemy casualties in the Dieppe action were 93 aircraft; Allied aircraft losses were 98 (30 of the pilots being rescued).

On 23 August, 412 Squadron moved to RAF Station Tangmere and began to function as part of Tangmere Wing. The Squadron was by now operating in high gear, and its operational hours for the month, in excess of 500, were double the total of training hours logged.

Over the Heart of Hitler's Impregnable "Festung Europa"...

From September through November, the Falcons flew numerous rhubarb missions to northern France. Flying in pairs, the pilots harassed communications and strafed locomotives and other ground targets. Among these days was a memorable 25 October 1942 when eight Squadron Spitfires thoroughly strafed a hutted camp in the Abbeville area. The attack brought congratulations from Air Marshall T.L. Leigh Mallory, C.B., D.S.O., A.O.C. No. 11 Group.

When the aerodrome at Tangmere was rendered unserviceable by the frequent drizzles of the English autumn, the Squadron continued operations from Kenley. In November, enemy flak cost the lives of 412 pilots Sgt. W.D. Pagan and Sgt. H.D. Spence.

In mid-December the field at Kenley became soggy and virtually useless for 412 Squadron, now under the leadership of Sqn. Ldr. F.W. Kelly. The Squadron moved about half its ground crew to Friston and based some of its operations there. By now the strafing missions had given way to support of the bombers which were pounding Abbeville and Beny-Sur-Mer.

After the start of the new year, bomber escort operations continued over the Sherbourg in company with 401, 402 and 416 Squadrons. Sqn. Ldr. Kelly was awarded a D.F.C. for his exploits on these missions. On 29 January 1943 the Squadron, which had

Squadron Leader Fred Kelly-CO of 412 Squadron from November 1942 to June 1943, enjoying some bread and butter. (Courtesy of 412 Squadron)

operated under 11 Group since 1 May the previous year, moved to Angle in South Wales, coming under 10 Group. During the nine months it had spent under 11 Group at Martlesham Heath and a number of different airfields near the south coast, the Squadron had averaged roughly 345 hours per month on operations.

It had redressed the balance sheet somewhat in regard to pilot losses versus enemy aircraft claims. Seven of its own pilots had been lost while it had claimed eight enemy aircraft destroyed, two "probables" and nine damaged during rhubarb operations.

From Angle, the Squadron began a round of patrols and on 8 February 1943 was shifted to Fairwood Common, Glamorgan, remaining under 10 Group. The Squadron was taken off operations 10 February to participate in Exercise Spartan, which developed squadron mobility and cooperation with the army. It was more than two months before the Falcons returned to operational flying.

Following completion of the exercise, 412, still under 10 Group, moved to Perranporth, Cornwall on 12 April 1943. On arrival there, or shortly afterwards, it received a number of Spitfire LF Mk VCs, the long range versions of the variant. It continued to fly both VBs and VCs for the next couple of months.

412 Squadron on maneuvers in England changing a tire the hard way, March 1943. (Courtesy of Ken Robb)

F/O Dave Boyd and F/O Ken Robb at the bread line with 412 Squadron on maneuvers somewhere in England. March 1943. (Courtesy of Ken Robb)

Returning from "train-bustin" over enemy territory F/O L.W. "Pip" Powell describes to LAC W. Coults (ground crew) how 412 found a perfect target, March 1943.

The Squadron flew two sea patrols from Perranporth on 13 April, its first operational flights since 9 February, and continued to operate from Cornwall until the second half of June. As part of Perranporth Wing, 412 flew 221 operational sorties; most of the operations were sea patrols with a number of shipping reconnaissances and strikes. Utilizing other airfields as advanced landing grounds, it also took part in rodeos, circuses, ramrods and flew a series of rhubarbs over occupied France.

During one mission, on 7 May 1943, in the Ile de Batz-Ushant area, Flying Officer L.W. Jones was shot down, but Flt. Sgt. (later Warrant Officer 1st Class) E.J.V. Levesque, though hit in the cannon magazine, managed to coax his craft home on a damaged mainplane. His luck ran out though on 7 June. While strafing rail targets on the Brest peninsula between Morlaix and St.- Brieus, Levesque was knocked down by flak.

In May, Flying Officer L.W. Powell brought down an FW 190 and earned himself a DFC in an operation with 610 and 65 Squadrons in support of a dozen Venturas attacking the aerodrome at Morlaix. F/O Powell and S/L Kelly attended the investiture at Buckingham Palace on 25 June and received their decorations from H.M. the King.

Also in May, 412 Squadron was selected to train 12 pilots for aircraft carrier landings. This included each pilot doing 2 hours slow flying, doing turns with wheels and flaps extended. Next there were five hours doing dummy deck landings on a specially marked-off portion of the runway at home base. A Royal Navy officer was attached to the Squadron as the landing controller, called a batsman. Each pilot was rated by the batsman and all passed as acceptable.

On 30 May the pilots were ferried north to RAF Station Ayr in Scotland in an RAF Harrow aircraft. On 31 May they were flown about 10 miles out to sea and landed on the Royal Navy aircraft carrier ARGUS, the smallest aircraft carrier in the British Navy. Using Royal Navy Spitfires modified with a hook controlled from the cockpit, each pilot completed 4 deck landings using a batsman located on the port side of the rear deck.

The Squadron left the southwest in June and returned to Friston for more action in the "Hell's Corner" of Southeast England. In July, 412 Squadron pilots flew ramrod and rodeo operations from Redhill. On 5 July the unit became part of No. 126 RCAF Airfield Hq., which came under No. 83 Group, Tactical Air Force, (TAF), Fighter Command.

As part of TAF 83, the Squadron was preparing to go to France, or wherever the second front opened. The pilots with their flying up to a high standard were able to relax, but the lot of the groundcrew was a different story. Both fitters and riggers had to take extra courses on ground defence and truck driving, as the unit was becoming totally mobile. It was surprising to see fitters and riggers taking rifle drill and instruction in the art of ground defence from RAF Regiment personnel. They were to make up the nucleus of a "backers-up" force which was to help the RAF Regiment in case the aerodrome was attacked while on the continent. They were also taught the necessity for ground defence during the air raid attacks. The squadron was intensifying its training both on the ground and in the air. On 7 August 1943, the Squadron moved to Staplehurst in Kent.

In the Skies of France...

The aircraft were now carrying the war closer to the enemy as the Spitfires were equipped with long range fuel tanks, either 45 or 90 gallons depending on the operation. Flying escort for USAAF heavy bombers, which were now carrying out daylight bombing raids, required maximum fuel.

In November 1943 the great bomber strikes commenced in earnest against the threatening rocket installations and other significant targets at Calais, Triqueville, Minoceyque, Lille, Venderville, and the vast aerodromes at Cambrai and Chievres. 412 Squadron flew close escort to the 72 bomber armadas of Marauders and Mitchells. They also conducted fighter sweeps of the Hardelot, St.-Omer, and Bethune sectors. No enemy aircraft were in evidence, but flak sent down F/L A.C. Coles to share the fate of the Kriegesgefangenen partaking of the meagre amenities of Stalag Luft IV. F/L D.B. Wurtele stretched his luck successfully and limped back to a safe let-down in his damaged aircraft.

December was marked by increasing demands upon 412 Squadron to supply cover for bombers pounding French airfields and returning from attacks on the Schipol airport at Amsterdam, but in a hectic month of ramrod operations, the Squadron suffered no casualties while only its most outstanding fighter, F/L G.F. "Buzz" Beurling, scored. It was his only kill with 412 Squadron and the 31st entry in his amazing wartime record.

Early in November 1943, 412 Squadron began receiving Spitfire LF Mk IXBs and was completely re-equipped with this variant by month's end. By the end of 1943, the Squadron had 3,200 hours of operation. The future was to hold even more interesting work.

The Falcon Squadron began the eventful year of 1944 unspectacularly with a week of air-firing practice at Hutton Cranswick. They then returned to the routine attacks on Noball targets, and bomber escort assignments.

The Squadron shifted briefly to Yorkshire early in January 1944 for an air-firing course and to Wales at the end of March 1944 for air-firing and bombing courses. Apart from these absences, it operated from a number of South Coast airfields until shortly after D-Day.

On 13 October, 412 Squadron shifted from 126 Airfield to RAF Biggin Hill's main mess and taxied its aircraft over to the nearby dispersal area previously used by 411, the "Grizzly Bear" Squadron. 412 thereby inherited more creature comforts, including F/L R.S. Hyndman's murals in No. 411's elaborately decorated dispersal hut.

On 2 February the Canadian High Commissioner, the Honourable Vincent Massey, visited the Squadron during his inspection of the wing. He was accompanied by Air Vice Marshall N.R. Anderson (Second in command of the RCAF overseas) and Group Capt. W.R. MacBrien, C.O. of 17 Wing. The Hon. Mr. Massey showed keen interest in 412 Squadron as his son, F/L Hart Massey, had served for some time on the unit as intelligence officer.

Bomber escort duties in the Pas de Calais sector, sweeps of Astend-Bethune-Abbeville, fighter umbrellas for Mitchells and Bostons pounding Noball installations at Tocqueville and south of Dieppe, support of heavy attacks in the Eindhoven area, and rendezvous near Brussels with B-17s returning from Germany made February a busy month. In all these operations the Squadron experienced only light flak and no fighter opposition. The month's tally was 291 sorties; the casualties were nil. Air supremacy had been realized.

Top row (L to R): SGT. Dunning, SGT. Tape, SGT. Ketterson, SGT. MacLean, SGT. Bullion, P/O Powell, F/SGT Levesque, F/LT Massey (Intelligence Officer), P/O Pearce, P/O Needham, W/O MacCrimmon, F/SGT. Edwards, P/O Richards. *Center (L to R):* F/SGT Aldcorn, P/O Earle, W/O Harwood, P/O Thompson. *Bottom (L to R):* P/O Robb, F/LT Jolly (Squadron Padre), F/LT Kelly, S/LDR Fee, F/LT Green, F/LT Godfrey, P/O McKay.

(R to L): Doug Thomson, Hank Winterburn, Jack Mugridge, L.A. C. Wood, Bill Roberts, Gord Bowley, L.A.C. Klippentum and Murry Monery, at 126 Airfield-412 Squadron, Biggin Hill on Jan. 20, 1944. (Courtesy of W. Roberts)

Engine trouble, not the Luftwaffe, accounted for Flying Officer A.B. Ketterson's death on 4 March. It was not until 23 March, despite the continued fast pace of operations, that the Germans were sighted again. F/O Laubman and F/L Needham shared a Ju 88 on that occasion. During ramrod 661 on 16 March against Abbeville, F/O T.M. Saunderson experienced engine trouble over the Channel and glided in toward the French coast, bailing out at 2,500 feet about a mile from the Somme Estuary. He spent an hour and a half in the water, with F/L Laubman circling overhead to provide protection, before Air Sea Rescue managed to land a Walrus and pick him up.

Following bombing practice in March and April, 412 Squadron flew its first dive bombing operation on 18 April. Fourteen of its Spitfires, each carrying a 500-pound bomb, attacked a Noball target southwest of Abbeville and eight bombs were reported to have fallen in the target area. The "softening up" of occupied France continued, with 412 dive-bombing rail and road communications along with flying-bomb sites. These operations were sometimes flown with 90-gallon drop tanks which the Squadron used during April. Its Spitfires also received the new gyro gunsight.

Throughout the July 1943-May 1944 period, the Squadron averaged 324 operational hours per month, with September 1943 and May 1944 being the two busiest months. During this period, enemy aircraft opposition was sporadic. The Squadron lost seven pilots while claiming 11 aircraft destroyed, possibly destroyed, or damaged.

Operations in May brought the Falcons some casualties. On the 10th, at 6,000 feet over Rheims, two FW 190s were attacked by Flight Lieutenants E.C. Likeness and J.A. Crimmins. Both the Falcons were shot down - a rare occurrence in this period of the war. Likeness, hit by enemy fire, was forced to bail out three miles inland from Treport. He evaded capture and was soon back with the Squadron. Crimmins crashed and was buried by the commune of Beauvais in the department of Oise. The next day, in a dive bombing show on a Noball site, Flying Officers J.S. Hamilton and R.W. Thatcher collided in mid-air over the target. Hamilton, who had fought through the dark days of Malta, found that his luck held once more. He bailed out and was picked up almost immediately by Air/Sea Rescue. Thatcher was taken prisoner of war.

Over the Beaches of Normandy...

Once a measure of air superiority had been attained, the invasion of the Continent was launched. After a foothold was gained, the ground forces began their push across France. The Allied air forces, which had helped to make that initial landing possible by months of "softening up" the enemy and disrupting communications, then complemented and protected the army's gains with invaluable air support. The Falcon Squadron went to work too, and from D-Day to the end of March 1945, it bagged 230 mechanized transports (METs) and damaged another 574; destroyed 20 locomotives and 27 carriages (crippling 72 and 75 respectively), and put nine tanks out of commission. It also cut vital rail lines in 86 places. The Falcons harassed enemy troops and battered supply lines. 412 Squadron rained down more than one half million pounds of high explosives on important targets, blasted communications and hardpressed the foe.

This long list of accomplishments began on 4 June 1944, when orders were received during the evening to paint invasion stripes on the Squadron's Spitfires. The next day, several convoy patrols were flown. Later in the evening there was a briefing at 2330 hours to inform the pilots of 412 that the invasion was under way. The convoys which they had guarded throughout the day were now steaming across the Channel toward the beaches of Normandy. The Falcons had less than two hours sleep before being called to readiness at 0330 hours on 6 June, D-Day. The invasion of Hitler's "Festung Europa," Operation Overlord, had begun.

The Squadron flew four beachhead patrols during the day for 49 sorties; take-off times ranged from 0810 to 2135 hours. It was a long and exciting day, but had one disappointing feature: no enemy aircraft were encountered and the missions were uneventful. More importantly, a toehold on the beaches had been gained by Allied troops.

Further beachhead patrols were flown during the next two days. On the 7th, the Falcons, flying with the other two squadrons of the wing, ran into a dozen Ju 88s between Caen and the sea. Some of the Junkers dove at the congested beaches while the others turned to regain the cover of the clouds as the Spitfires closed in. Few of the Ju 88s escaped; eight were destroyed, another probably destroyed and two damaged. From this total, Flying Officer P. Charron of the Falcons destroyed one of the 88s while the Squadron claimed both damaged. The aggressiveness of the Germans was short-lived, however, and three weeks passed before the Luftwaffe were encountered again in any strength.

Bad weather grounded the Squadron on 9 June, but the next day the Falcons helped to escort Halifax and Stirling bombers dropping supplies to forward troops, and flew a fighter sweep over the Evreux-Chartres-Argenton area. On the second operation of the day, four of their Spitfires put down at a Normandy landing strip. Another time, a dozen 412 aircraft, in company with 401 Squadron Spitfires, flew to a Normandy landing strip in the early morning of 14 June. Later in the afternoon they flew a fighter sweep over the Le Mans-Chartres-Evreux area to strafe military road traffic.

Landing on the Normandy beachhead was an experience which none of the Spitfire pilots would forget. The landing strips were inches deep in dust. Whenever aircraft landed or took off, tremendous clouds swirled up. The Spitfires and personnel were coated with dust. When rain fell, as it so often did during the summer months, runways became stretches of sticky mud.

The airstrip was located about a mile from the Canadian landing site of Juno Beach, once the scene of bitter D-Day fighting. The nights at the airfields were noisy with the off-loading of landing craft and German aircraft trying to bomb the ships while ack-ack batteries hurled thousands of shells into the night sky. Near the runways, tents were erected and slit-trenches dug.

A landmark move occurred 18 June 1944 when the Squadron relocated to landing strip B-4 at Beny-sur-Mer, France, inland from Courseulles. Henceforth, its wartime flying in support of the British Second Army was done from landing strips and airfields in France, the Low Countries and Germany. The move to France was followed by a drastic change in its fortunes regarding successes against the Luftwaffe and ground targets, balanced against pilot losses. From August 1941 through June 1944 the Falcons claimed 40 enemy aircraft destroyed, possibly destroyed, or damaged, while losing only 33 of its own pilots. From July 1944 to the war's end it lost 24 more pilots but claimed 122 enemy aircraft destroyed, possibly destroyed, or damaged.

The Falcons resumed dive bombing when one dozen aircraft attacked the Caen marshalling yards. By the month's end they had logged 1034 hours while flying 673 sorties, its largest monthly total of flying time to date. Operations continued at the same pace through July as the Squadron flew a busy round of armed reconnaissances, dive bombing attacks and defensive patrols, with occasional escort jobs for day bombers. Allied air supremacy was firmly in their favour throughout the six weeks of June and July.

Even though the Allied armies had moved off the beaches, they had been stopped shortly inland. The Canadian landing forces had been halted ten miles from the beach outside Caen, France, by German Tiger tanks. A stalemate began that would continue until August.

In armed reconnaissance . . .

On 2 July 1944 the Squadron engaged 10 enemy fighters while escorting Mustangs bombing a bridge. The Falcon pilots claimed four destroyed and five damaged for the loss of one of their own. Two armed reconnaissances on 7 July resulted in air combats in which four enemy aircraft were claimed as destroyed and one damaged. One Falcon pilot, F/L Needham, the B Flight Commander, went missing. He was taken prisoner, treated in a French hospital for burns and later released when American troops liberated the area. He was returned to Allied military personnel in Britain in early August.

(L to R): Sgt. Cornwall, Sgt. Murray, Sgt. Leggett, and F/Sgt. Goldberg enjoying a meal between missions.

Sqn. photo at Redhill (July-August 1943).

On 11 July 1944 a new Squadron policy was instituted so that armed reconnaissances (recces) were flown with some of the aircraft carrying a 500-pound bomb each. The Squadron, along with other squadrons of 126 Wing, assisted the British-Canadian push at Caen on 18 July, helping to provide cover for an early-morning bombing by Lancasters and B-17s. Two armed reconnaissances were also flown during the day, as well as a defensive patrol while the Spitfires went down to strafe ground targets. A tank, various mechanized transports and enemy troops were included in the day's bag of ground targets. Roads and rail lines, gun positions and troop concentrations were among the ground targets successfully strafed and bombed during July. Meanwhile, the Squadron enjoyed spectacular successes against the Luftwaffe in the air.

On 24 July, four Falcon Spitfires on an afternoon weather reconnaissance engaged 40 or more FW 190s and Me 109s at 10,000 feet over Lisieux. Seven of the enemy fighters were confirmed as having been destroyed for no 412 losses. In all, the Squadron claimed 19 enemy aircraft destroyed and six damaged during July, logging 1,092 hours during the month while flying 902 sorties.

In the period of June-July, 412 Squadron recorded four losses of its own: Warrant Officer II L.W. Love was killed over Bavent on patrol on June 17, Warrant Officer II A.E. Seller was forced down near Caen and became a POW on 28 June, Flying Officer H.W. Bowker was killed in action southeast of Caen on 2 July and Flight Lieutenant Needham had to bail out near Falaise on 7 July. Needham, the B-Flight Commander, turned up safe in the United Kingdom a month later.

On 2 August 1944, the O.C., Squadron Leader J. Sheppard, crash-landed behind enemy lines a few kilometres northwest of Les Chapelles. The aircraft was badly damaged upon landing and Sheppard was wounded in both legs. He fell into the hands of a German patrol and was taken to a hospital at Alencon from which he escaped in the company of a Royal Marine on 6 August. He returned to the Allied lines a week later after a harrowing series of exploits. Meanwhile, Flight Lieutenant D.H. Dover, a 412 flight commander, was made acting Squadron Leader and took over command of the Falcons. Both he and Flight Lieutenant O.M. Linton, the B-flight commander who had distinguished himself on 24 July 1944, were soon granted Distinguished Flying Crosses.

The rapid advance of the Allied ground troops made possible the frequent moves of 412 Squadron to a succession of front-line airfields. On 8 August they left Beny-sur-Mer for Cristot and soon moved on to Illiers L'Eveque, Poix, Evere, the large airport six miles from Brussels, and later to Le Culot, also in Belgium. October took them across the borders of the Netherlands to Rips and then Volkel. Although the Outfit began to take on some of the aspects of a travelling tent show, their usefulness always increased as evidenced by the successful operations of the fall months.

In August, a new offensive was planned for a "Break-Out" from the beach areas and a push into France. The Canadian forces had pinned down the German tanks at Caen, and with the new offensive, they took Caen and the surrounding area.

Throughout most of August 1944, the Squadron concentrated on harassing the retreating German forces by dive bombing and strafing, claiming nine enemy aircraft during the month. The Falcons bombed barges and other targets on the Seine on 4 August and four days later moved forward to B-18 at Cristot, France, where they operated for the remainder of the month. By 12 August the continuing attacks on the German forces were beginning to reach a climax. On that day, 412 pilots flew 47 sorties in a trio of armed recces and a fighter sweep which left a dozen METs in flames or smoke, plus 24 more damaged. The Falcons' strafing and dive bombing attacks continued for the next week and reached a high point on 18 and 19 August as German transport and other vehicles were attacked in the Falaise pocket. Many were also destroyed trying to escape the pocket through the narrow neck between Falaise and Argentan. The Falaise pocket was created by a pincer movement of Canadian and American forces around the town of Falaise southward from Caen.

The Allied air strength was so mighty against the German forces that a captured German General admitted, "The fighter bomber attacks were unbearable." By day, the Panzer units had to remain hidden under camouflage nets. Any attempt to counterattack failed because of the intensity of the fighter-bomber attacks, even causing Tiger tanks to halt or become burned out hulks. The German losses exceeded 50% of strength for most units

On 18 August two Falcon pilots returned from an early afternoon reconnaissance patrol to report that between 1,000 and 1,500 enemy transports were crowded within a wooded area and lined bumper to bumper on the roads near Argentan. Two armed recces, each in squadron strength, left 48 METs in flames or smoke with 54 more damaged. A body of troops was also shot up and a tank damaged. Four more armed recces and 40 sorties were flown the next day. Sixty METs were claimed as having been left burning and an additional 65 damaged as well as nine armoured fighting vehicles hit and two tanks damaged.

On the 20th of August the Squadron was on readiness and restricted its flying to front line patrols but two days later returned to ground targets, bagging 23 METs destroyed or smoking and 16 damaged. During August the Squadron logged 854 hours while flying 715 sorties and claimed 257 METs left ablaze and 271 damaged, plus hits on tanks, armoured fighting vehicles, barges, and many other ground targets. Four enemy aircraft were claimed as destroyed during the month and five were damaged.

By the end of August 1944 the battle front had shifted too far from 412's airfield for the Squadron to be effective against the enemy; so during the first three days of September, the Falcons made a trio of forward moves, halting briefly at B-44, Poix, France. Several uneventful front line patrols were flown over the Brussels-Antwerp area on 5 September and the following day the Squadron moved on to B-56 at Evere, Belgium, six miles from the centre of Brussels. There, Falcons flew a series of patrols and armed reconnaissances in which they concentrated on rail targets before moving to B-68, Le Culot, Belgium, on 21 September. The Falcons arrived at Le Culot in time to take part in the heavy air fighting that followed the British airborne landings at Arnhem and Nijmegen. 412 Fighter Squadron immediately began an intensive series of patrols over the areas, temporarily halting its attacks on the enemy's rail system.

Over Arnheim . . .

The remaining days of September brought the Falcons their most spectacular string of success against the Luftwaffe. On the 25th, two fighters were destroyed during patrols. Then a dozen Falcon Spitfires, on an early-afternoon low-level patrol over Nijmegen the next day, ran into two gaggles of 12 or more Me 109s and 25 or more FW 190s flying on the deck eastwards along the Rhine. In the combat that followed, the squadron claimed eight of the enemy fighters destroyed while later in the afternoon a patrol of 10 Falcon Spitfires encountered a like number of enemy fighters in the Nijmegen area, claiming two destroyed and two damaged. There were no 412 losses during the day.

The Squadron's record of 26-27 September 1944 was a highlight of all its outstanding feats. The Luftwaffe was out those days in unaccustomed strength for the Nijmegen area, yet 13

First Canadian Cemetery in France at Beny-Sur-Mer-412 internees located near the fence, July 1944. (Courtesy of W.O. Roberts)

Bud Bowker in damaged aircraft that Eddie Levesque nursed home from France. (Courtesy of W.O. Roberts)

pilots of 412 Squadron destroyed 30 enemy aircraft, probably destroyed another and damaged seven more.

On 27 September 1944 the Luftwaffe made its greatest effort to knock out the Nijmegen bridge. But it was a record day for the Squadron too, concerning enemy aircraft claims. The Falcons flew low patrols over the Nijmegen area. The first, carried out with 45-gallon drop tanks, took place in the early morning. Between 10 and 15 Me 109s were engaged and two were claimed as destroyed and two as damaged. Not one of the 12 Falcon aircraft received a single hit. During the late morning, 20 or more Me 109s were engaged with two claimed as destroyed and four damaged for the loss of one pilot. In the late afternoon, a dozen 412 aircraft fought between 12 and 15 FW 190s, destroying four and damaging one for yet the loss of another pilot. The day's score came to 14 destroyed and seven damaged against the loss of two pilots. One of the Squadron's flight commanders, Flight Lieutenant D.C. Laubman, D.F.C. (later Lieutenant General Laubman, Chief of Personnel, Canadian Armed Forces), was credited with four Me 109s destroyed and two damaged during the day's fighting.

The Falcons exchanged their Spitfire LF Mk IXBs for LF Mk IXEs on 28 September. Their new aircraft had a pair of 20 mm cannon and two .50 calibre machine guns in place of the two 20 mm cannon and four .303 calibre machine guns in the Mk IXBs. The heavier-armed Spitfires were flown the next day when a 412 patrol ran into 50 or more FW 190s; three of the enemy were destroyed with no losses.

During September, the Squadron logged 658 hours while flying 408 sorties and, on four days alone - the 25th, 26th, 27th, and 29th - destroyed 29 enemy aircraft and damaged 10, losing two pilots.

A lull in October checked this rapid pace and gave the Squadron a little time to settle into its new quarters. There still was plenty of action, however, with 401 Squadron destroying an Me 262 on 5 October. It was thought to be the first enemy jet shot down by any RAF or RCAF squadron. This gave the 412 pilots plenty to talk about.

October saw the Squadron on the move again. On 4 October the Falcons moved their base to B84, a grass strip at Rips in the Netherlands where it immediately resumed Arnhem-Nijmegen patrols. Bad weather and airfield unserviceability hampered flying, so the Squadron saw little action until the end of the month.

On 14 October 1944, the Squadron moved its base again, this time to B80, Volkel, the Netherlands, resuming operations the next day. On 18 October the Squadron Spitfires began carrying 1,000 pound bomb loads - one 500-pounder under the fuselage and a 250-pounder under each wing. On that day, two bombing attacks were made in squadron strength on a rail junction near Coesfeld, Germany, and another on a rail bridge over the Dortmund-Ems canal. On such rail target attacks, the pilots, after having released their bombs, sought targets of opportunity to strafe before returning to base. The score on that day counted three locomotives damaged, three METs destroyed and three more damaged.

Bombing of the enemy's rail system continued through the remainder of the month with the 28th seeing October's first major action. The Squadron flew nine separate bombing operations, with Pilot Officer W.C. Busby joining aces Laubman and Charron on the kill scoreboard; between them they destroyed four enemy fighters and counted one "probable."

On 3 November, the Squadron moved to Warmwell, Dorset, for an air-firing course, returning to Volkel on the 13th, but the pilots were not able to fly back until the 18th due to bad weather.

One of the Squadron's worst days came on the 19th of November. Nine separate bombing attacks on rail targets were flown during the day. Each attack was flown by four Spitfires with a 1,000-pound payload. In the Bocholt area, a whole section of 412 pilots was wiped out. Flying Officers J.W. Johnston, W.H. Bellingham and the stalwart F/L Charron were all killed while WO1 J.A. Comeau was severely wounded, later losing his right leg by amputation.

The Squadron continued to concentrate on dive bombing the enemy's rail systems throughout the remainder of the month. Flying Officer F.T. Murray was credited with the month's sole victory during a patrol over Venlo on 26 November.

On 5 December 1944 the Squadron flew 34 sorties, claiming two enemy aircraft destroyed and three probably destroyed. On 6 December the squadron moved to Heesech, the Netherlands, for the winter and continued to run up its tally of enemy aircraft as they were encountered. But victories would not be without a price tag. Flight Lieutenant R.N. Earle, one of the squadron's outstanding pilots, was killed by flak that month and Flying Officer D.W. Glithero became a P.O.W. for the rest of the war.

On the 14th of December, two enemy fighters were destroyed and another damaged by Falcon fighters. The day's victories put 412 Squadron in first place within the 2nd Tactical Air Force in regard to enemy aircraft shot down or damaged.

The winter quarters at Heesch were a former workers camp near Nijmegen. The airstrip had been hastily constructed on porous sandy soil. However, wooden barracks provided a degree of comfort that had been unachievable in the previous tent villages.

About this time many of 126 Wing were having encounters with some of Hitler's "Wonder Weapons," in particular the jets, Me 262 and 163. Flight Lieutenant C.W. Fox recorded in his logbook having sighted an ME 262 on 30 September 1944. The ME 262 had first been placed into service as a jet bomber in August 1944, but not to good effect. It was later used as a fighter, but too late to have any effect on the outcome of the war. The Me 163, also known as the Komet, did see limited use against daylight bomber raids in 1944, but they were no great menace to either the bombers or the escort fighters, the reason being that they were simply too fast and too poorly armed to deliver a lethal cone of fire except at a self-destruct range.

During the middle two weeks of December 1944, almost the whole European continent was blanketed by low cloud and fog. Little or no flying was possible, as even the bomber and fighter forces based in the U.K. were unable to move. On 16 December the Germans launched a counter-offensive against the Allies whose front had been left thin in the Ardennes region. The attack, directed by Von Rundstedt, was a desperate attempt to split the Allied armies and disrupt their supply system by capturing Liege and Antwerp. The attack caught the Allies by surprise and, aided by the lack of opposition by Allied air forces made possible by the bad weather, the German penetration had become so deep that by 19 December, communications had become impaired. U.S. troops on the northern part of the salient were placed under Montgomery's command. By Christmas the weather improved, the Allies recovered, and by 25 January 1945 the original front had been re-established. The effect of the German effort was a delay in the Allied operations of perhaps six weeks and a great loss to the Germans of personnel and material.

Von Rundstedt's counter-offensive in the Ardennes, later called the "Battle of the Bulge", would change 412's missions for the remainder of the month as fighters flew sweeps over the battle area and armed reconnaissances behind the German positions, strafing road and rail transports. During the month, the squadron logged 567 hours (424 sorties) tallying rail and other ground targets plus 14 enemy aircraft destroyed, probably destroyed or damaged for the loss of two pilots.

412 Squadron had ended the year with the opportunity to look back with pride on the accomplishments of the previous years. However, the Luftwaffe was ever-present and on New Year's Day, 1945, they attempted to catch Allied airmen off guard by attacking airfields of the Netherlands and Belgium in force. RCAF wings in Eindhoven, Evere and Heesch sustained losses in aircraft and personnel, but took a heavy toll on the enemy.

The Falcons, however, sustained no damage to their aircraft on the ground and were able to mount three fighter sweeps and 29 sorties. During the day, 40 enemy aircraft were destroyed and at least a dozen more probably destroyed or damaged. 412 Squadron alone netted seven, all fighters except for one Ju 88, for the loss of one pilot. The victors were Squadron Leader D.H. Dover, Flight Lieutenants J.B. Doak, B.E. MacPherson, W.J. Banks, J.A. Swan and Flying Officers V. Smith and E.D. Kelly.

During the next three weeks of the new year, inclement weather permitted a mere eight days of flying. When 412 finally did get back into action, there was a tragic loss of an entire section of four aircraft. On the 20th, the section failed to return from an armed reconnaissance flown in squadron strength over the Munste-Emmerich-Osnabruck-Lingen area. Bad weather forced 412 to patrol down to 500 feet as it was returning to base, and the Spitfires were fired at by light anti-aircraft guns in the Nijmegen area. The one section climbed into cloud and was thereafter not sighted. Later it was learned that all four had been forced down within enemy territory: F/L MacPherson, Pilot Officers B.S. McPhee and W.J. Walkom, and F/L F.H. Richards disappeared in snow flurries. The first three respectively, became POWs at Stalag Luft XIII. F/L Richards, knocked down by flak, was slightly wounded but made his way back in April with the aid of the Dutch resistance.

Dive-bombing and armed recce operations, unopposed but for occasional flak, continued throughout the month. Usually six aircraft composed a section for dive-bombing operations, and 500-pound bombs were carried. The 45-gallon extra fuel tanks were often used and afforded valuable added range. Although the fuel tanks tended to render the aircraft a little less manoeuvrable, this was unimportant due to the relative absence of enemy fighters.

Throughout February and most of March 1945, the Falcons returned to dive bombing the enemy's rail system while flying armed reconnaissances, fighter sweeps and patrols. Two pilots, Pilot Officer L. Dunkleman and Flying Officer A.T. Gibb, were brought down by flak on 11 February. Both made their way back to safety unharmed. Engine failure claimed the life of Pilot Officer Cowan on the 22nd when he was within only six miles of

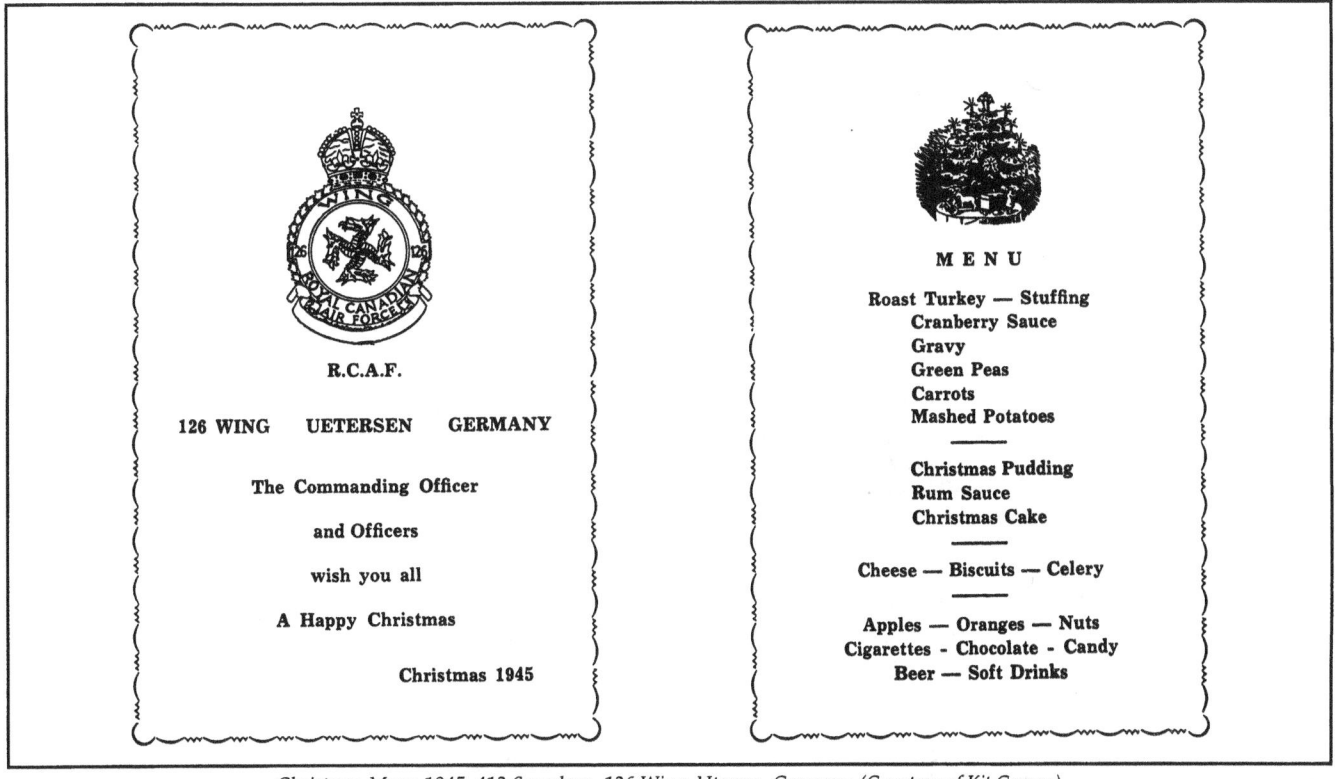

Christmas Menu 1945, 412 Squadron, 126 Wing, Utersen, Germany. (Courtesy of Kit Carson)

the base. During February, F/L C. Fox, who had recently completed his tour with the Falcons, received a bar to the DFC that he had previously won with them. F/L Banks also was honoured.

Over the Rhine . . .

The Squadron was released for 24-hour periods in March on several occasions as part of the wing's policy of restricted flying. Only twice that month was the Luftwaffe encountered; 412 Squadron knocked down five aircraft. With the successful completion of the first stage of the Rhine crossing, 412's role became armed reconnaissance aimed at harrying transportation and disrupting communications. Subsequent operations were conducted in the Dorsten-Haltern-Ham-Munster area with very favourable results; the Squadron logged 601 operational sorties in March, twice the February score.

German resistance was crumbling by April, but that didn't mean a slowdown for 412. On the contrary, the month was one of the busiest with 642 sorties. For the first six days of the month, the Falcons flew six patrols and through the following weeks concentrated on armed recces over Germany.

April also saw the move of the Squadron base onto German soil for the first time. The Falcons first went to B108 at Rheine on 12 April and then to B116 at the old Luftwaffe permanent air station in Wunstorf on the 15th. Already 412 Squadron was enjoying the spoils of war; the leaky tents and Spartan accommodations of the previous residences gave way to brick buildings, crystal chandeliers, bowling alleys, and wine cellars. The accommodations made the war seem farther away. However, the move enabled 412 Spitfires to mount a round of armed recces that took a heavy toll on rail, road, and other targets. The move into Germany also brought a lengthy list of enemy aircraft claims, following a relatively lean three-and-a-half month period.

On 19 April, five armed recces were flown over the battle area and during one of these, a patrol of 11 Falcon Spitfires engaged half a dozen FW 190s over Hagenow airfield, destroying four.

Flak was the major enemy, with road convoys throwing up heavy barrages to protect themselves; railway flak cars were particularly dangerous. In addition, the Germans had set up camouflaged flak traps in the fields, often baiting them with dummy aircraft. Flak brought down Flight Lieutenants W.J. Anderson, who was killed, and W.R. James, who was taken prisoner of war, at the end of March. But as the squadron began to operate closer and closer to Allied lines, the chances increased that if one had to hit the silk, one could return to the squadron. Flying Officer V. Smith and Flight Lieutenants B. Barker and L.A. Stewart were brought down, only to be back with 412 in a matter of hours.

The accurate pinpointing of Flying Officer G.N. Horter's crash on 28 April 1945 made possible a spectacular rescue. After his plane had been damaged, F/O Horter "had ridden it down" in No Man's Land about two miles southeast of Marschaht. At first the other members of his section thought he was a goner, for upon landing, the jettison tank of the plane caught fire, leaving a 50-foot trail of flame before the aircraft blew up. The Operations Record Book reveals, "It is strongly believed that he was instantly killed, unless he was miraculously thrown clear." They were wrong. Two days later, the squadron medical officer, Flight Lieutenant E. McAllister, arrived on the scene and found Horter still strapped in the cockpit, wounded, but semi-conscious. An army unit nearby had seen the crash and the aircraft in flames but "were not anxious to investigate," explaining that snipers in the area had earlier caused the deaths of a lieutenant and a sergeant.

Flying Officer Horter's life was saved by the Squadron's loyal concern for its own and by the fact that he had not been thrown clear. In his injured state he would surely not have been able to keep his head above water in the deep pool nearby, where he most likely would have landed.

On 29 April 1945, airmen guarding the Squadron's aircraft were surprised when a Ju 52 landed at the airfield during the early hours of the morning, and a crew of five gave themselves up. The event was indicative of the winding-down of the war; even many of the Germans saw defeat as imminent. When Flight Lieutenant J.G. Burchill was hit by flak and forced to bail out, he fell into Nazi hands and was held prisoner at Handorf airfield. One of the guards, with an eye to the future, helped him escape, hid him in an air raid shelter and contacted 9th USAAF troops.

"He had fed me and kept up a continuous recce during this period." Burchill would later report to the intelligence officers, describing the couple of days in which he hid from the Germans in their own camp. "I signed a paper for him."

The April tally was 13 enemy aircraft destroyed and two damaged. Ground targets included 52 MET destroyed and 147 damaged, two locomotives annihilated and 12 disabled, 15 trains blown up and 60 damaged, three horse-drawn transports destroyed and seven damaged, one ferry boat wiped out and two tanks demolished.

The end was near, and as pilots continued to mount impressive "kills," the ground and servicing crews performed better. An average of 79 percent of the aircraft was kept ready for use at all times. In any estimate of the factors directly contributing to the Squadron's enviable place among the top fighter units, all pilots would give an enormous amount of credit to the ground crews who "Kept 'em flying."

In functioning under mobile field conditions, the servicing crews worked wonders and earned the highest praise. Lacking the glamour of the pilots, and some of the amenities and privileges afforded to their officers, these "erks" nonetheless worked with high efficiency.

Flying Officer D.M. Pieri, DFC, one of 412's outstanding pilots, was brought down by flak northeast of Hamburg on 3 May. He became the squadron's last wartime casualty. Pieri had three-and-a-half enemy aircraft destroyed to his credit while with 412, plus another two-and-a-half scored with another squadron.

The Falcons only operated during the first four days of May, flying a few hours on armed reconnaissances and patrols. The end of the war in Europe was happening quickly. At 0241 hours on 7 May 1945, the surrender was signed by German General Alfred Jodl, to become effective at midnight 8-9 May. The act was ratified at Berlin on the night of 9 May. The collapse of Nazi Germany was complete, and 412 Squadron had played a large part in that collapse.

Finally, word was received that the Third Reich had been toppled. For 412 Squadron and other Allied servicemen, that meant a brief period of rejoicing and celebration. But even after the war, the Falcons were to lose two more pilots. Pilot Officer J.E. Taylor was fatally injured on 1 June 1945, in a high-level bombing practice at Warmwell, and Flight Lieutenant J. MacKay was seriously injured in a crash-landing while on course at RAF Station Sylt, Germany, on 19 December 1945.

412 Squadron had claimed an impressive 109 enemy aircraft destroyed, 11 probably destroyed and 41 damaged. The list of ground targets hit by Falcon bombs and bullets was equally impressive: thousands of enemy transport vehicles, locomotives, rail cars, flak cars, barges, and armoured vehicles were destroyed. In all, more than 200 tons of bombs were dropped.

The victories were not without a high toll, however. 412 Squadron lost 57 pilots, and another pilot was killed in a flying accident after V-E Day; 49 of those lost were killed and 15 of those posted as missing survived as POW's or evaders. The fate of one missing pilot, the USAAF officer, was never determined.

Post-War...

412 Fighter Squadron, with other units of 126 Wing, moved after V-E Day to Fassberg, Germany, one of the largest and most comfortable aerodromes in Germany. In July, they moved to Utersen, near Hamburg, as part of the British Air Forces of Occupation.

During this time, many of the pilots were able to take advantage of flying some of the captured German aircraft. Some of the reactions to the aircraft were not always favourable. In Flight Lieutenant C.W. Fox's Pilot's Flying Log Book, he remarked after flying a FW 190, that it had a noisy motor and was lousy to land; however, "It was nice for low flying." He was also able to fly a Me 108, which was a trainer. Fox's reaction was that it was a "nice all-metal plane."

Other pilots were able to try other types of fighters and light planes. Everything that followed was anti-climactic. The burning question in everyone's mind was, "When does everyone go home?"

Homeward Bound...

On 19 March 1946, 18 Spitfires were returned to the RAF. They were flown direct from Utersen, Germany to Manston Airfield in England and then - after refuelling and Customs inspection - inland to Collerne Airfield. The pilots proceeded first to London and then to Topfield, Yorkshire by train. Finally they boarded the Ile de France Passenger Liner for Canada. Goodbye Spitfires!

FLYING WITH 412 (F) SQN
by Bill Burley, Pilot, 1944-45

I joined the Squadron during the Battle of the Falaise Gap. After that was over, we chased the Germans back to Germany with little contact with fighters, except for the few days excitement around Arnhem and Nijmegen when our boys got a few in September 1944. The Germans were saving their fighters to attack the American day bombers according to books I have read about American fighter pilots. Of course, the German fighters took one last crack at us on New Year's day of 1945 when they beat up on Brussels and Eindhoven airports.

From August of 1944 to the end of the war, it was just routine patrols, dive bombing and armed recces (strafing anything that moved). For example, I took part in 160 sorties for about 204 hours and we never lost a pilot or aircraft on any of them. Except that I pancaked one near Eindhoven when I ran out of fuel after chasing a German back into Germany from Arnhem - "Tough luck!" I finished my tour in May and the Germans gave up the next day.

Two thrilling events for me were the trip into Paris the day after it was liberated. We had the day off and F/L Mo McPherson took four of us into Paris in his jeep. The crowds were cheering everyone in uniform as they rode through - and when I rode through London the day after "V" day and the crowds were celebrating as they had in Paris. 412 Squadron did its part to help make both events possible.

412 Fighter Squadron Pilots-May 1945. **Standing (L to R):** *F/O L. Dunkleman, F/L R. Hazel, F/L R. Barker, F/L C. Johnson, F/O D. Murchie, F/L D. Dewan, S/L D. Boyd, F/L J. Trist, F/O G. Marshall, F/O A. Gibb, W/O H. David, F/O H. Grant.* **Sitting on aircraft:** *P/O J. Taylor, P/O J. Sutherland, F/O M. Lepard, F/O R. Carew, W/O I. MacDonald, F/O V. Smith, F/L H. MacLean, F/O P. Lapoint, F/O J. Allen, F/O A. Keats, F/O F. Roberts.*

In Memory of John Magee
Holy Cross Parish Church
Scopwick, Lincolnshire
by The Reverend Gerald Smith, Vicar
P/O John Magee, RCAF

It is almost two years since a small plot of ground in our church graveyard here in this small village was suddenly thrown into the world spotlight and millions became aware, myself included, of the location of the grave of young John Magee.

I had just been appointed to this living and suddenly sat up as a grave in Scopwick appeared briefly on the television screen. It was the day after "Challenger" blew up, and President Reagan had quoted "High Flight," and suddenly John Magee achieved a kind of immortality which so few achieve, and then, more often than not, by circumstance, rather than by their own achievements, which, in the case of John Magee were not inconsiderable, albeit he did but live nineteen years.

It is not for me to recall the brief, but moving history of this young poet and flier who, if anything, belonged to an age now all but obliterated. His conflict and the ethos of his writing looked to Rupert Brook and an era which was, at the very moment of his death, being erased for ever.

There is no way I can briefly encompass this - which Ivan Henson has gathered together in incredible detail - to a degree which makes one realize the enormous task which faces all historians. If such a huge collection of material exists on a young man of nineteen, how much more is there to sift through on the life of a person of age and substance, no matter how little "known?"

As Ivan has pointed out to me, John Magee was, and is, far better known in the United States and Canada when he returned to the UK to fly in the war after schooling at Rugby. He was then already a prolific poet and his death was given media coverage across the Atlantic to a degree unknown in this country in time of war.

The "Challenger" disaster revived, if you like, or newly kindled, a world-wide interest in John's story and in particular his poem "High Flight."

Ivan kindly let me have a copy of the original manuscript of the poem now in the Library of Congress. We have had an extract of "High Flight" in our Church Porch for some time. But, to Ivan, an extract was less than John deserves at the place at which and from where he was buried. His funeral was here, at Scopwick Church, on Saturday 13th December, 1941 at 2:30 p.m. I have here the Order of Parade, although I still have to research the service and burial registers for the service in the Diocesan Archives. Ivan has suggested, and it is a timely suggestion, that quite a number of people visit Scopwick to see the War Graves, and now to see John's grave in particular, and they more often than not arrive at the Church first to find that the grave and graves are, apparently, not here. We know that they are - but in the new Graveyard - and Ivan suggests a public signpost to the Graveyard and War Graves. In due course I hope the Parish Council can follow this up and see to the provision of such a signpost or signposts.

But, Ivan, being the sort of person he is, hasn't stopped at making suggestions. He would like to make a more permanent exhibition of John Magee's background in the village, possibly in the Village Hall and he has made a start on this by beginning where John's funeral was held - here in this church. To this end he has presented us with a magnificent hand-scrolled, framed copy of John Magee's poem, "High Flight", to be displayed in church. He has it with him now and in a moment I will ask him to present it and show it to us. For our part I can assure him that we will see that it is properly and safely displayed here, with a suitable explanatory notice, which will also direct enquirers to the Graveyard. Those of you who are visitors should know that the church is open every day from about 9:00 am to 5:00 p.m.

Battle Honours

Defence of Britain
1940 - 1945

For interception operations subsequent to the Battle of Britain in defence of Great Britain and Northern Ireland against enemy aircraft and flying bombs.

Fortress Europe
1941 - 1944

For operations by aircraft based in the British Isles, against targets in Germany, Italy, and enemy-occupied Europe from the fall of France to the invasion of Normandy.

Dieppe

For squadrons which participated in the combined operation against Dieppe on 19 August 1944.

Arnhem

For squadrons participating in the operation of the Allied Airborne Army (17 to 26 September 1944).

English Channel and North Sea
1942 -1943

For ship attack, anti-submarine and mining operations over the English Channel and North Sea from the outbreak of War to VE Day.

France and Germany
1944-1945

For operations over France, Belgium, Holland and Germany during the liberation of Northwest Europe and the advance into the enemy's homeland from initiation of air action preparatory to the invasion of France to VE Day.

Normandy
1944

For operations supporting the Allied landings in Normandy, establishment of the lodgement area, and the subsequent "break-through."

Rhine

For operations in support of the battle for the Rhine crossing, 8 February to 24 March 1945.

412 Fighter Squadron

Officers Commanding & Commanding Officers

Squadron Leader C.W. Trevena
30 Jun 1941 - 11 Nov 1941
Squadron Leader J.D. Morrison
12 Nov 1941 - 24 Mar 1942
Squadron Leader R.C. Weston
1 Apr 1942 - 27 Jul 1942
Squadron Leader C.J. Fee, DFC
28 Jul 1942 - 26 Nov 1942
Squadron Leader F.W. Kelly, DFC
27 Nov 1942 - 24 Jun 1943
Squadron Leader G.C. Keefer, DFC & Bar
25 Jun 1943 - 11 Apr 1944
Squadron Leader J.E. Sheppard, DFC
12 Apr 1944 - 1 Aug 1944 (MIA)
Squadron Leader D.H. Dover, DFC & Bar
2 Aug 1944 - 28 Jan 1945
Squadron Leader M.D. Boyd, DFC
29 Jan 1945 - 29 May 1945
Squadron Leader D.J. Dewan, AFC
30 May 1945 - 21 Mar 1946

Squadron Bases

Digby Lines	30 Jun 1941 - 20 Oct 1941
Wellingoore, Lincs	20 Oct 1941 - 1 May 1942
Martlesham Heath, Suffolk	1 May 1942 - 3 Jun 1942
North Weald, Essex	3 Jun 1942 - 18 Jun 1942
Marston, Sussex	18 Jun 1942 - 10 Aug 1942
Martlesham Heath, Suffolk1	Aug 1942 - 14 Aug 1942
Marston, Sussex	14 Aug 1942 - 23 Aug 1942
Tangmere, Sussex	23 Aug 1942 - 23 Sep 1942
Redhill, Surrey	23 Sep 1942 - 7 Jan 1943

All pilots and 80% of ground crew at Kenley, Surrey, 1 to 25 Nov 1942 - Redhill airfield unserviceable during this period because of heavy rain. All pilots, serviceable aircraft and 50% of ground crew at Friston, Sussex, 18 Dec 1942 to 5 Jan 1943 - Same reason. Pilots and groundcrew proceeded from Friston to Kenley 5 Jan 1943.

Kenley, Surrey	7 Jan 1943 - 29 Jan 1943
Angle, Pembroke	29 Jan 1943 - 8 Feb 1943
Fairwood Common, Glamorgan	8 Feb 1943 - 12 Apr 1943
Perranporth, Cornwall	12 Apr 1943 - 21 Jun 1943
Friston, Sussex	21 Jun 1943 - 13 Jul 1943
Redhill, Surrey	13 Jul 1943 - 7 Aug 1943
Staplehurst, Kent	7 Aug 1943 - 13 Oct 1943
Biggin Hill, Kent	13 Oct 1943 - 6 Jan 1944
Hutton Cranswick, Yorks	6 Jan 1944 - 20 Jan 1944
Fairwood Common, Glamorgan	30 Mar 1944 - 7 Apr 1944
Biggin Hill, Kent	7 Apr 1944 - 15 Apr 1944
Tangmere, Sussex	15 Apr 1944 - 18 Jun 1944
B.4 - Beny-Sur-Mer, France	18 Jun 1944 - 8 Aug 1944
B.18 - Cristot, France	8 Aug 1944 - 1 Sep 1944

Bases continued ...

B.24 - St. Andre de l'Eure, France	1 Sep 1944 - 2 Sep 1944
B.26 - Illiers-Marcilly la Campagne	2 Sep 1944 - 3 Sep 1944
B.44 - Poix, France	3 Sep 1944 - 6 Sep 1944
B.56 - Evere, Belgium	7 Sep 1944 - 21 Sep 1944
B.68 - Le Culot, Belgium	21 Sep 1944 - 4 Oct 1944
B.84 - Rips, Netherlands	4 Oct 1944 - 14 Oct 1944
B.80 - Volkel, Netherlands	14 Oct 1944 - 3 Nov 1944
Warmell, Dorset	3 Nov 1944 - 13 Nov 1944
B.80 - Volkel, Netherlands	13 Nov 1944 - 6 Dec 1944
B.88 - Heesch, Netherlands	6 Dec 1944 - 12 Apr 1945
B.108 - Rheine, Germany	12 Apr 1945 - 15 Apr 1945
B.116 - Wunstorf, Germany	15 Apr 1945 - 13 May 1945
Warmell, Dorset	13 May 1945 - 6 Jun 1945
B.152 - Fassberg, Germany	7 Jun 1945 - 5 Jul 1945
B.174 - Utersen, Germany	5 Jul 1945 - 7 Dec 1945
Sylt, Germany	7 Dec 1945 - 24 Dec 1945
B.174 - Utersen, Germany	24 Dec 1945 - 21 Mar 1946

Squadron Aircraft
30 Jun 1941 - 21 Mar 1946

Spitfire 2A	Jul 1941 - Oct 1941
Spitfire 5B	Oct 1941 - Nov 1943
Spitfire 9B	Nov 1943 - Sep 1944
Spitfire 9E	Sep 1944 - May 1945
Spitfire 16	May 1945 - Jun 1945
Spitfire 14E	Jun 1945 - Mar 1946

Squadron Honours And Awards

Seventeen Distinguished Flying Crosses, seven bars to that decoration, one Air Force Cross and four Mentions in Despatches were awarded to members of the Squadron.

S/L C.J. Fee, DFC and Bar
S/L G.C. Keefer, DFC and Bar
S/L D.H. Dover, DFC and Bar
F/L D.C. Laubman, DFC and Bar
F/L C.W. Fox, DFC and Bar
F/L W.J. Banks, DFC and Bar
F/O D.R.C. Jamieson, DFC and Bar
S/L M.D. Boyd, DFC
S/L J.L. Fee, DFC
S/L F.W. Kelly, DFC
F/L F.E. Green, DFC
F/L R.A. Ellis, DFC
F/L R.B. Barker, DFC
F/L D.M. Pieri, DFC
F/L R.A.I. Smith, DFC
F/O L.F. Berryman, DFC
F/O L.W. Powell, DFC
S/L D.J. Dewan, AFC

Squadron Badge

In September 1944, His Majesty the late King George VI approved the 412 Squadron Badge. The Badge has as its central device a Falcon colant. The Falcon was selected to represent 412 Squadron as it is a bird indigenous to all parts of Canada. Known for its skill and aggressiveness in dealing with its enemies, it has been used for hunting from an early date in history. The Squadron motto appearing on the badge is "Promptus Ad Vindictam," "Swift to Avenge."

Squadron Standard

On 25 September 1964, the Squadron Standard was presented to 412 Squadron by the Honourable W. Earl Rowe, Lieutenant Governor of the Province of Ontario. No. 412 Squadron was the first Regular Force Squadron to celebrate the twenty-fifth year of continuous service and thus received its Standard. The 412 Squadron Standard bears the maximum possible number of eight Battle Honours.

SQUADRON WORLD WAR II CODE LETTERS
VZ (··· – – ··)

412 Squadron Badge

412 Squadron Standard

Three of the 412 Squadron pilots who went to London for training courses in 1958 on the Napier Eland engine (the original engine on the CC109.) 412 pilots from left: 2nd from left George Dungey, 3rd from left: Chuck Lockwood, 5th from left: Bob Decher. (Courtesy of Chuck Lockwood.)

Group of ex-412 Sqn pilots attending a Canadian Fighter Pilot Association reunion held in Ottawa in 1983. Left to right: Al Keats, Bob Walcom, George Keefer, Arnold Gibb, Barry Needham, Lloyd Stewart, Rod Smith, Joseph Richards, Bill Bliss, Dewy Dewan, Dean Kelly, Moe McPherson, Dean Dover, Dave Boyd, Murray Lepard and Fred Green.

412 Transport Squadron

A New Career

VIP Transport
A New Career

On 1 April 1947, No. 12 Communications Squadron, which had operated out of Rockcliffe since 10 September 1939, was reorganized to place more emphasis on the unit's transport responsibilities. In June 1955, after a record 16 years of tenure at the same Rockcliffe station, the Squadron moved to Uplands, its new home base, where its aircraft were to fly to all parts of the globe.

In the post-war reorganization of the Royal Canadian Air Force (RCAF) it was thought that 412 (Fighter) Squadron should not fade away into the history books of the RCAF. Number 12 Communications Squadron had achieved such success in the air transport field that it was selected to perpetuate the name of 412 (Fighter) Squadron. On 1 April 1947, it was re-designated 412 (Composite) Squadron, its name reflecting a dual purpose of providing air transport and training. The training role was deleted on 1 April 1949. Having dropped its functions of providing practice flying facilities for AFHQ and AMCHQ a year and a half previously, the unit assumed its present identity, 412 (Transport) Squadron, and became a unit of Air Transport Command.

Thus began a new career for 412, which had distinguished itself during World War II as one of the best-known units in the Royal Canadian Air Force. International developments during the post-war years greatly increased the transport commitments of the RCAF as a whole, and of 412 in particular. The passenger manifests have included royalty, Governors-General, Prime Ministers, statesmen, distinguished military leaders and others who

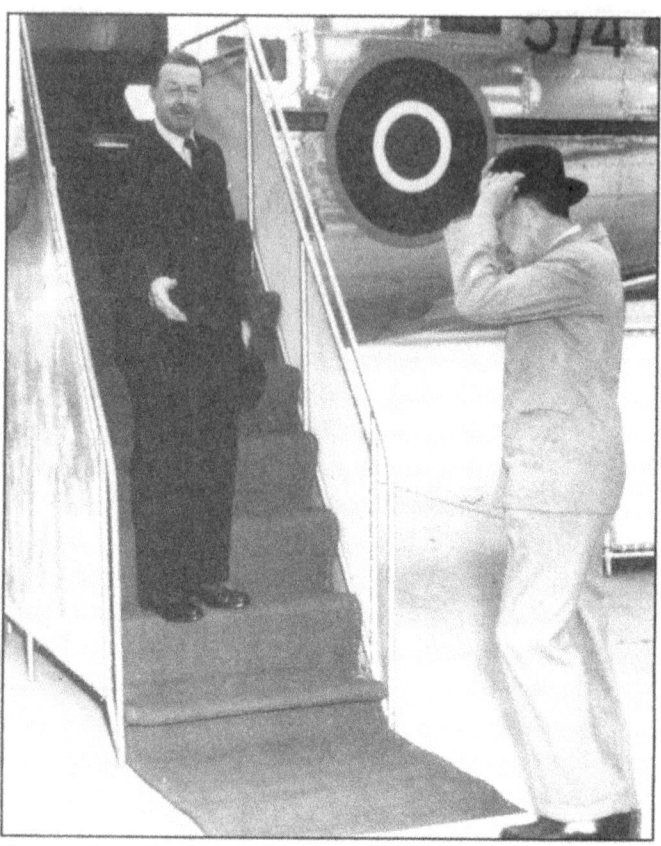

Governor General Lord Alexander of Tunis returning from a trip on the 412 (T) Sqn. Liberator No. 574, Spring 1946.

*Arrival back at RCAF Station Rockcliffe, Ontario in September 1946 are: **L to R:** June Olsen, Stuart Olsen, Eve Reeves and Bill Reeves. They served during the one-month tour of Canada with Field Marshal Bernard Montgomery who visited most Canadian cities to honour Canadians who served in World War II. (Courtesy of Stuart Olsen)*

have had great impact in world affairs. The notables who have been entrusted to its care have been Her Royal Highness Queen Elizabeth II and H.R.H. Prince Phillip, H.R.H. Princess Margaret, H.R.H. Prince Charles and others of the Royal Family. Also, Sir Winston Churchill, Sir Anthony Eden, The Right Honourable Vincent Massey, Field Marshall The Viscount Montgomery of El Alamein, Secretary-General of NATO Paul Henri Spaak, Marshall of the Royal Air Force Sir John Slessor, Bob Hope and many others have been passengers on the Falcons.

New Responsibilities

With the changes to Air Transport Command came broader air transport responsibilities. In 1946, the squadron made its first VIP intercontinental trip — a Dakota flight to South America. In June 1947, a squadron Liberator aircraft flew to Nanking, China, the squadron's maiden trans-Pacific flight. Its first trans-Atlantic crossing was the following April. In April of 1949, the squadron acquired its first North Star. Thereafter, intercontinental flights became routine. A North Star took off from Rockcliffe in January 1950 on the first round-the-world flight. The distinguished passenger aboard was the Honourable Lester B. Pearson, the Minister of External Affairs then attending the Commonwealth Foreign Ministers Conference in Ceylon.

The 'one and only' C5 aircraft, number 10,000, joined the squadron on 21 June 1950. Similar to the North Star, but slightly larger and powered with radial engines instead of in-line, the C5 was especially fitted for the transport of distinguished passengers both in Canada and abroad. In the summer of 1958, the squadron transported H.R.H. Princess Margaret on her cross-

Prime Minister Winston Churchill departs for Washington on a C5 in 1954. (Courtesy of 412 (T) Squadron)

Governor General Vincent Massey on his Canadian-Arctic Tour, March 1956. (Courtesy of Robert Cameron)

*Fifteenth birthday celebrations for the "Charlie 5" held at Uplands, June 21, 1965. Pictured second from right is Sgt. Beauchamp who was called out of retirement for the occasion. **L to R:** F/S Mignault, Uplands Base CDR, Sgt. Beauchamp and F/L Budgeon.*

Canada tour in the C5. It was also used by Queen Elizabeth II and Prince Philip during their famous Canadian tour in 1959. The C5 retired on 30 April 1966 after many outstanding years of service.

With the acquisition of the deHavilland Comet aircraft on 29 May 1953, the squadron entered the pure jet transport field and pioneered the operation of pure jet transport aircraft across the Atlantic Ocean. The Comet was the first jet transport in the Royal Canadian Air Force.

By the summer of 1955, the squadron aircraft had outgrown the airfield facilities at Rockcliffe and a move was made to Station Uplands, thus ending residence at Rockcliffe.

The tradition of presenting a Squadron Standard began in 1943, when His Majesty King George VI graciously observed the 25th anniversary of the Royal Air Force by proclaiming that all Squadrons, upon their 25th anniversary, would be entitled to be presented with a Squadron Standard. In 1958, this honour and privilege was extended to Squadrons of the Royal Canadian Air Force.

On 25 September 1964, the Honourable W. Earl Rowe, Lieutenant Governor of Ontario, presented the Squadron Standard to 412 Squadron. While four Squadrons of the R.C.A.F. Auxiliary had been previously honoured (400, 401, 402 and 424) 412 Squadron became the first Regular Force Squadron to celebrate 25 years of continuous service and thus received its Standard. The Squadron Standard was received by Wing Commander M.G. Bryan, Officer Commanding 412 Squadron. W/C Bryan's acceptance speech follows :

*Ottawa Airport and RCAF Station Uplands. **Crew (top to bottom):** Flt./Lt. Ralf Herbert (Pilot); Lt. Don Stewart (Navigator); Flt./Lt. Russ Chalk (Radio Operator); Squadron Leader Stuart Olsen (Pilot); and Honourable Brooke Claxton. Two Comet 1A aircraft were purchased by Canadian National Defence in 1953. This is the first one to be delivered to Canada and No. 412 Squadron, it was the first jet Transport Aircraft to be operated in North America. (Courtesy of S. Olsen)*

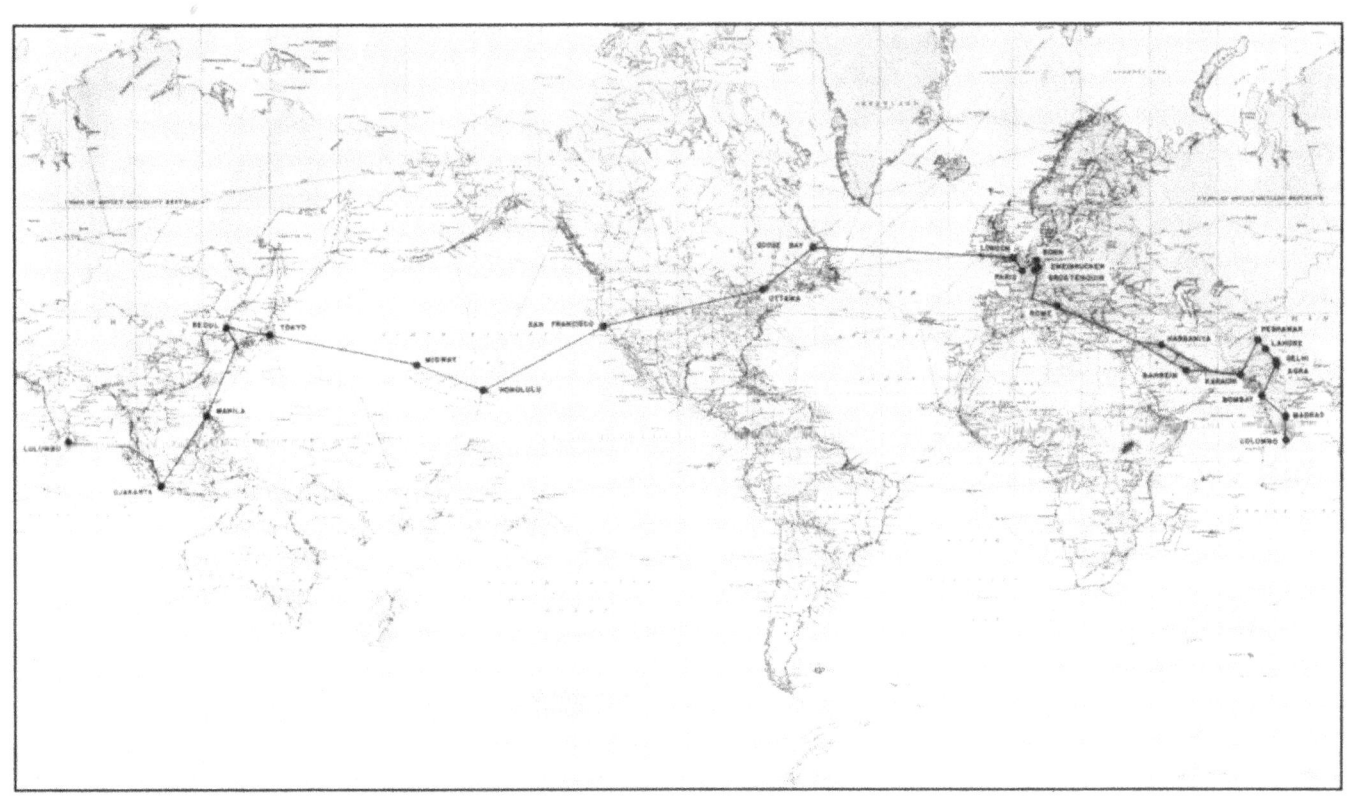

Route of the first Round-the-World flight by the 412 Sqn. January 2, 1950.

Quote: The Honourable W. Earl Rowe;
The Honourable Paul T. Hellyer;
Air Chief Marshall Miller;
Air Commodore Lane;
Group Captain Gillespie;
Honoured Guests;
Ladies and Gentlemen

It is with deep and humble pride that we, the present members of 412 Squadron, Royal Canadian Air Force, accept our Squadron Standard on behalf of all members of the Squadron-- past, present, and indeed future.
In accepting our Standard for safekeeping and safeguarding, to be handed on to airmen who will succeed us, we are most mindful of the fine traditions and heritage that have been founded so well by those who have preceded us over the past 25 years of continuous service by the Squadron.
We acknowledge our debt to them; we are proud to join their ranks.
In this era of troubled peace we, as are all members of the Royal Canadian Air Force, dedicated to the cause of maintaining world peace. Thus, we fervently hope that no future occasion will arise that need bring about the placement of further Battle Honours on our Squadron Standard.
If, however, our efforts for peace prove to be in vain, then we pray that with the help of God, we will have the necessary skills, personal fortitude, and courage to meet any challenge that may confront us to ensure that the Standard of 412 Squadron continues to fly victorious with pride and honour.
Thank you.
Unquote

Comet crew at Baalbeck, Syria, 1953. **Front:** *F/Ls A. James, J. Menton, H. Wright, unidentified.* **Back:** *R. Edwards, T.M. Hall, L.W. Hussey, unidentified, R.W. Lloyd. (Courtesy of R.M. Edwards)*

Wing Commander Jim Borden signs over the command of 412 (Transport) Squadron to Wing Commander Mel Bryan; RCAF Station Uplands; August 1963.

Centennial Year, 1967, was particularly noteworthy because of the primary role the Squadron played in the airlift of visiting representatives from more than 50 countries. As a special Centennial project, a Yukon from the Squadron flew over the North Pole, dropping a Canadian flag to mark the country's 100th birthday. The Yukon flight on 25 August 1968 was the last mission flown by this aircraft with the Squadron.

With the departure of the Yukons, and owing to the limited range of the remaining Cosmopolitan aircraft, the Squadron became almost exclusively North American-oriented. Global missions were once again made possible by the acquisition in 1969 of seven Falcons to complement the Cosmopolitan fleet. The Falcon allowed 412 to again offer service worldwide. Both aircraft have continued to break new ground for their types with trips into the Canadian Arctic, Africa, Middle East, Europe, Asia, the Caribbean and South America.

In 1969, Falcon 117505 participated in the England-to-Australia air race, setting a class speed record under the command of Major D.B. O'Connor. In 1971, Falcon 117501, captained by Lieutenant Colonel C.R. Hallowell, flew from London to Victoria in the air race to commemorate the British Columbia Centennial.

In August 1975, a permanent squadron detachment, equipped with Cosmopolitan aircraft, was established at Canadian Forces Base (CFB) Lahr in Germany. On 23 January 1980, the Cosmopolitan departed for Canada, signalling the completion of the transition of the Lahr detachment to a deHavilland Dash-7 operation. In addition, a permanent detachment with a Cosmopolitan aircraft was formed in July 1980 at CFB Winnipeg in support of Air Command.

In 1983, two Canadair Challenger 600 series aircraft were taken on inventory by 412 Squadron. The acquisition of these aircraft reoriented the squadron to its former global VIP role.

The year 1985 saw the retirement of the Falcon aircraft after 17 years of service with the squadron. As well, the year marked the silver anniversary of the Cosmopolitan. This aircraft was finally retired from service in 1994.

During the same time period, the Challenger fleet was expanded to its current level of eight aircraft. The expansion, in combination with the acquisition of the VIP mandate from Transport Canada, ensured a sustained high level of worldwide operations.

The consolidation of responsibility under Department of National Defence (DND) for VIP administrative flight service substantially increased the squadron manning levels. Total squadron personnel strength reached 120. In addition, changes to the Challenger fleet continued with the replacement of four

600 Series Challengers with four 601 Series aircraft. Royal visitors continue to utilize the service of 412 Squadron. Their Royal Highnesses the Duke and Duchess of York and His Royal Highness Prince Edward flew on Challenger trans-Atlantic missions during 1987.

The replacement of deHavilland Dash-7 aircraft in Lahr by two deHavilland Dash-8 aircraft occurred during May 1987, thus continuing a 412 Squadron presence in Europe. In April 1990 the DH-8s were returned to CFB Winnipeg and replaced with a single Cosmopolitan. The end of an era for the air force, and for 412 Squadron in Europe occured on 28 July 1993, when this, the last European-based Canadian air force aircraft, was repatriated to 412 Squadron for the final time. Throughout 1990 and 1991, members of 412 Squadron once again led the way by pioneering VIP aircraft missions into the Persion Gulf area during Operation Desert Storm, and throughout the former Soviet Union and Eastern Bloc countries.

The Flying Falcon Squadron continues to add honour to a proud heritage — in a vastly different role than that to which it was born. The present Squadron personnel reflect with great pride a unit with an unbroken record of service since 1939. They face the future with confidence, optimism and enthusiasm based on over fifty years of service and tradition.

Nostalgia
by S/L Paul Webb, Navigator
1949-54

In 1984, Korean Air Lines flight 007 strayed over Russian airspace while enroute from Alaska to Korea. The Boeing 747 was shot down. The incident reminded me of the time that I found myself over the Russian-occupied Kurile Islands while navigator of North Star 17520 on a flight from Shemya, Alaska to Misawa, Japan. My log book shows that this occurred on 6 Jan 52, the captain was S/L Stu Cowan and the flight duration was 11 hours.

The route was notorious for bad weather and absence of navigation facilities. Unlike today's transoceanic aircraft, we didn't have Doppler and inertial navigation systems. We used celestial sights when the stars were visible, which wasn't often on that route while cruising at 10,000 feet in almost continuous cloud. So it was mostly dead reckoning, aided by radar altimeter pressure drifts. We obtained a fix from a weather ship stationed about halfway along the route. However, these ships didn't know their own positions too accurately, often spending days or weeks without celestial fixes themselves. No GPS satellite systems in those days!

About two hours from ETA, a break in the clouds showed that we were over land, over one of the Kuriles in fact, and 100 miles west of track. Since the Korean War was very active, the Soviet Union was considered hostile territory, so we got out fast. At least we now knew where we were! It made for lively conversation as we sat in the Marounouchi Hotel bar in Tokyo sipping brandy alexanders (at ten cents a piece). We were told that this was not an uncommon experience for crews flying the busy Korean airlift route, but it made an impression on me at the time.

The flight home via Hawaii and San Francisco was a navigator's dream. We had a crew rest in Honolulu at the Moana Hotel on Waikiki Beach (special rates for servicemen of $1.50 a day). I recall that we had the beach to ourselves with a view of Diamond Head and not a tourist in sight. Hawaii Five-O was never like that. My fellow crew members on that flight included F/O Mac Hall and Maurice Murphy, pilots, and F/O Don Stewart, navigator. I was also a Flying Officer then.

The most interesting trip I made as navigator was taking CD Howe and a Canadian Trade Mission on a tour of South America. The aircraft was the Canadair C5, a modified North Star with pressurized fuselage and Pratt & Whitney R-2800 engines, very similar to the Douglas DC-6. F/L Jack Reid was captain. We left Rockcliffe in a snowstorm on 5 Jan 53 and landed at San Juan, Puerto Rico, where we were greeted by trayloads of Daiquiris to mark Epiphany. For the next five weeks we visited eleven countries down to Argentina. The crew were given VIP treatment and wonderful hospitality everywhere. A personal touch was circling the place where I was born in the interior of Trinidad. I enjoyed Rio de Janeiro best and recall spending a pleasant afternoon on top of the Sugar Loaf drinking the good Brazilian beer and enjoying the view.

Another flight into adverse weather occurred in October 1954. C5 aircraft number 10,000 captained by F/L Les Hussey with myself as navigator, left Shannon, Ireland, for Gander, New-

August 6, 1958 Princess Margaret chats with W/C Carr over the St. Lawrence Seaway, on her cross-Canadian tour in the C5.

LAC R. McKittrick, Cpl. K.H. Sjolin, Sgt. J.O. Mignault, and F/Sgt. E.J. Benoit taken at the Taj Mahl in India in 1954. Prime Minister St. Laurent's Round-the-World Tour. (Courtesy of K. Sjolin)

L to R: Cpl. K. MacDonald, Maj. D. O'Connor and Capt. R. Day visit the Pan American Airways terminal at Kennedy Airport to make preparations for the London to Adelaide, Australia 1969 Air Race. During the actual race, the crew set two world and three class records for sections of the trip.

foundland. The VIP on board was Lester B Pearson, Minister of External Affairs. The weather forecast had predicted a hurricane to move from the eastern seaboard out into mid-Atlantic but well south of our track. As the flight progressed, it became apparent that we were getting headwinds in excess of 150 knots and would not make Gander. The hurricane had moved well north of its forecast position and was directly in our path. The prudent decision was made to return to Shannon. The VIP was sound asleep so was not awakened. After 10 hours and 15 minutes in the air we touched down at Shannon.

Mr Pearson had set his watch back 4 1/2 hours to Newfoundland time at takeoff. When he awoke prior to landing he was heard to say, "I've never seen the sun rise over Newfoundland in October at two thirty in the morning!" We got Mr Pearson back to Canada the following day, taking the southerly route through the Azores to avoid the offending hurricane. This, by the way, was the infamous Hurricane Hazel which caused so much damage to Southern Ontario.

In 1950, the Squadron was trained for air transport support of army operations, including paratroop dropping. We practised regularly with the Royal Canadian Regiment at Petawawa and the Royal 22nd Regiment (the "Van Doos") at Valcartier. On one occasion in September 1950, we were guests of the Van Doos at a mess dinner in the Citadel, Quebec City. The parade square at the Citadel was graced by an ancient cannon, dating I believe, from the War of 1812.

During the course of the evening, some intrepid souls among the 412 contingent borrowed a truck and spirited the cannon from its pride of place to one of our Dakota aircraft at Valcartier. The following day it appeared outside the 412 hangar at Rockcliffe, an exotic object of much curiosity and interest. Meanwhile, back in Quebec, the cannon had been missed and the reason for its disappearance deduced with the applica-

The 412 (T) Squadron Falcon crew of the England-Australia Air Race, 1969. L to R: S/L Roger Landry, S/L Doc O'Connor, Cpl. Ken McDougall, F/L Bob Brinkhurst and F/L Midge Pennington. (Courtesy of Doc O'Connor)

Carrying Honourable James Richardson, Minister of National Defence, for an official visit to North Bay, March 2, 1973. Intercepted and escorted en route.

Their Royal Highnesses, The Prince and Princess of Wales pose with their Cosmopolitan Crew, July 1983.

tion of Gallic logic. A prank was suspected, with 412 the prime suspect.

Unfortunately, the Colonel of the regiment took rather a poor view of the affair and took his complaints to a high level in Ottawa. The situation was saved by a combination of good humour and an apology, and the cannon was returned speedily to Valcartier (some 412 members wanted to drop it on the Citadel, with or without a parachute, but the CO vetoed this idea). All ended amicably and the Van Doos had a special model cannon made and presented to 412 Squadron to commemorate the event. I wonder if it is still around today?

We had a USAF exchange officer on Squadron, Major Bob Leighty, who used to fly the American ambassador's B-17 on weekends. This aircraft was a standard World War 2 bomber converted to a VIP interior. I was sometimes invited along as navigator and enjoyed the view of the world through the big plexiglass nose. The most memorable of these weekend jaunts was the time when the brakes failed on landing at Edmonton. We ran right off the end of the runway and rolled to a stop at the boundary with the nose pointing over the fence adjoining the busy Kingsway. The sighs of relief were audible. This happened on 26 July 52 and rated a mention in the Edmonton Journal.

I should mention the fishing trips we made in the Squadron Grumman Goose, number 386, piloted by F/O Bill Collins. We flew into lakes about an hour's flight north of Rockcliffe, then sat on the wing and fished. I've never caught so many speckled trout since. On a summer days of 1953 we even had a social visit from retired A/V/M Bob Leckie who had a cottage nearby. Leckie was a veteran of the Royal Flying Corps and won his DSO by shooting down a Zeppelin over London in WWI.

As I think back to those days from the vantage point of my late sixties, many episodes come to mind, single isolated instances which are nevertheless retained in the memory. Like the blind take-off we made from Dorval on 13 March 52 with F/L Howie Russell at the controls of Dakota 291. We were the last aircraft out before Dorval was closed by dense fog. Visibility at the runway button was just about zero. Howie set his gyro to the runway heading, ran up to take off power with brakes full on and then released them. It felt a bit like being catapulted from an aircraft carrier, but we got back home that night. Another demonstration of Howie Russell's superb airmanship was landing North Star 17520 at North Island Naval Air Station, San Diego, on 22 March 54, in a tropical storm. The field was flooded and the runway was indistinguishable from the Pacific Ocean into which it ran. Even the USN were impressed with that landing!

I think that the most violent weather I experienced was on a flight from Gander to Rockcliffe on 9 October 1949. I was on Dakota 657, with F/Os Frank Steele and Mac Hall as pilots. The flight took eight hours, much of it through severe thunderstorms. At 8,000 feet, we were tossed about like a cork, with severe turbulence, lightning strikes, St. Elmo's fire, the lot. Frank was singing his head off, thoroughly enjoying it. Mac was sweating it out at the controls. Our sole passenger was an Army Warrant Officer who needed a lift. He was on his knees with his rosary, certain that his last hour had arrived. The crewman and I did our best to comfort him, telling him that this was quite a normal flight and not to worry. He calmed down when we flew out of the worst of it but I doubt if he ever accepted a ride with the Air Force again!

The foregoing are just some of the more notable memories I have of my years flying on 412 between 1949 and 1954. I consider that my years with 412 Squadron are among the happiest of my life.

Grumman Goose of 412 (T) Sqn. in 1953.

The First 20 Years Of Support To 412 Squadron

by Air Traffic Assistants And Movements Controllers (Air)

In the mid-1940s, passengers and freight were processed by the Squadron traffic section, which was manned by aircrew officers and other ranks of the Air Traffic Assistant trade. The activities of the section included the reception and manifesting of passengers, the receipt, documentation, and loading of freight, calculation of weight and balance for aircraft, and documentation for Customs clearances. This was in addition to much cleaning and polishing of everything to be seen, as was befitting the reception of VIPs. These duties as carried out by the ATAs were sometimes considered less attractive than the task of flying on long-range trips where they acted as Purser (or general cabin handyman).

Over the years the tradesmen went through some trade name changes; Movements Controller (Air) was probably the least popular, as it seemed to invite comment from every amateur humorist that heard the name. At a press briefing for one Royal Tour, the title "Queen's Movement Controller" was commented on, and resulted in the crew position being changed to Flight Attendant for all publicity purposes. The NCO i/c the traffic section had an eminent position, the first being FS Butch Whalen; as a WAG he had done a Tour of Ops on Coastal Command in the UK and later served with 168 Squadron as a despatch/traffic officer. On R day, 1946, he mustered into the ATA trade. The next was Bill MacKay who had gained his traffic experience with 164 Squadron at Moncton and Dartmouth. Bill Kritsch had his wartime traffic experience with 168 Squadron at Rockcliffe and in the UK. Eric Irvine, a wartime pilot who had flown in the UK, returned to the RCAF in the ATA trade in 1946. Ed Grose, one of the first postwar ATAs, had been awarded a Queen's Commendation as an ATA crewmember on the Korean Airlift. Barney Barnett served in the Army in WWII and joined the RCAF as an ATA in 1946. Don Wood, another of the first postwar ATAs, had flown as an ATA on the Korean airlift.

Although the traffic section had evolved into No. 3 Air Movements Unit, it had operated as a Squadron section providing ground services and flight crew members. By the mid-1960s the Air Movements people employed on flying duties became a separate section, along with the Flight Stewards of the Squadron. (In the mid-1960s an Airman's Flying Badge was awarded to flying Air Movements personnel, and in the mid-1980s it was replaced by a distinctive Loadmaster flying badge).

Many Air Movements personnel had RCAF wartime experiences of note. A couple were: Charlie Fortier, an RCAF Airgunner who, as mid-upper gunner on a Lancaster returning from a raid on Berlin 13 December 1943, was the only survivor when the aircraft crashed in England. Bill Knox was an RCAF Airgunner on a RAF Squadron, and by the end of his tour had been involved with the shooting down of two German aircraft.

Many others had flying experiences in the war and in peacetime with 412 Squadron on worldwide operations. A few of the names are: Bergin, Holman, Winter, Verch, Clements, Thivierge, Cheeseman, Dear, Hudon, Murphy, Woodacre, Johnson (shoes), Weekes, Brien, Burke, Hatt, Aucoin, Kelloway, Coutlee, Hills, Varty, Graham, Poupart, Beaulieu, Conlin, Brien, Boyd, Kehoe, Savoie and Shipman.

3 AMU Uplands provided support to 412 Squadron and became a source of manpower for potential 412 Squadron loadmasters.

Magical Moments
by MWO Jerry Mignault

The C5 was carrying Her Majesty the Queen to meet the Dionne quintuplets. There had been a fairly good snowfall and the Royal shoes were damp. "What to do?" mused Jerry. "Why not pop them into the aircraft's spanking new oven?" he thought. Voila - the shoes were dried to a turn!

On another occasion, before an Asian trip which was to carry former Prime Minister John Diefenbaker, Jerry was ushered into the P.M.'s office for a discussion (Read advice) on the menus he would be preparing. "Sir," said Jerry, "If you eat what I ask you to eat, and drink some beer before each meal, we'll have no problems." The beer was important since it was thought to help prevent dysentery. Mr. Diefenbaker was so pleased with the results of Jerry's culinary expertise that he later invited Jerry and wife Madeleine to 24 Sussex Drive. In a light-hearted aside to Madeleine, the P.M. said, "Your husband saved my life by looking after me. Tonight, I'm looking after him!"

412 Transport Squadron Memories
by F/L David R. Adamson

It seems to me that our years at 412 Squadron provided an opportunity to not only broaden whatever flying skills we had, but more importantly, the special nature of the Squadron's operations provided personal growing experiences that became a catalyst in the development of our service careers.

Brushing shoulders daily, as we all did, with the senior political, diplomatic and military leaders of the free world provided a privileged insight into, and a respected acquaintance with, many dignitaries at levels beyond our imagination. That factor, and the crucible of high standards and strong competition, made service in 412 Squadron a unique and fulfilling experience. At the same time, one was always conscious of the consequence of even the smallest error, and human frailty being what it is, mistakes did occasionally occur, the results of which were sometimes far more personally disastrous than would have been the case in less conspicuous flying positions.

Notwithstanding, like all squadrons, there was always a great spirit of camaraderie - high esprit de corps - and when times got tough the Squadron family stuck together. Competition between members of a squadron was one thing, but competition between squadrons was fierce - never would it have been tolerated or accepted that 412 Squadron could not do anything that any other equivalent squadron could do - and as Wing Commander Howie Morrison would say, we would use twice as much finesse in getting it done.

The spirit that drove us on in all our accomplishments was, "Never let the squadron down in either your professional or personal conduct." That is not to say we didn't have fun - we did; indeed some of it perhaps testing the limits of the code. The following are some examples that come to mind.

The Battle of Bunker Hill, 1815-1951

A group of Squadron officers led by F/L Hugh Cram and F/O Maurice Murphy succeeded in liberating a small brass cannon from the Royal 22nd Regiment's enclave in the Citadel at Quebec City in July of 1951 and flying it out to Rockcliffe. This priceless object of Canadian history was naturally much revered by the Royal 22nd and indeed all Canadians, since it was inscribed with the words "Captured by the British from the American Forces at the Battle of Bunker Hill - 17 June 1775."

So audacious and effective was this act of liberation through the skill and daring of these 412 crews, that the missing cannon became a national cause celebre. The embarrassment of the Royal 22nd was even more acute as a result of similar activities that had reached the press concerning the Canadian and Australian armies raiding each other's lines in Korea and replacing each other's national flags with that of their own county. On top of this came the cannon debacle and the press took up the story non-stop.

Speculation ran wild. Some suggested that it might have been removed from the Citadel by an American tourist - all 250 pounds of it - so special checks were mounted at the border. Each day brought new speculation and the subject was at the top of the list of embarrassments that the Minister of National Defence had to defend each day during question period. To say the least, the cannon was a "hot item" and as it sat in front of the 412 hangar overlooking the Ottawa river, we daily prayed that someone would find it and bring an end to the national debate.

Finally, Wing Commander Bob Tricket, now deceased, called a friendly reporter and gave him the scoop. The Squadron was directed in no uncertain terms to return the cannon in an appropriately respectful manner to Quebec City and the Royal 22nd Regiment. My part in the proceedings is evidenced by an entry in my logbook dated July 25, 1951, Dakota 394, self & W/C Tricket, RC-QB-RC; return cannon. As I recall we were met with stony silence by a very military Major and three soldiers. The cannon was off-loaded and we returned to Rockcliffe. The cannon may be seen to this day outside the entrance to the Royal 22nd Officers Mess - the place from which it was liberated - through much daring by two dedicated 412 crews.

The sequel to the story is that since 412 Squadron obviously wanted a cannon and since the Royal 22nd was not likely to give us one, our other associated regiment, the Royal Canadian Regiment, presented the squadron with an ancient artillery piece at a full-blown ceremonial parade on the tarmac at Rockcliffe. That gun resided at the 412 Squadron hangar at Ottawa in a suitable place of honour. No doubt, the RCR takes regimental pride in having up-staged the Royal 22nd.

MEMORIES OF A 412 SQUADRON HANGAR GUARD
by C.D. (Doug) Pinhey

Most members of the wartime RCAF will recall having to perform some menial tasks such as perimeter/hangar guard duty, fire picket, closing (read cleaning) canteens, and so on. Well these same duties applied to post-war service as well, and on a miserable cold and wet early fall night, this particular AC2 happened to be at Rockcliffe, guarding Hangar 68, 412 (T) Squadron's aeroplane shelter, which could have challenged any World War I biplane as to the number of supporting cables it sported.

Sometime between 10 PM and 2 AM (that's 2200 and 0200) the AC2's tranquility was shattered by a very loud ringing similar to a fire alarm. After his initial heart-stopping fright, he responded by nearly breaking his neck exiting the hangar maintenance tower, thinking he was at ground level. All his perceptors now being fully functional, he proceeded to the source of the noise. This happened to be the main entrance/exit to the departure/arrival ramp, an area which to a man of his standing, had hitherto been considered sacred ground. "Out of Bounds" was the term that came to mind.

On approaching the door, he noticed a number of gentlemen wearing Airforce attire, so he unlocked, and invited them

Corporal Edith Cole, first RCAF stewardess on Royal Tour, 1959.

Madame Leger cuts her anniversary cake presented during the 1978 Royal Tour.

in out of the wet. Once they were inside he noted their badges of rank, getting a reading of one to four or five bars due to the shakes. One of the gentlemen (five bars) asked him if he was on duty and he replied, "Yes sir! I'm the hangar guard."

"Well," the gentleman said, "Do you see that little old Dak back there in the corner? I want it on the line in 15 minutes!" to which our AC2, having been warned of the dangers of arguing with someone who now appeared to have six bars, replied, "Right away, sir!"

Now, fellow Airforce-ians, we all know that 412 Squadron was a truly great transport squadron, and could transport just about anything, anywhere, and the proof was all stored on that side of the hangar. As the AC2 later declared, "The only aircraft missing was a Tiger Moth." First, he had to open the hangar doors, twelve in all. Then he had to seek out the various towing devices required for Harvard, Beech 18, Goose and Norseman. On viewing this array of aircraft, our AC2 thought perhaps the Squadron should be redesignated 412 (C) (For Compost, or is it Composite?) Squadron. Oh well, let us proceed. As this AC2 had a civilian driver's licence, he deduced that the towing trac-

General Eisenhower arrives in Ottawa on his official visit in 1950.

Loadmaster Flying Badge (Courtesy of E.C. Grose)

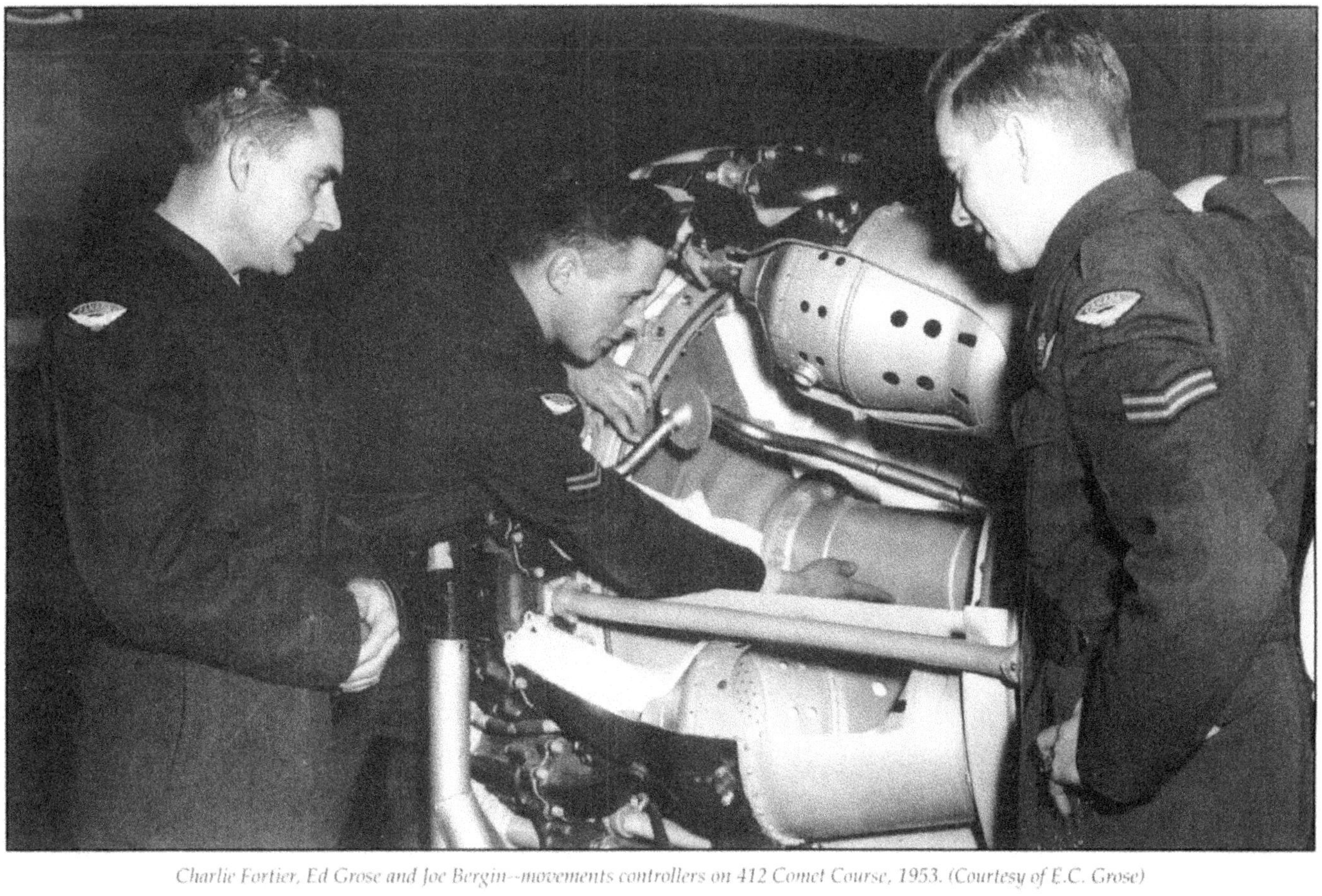

Charlie Fortier, Ed Grose and Joe Bergin—movements controllers on 412 Comet Course, 1953. (Courtesy of E.C. Grose)

tor must be similar to a car in its handling, so he fired it up and proceeded to clear the way to the Dak. Oh! It would be remiss not to mention the fact that the tarmac was covered with a thin coat of ice.

All went well for the AC2. Out came the Norseman, Harvard, Goose and Beech 18; now for the Dak! Now, as all good airmen know (Our AC2 Didn't), the Regs state that wingmen and brakeman are required to assist the shifting of aircraft from one environment to another (Indoors/outdoors), and a good story - or the description of a gal - wouldn't be complete without statistics. The stats in this case being that the wingspan of a Dak is ninety-five feet, six inches, and the hangar opening was slightly under one hundred feet. All of which adds up to a very shaky AC2, hooked on to one of the King's aeroplanes, and thinking maybe it could be entered in the King's Cup air race if he happened to shorten its wingspan sufficiently. However, it was not to be, as he managed somehow to get it out to the ramp between the hangars in one piece.

Well now, about this time, most bars and his jolly fellows climbed aboard, stowed the ladder, slammed the door and the AC2 was treated to a most refreshing breeze as the two P&W 1830s burst into life while he was disengaging the tow bar. That done, he drove to one side and watched the Dak trundle away, thinking it a little strange that it showed no lights all through taxi and take-off. "Oh well," he thought, "Lights don't provide much lift, so perhaps they're not needed in the heavy damp air."

When all became silent once more, the AC2 re-stored all the various flying machines, closed the hangar doors, and with the shakes having slackened, clear vision restored and with heart rate near normal, returned to his post in the maintenance tower. Being bushed, he decided that further studies of KR (Air), DROs and the funny looking bug that kept coming into view, could wait 'til - (what the heck) - ZZZZZZZ.

Only after our AC2 had become more familiar with the RCAF and its regulations did he start to wonder about that odd night. Was that flight authorized? If so, why were there no servicing personnel on duty? Where were the aircrew going? Why did they show no lights? These questions, and more, entered his young mind but since he now knew that he had broken a few regs himself that night, he wasn't about to discuss the situation with anyone else.

Let it be known that this stout fellow, this AC2, eventually took wing himself, and did engage in similar actions of his own to a lesser degree. And so ends one small chapter in a many-chaptered tale of 412 Squadron's operations.

Crew of C-5 Around-the-World 1950 Tour. Aircraft Commander G/C Lane.

The Emperor of Japan

In April 1953, Crown Prince Akihito, now Emperor of Japan, visited Canada, and 412 Squadron was sent to San Francisco in the C5 to bring him and his party to Victoria. Included in our crew was an inspector from the RCMP who may remain nameless. This was another of those privileged trips that offered yet another dimension to one's experience at 412 Transport Squadron.

Arriving in San Francisco, we were directed to a special security area at the airport, where we were welcomed by the Canadian and Japanese consulate staffs. Of special significance, the Japanese consulate had invited the crew to a Japanese gastronomic experience in one of San Francisco's best restaurants. We were delighted to accept and arrived en masse at the appointed hour to learn that the restaurant was, if nothing else, certainly up to 412 standards.

After going through a receiving line, we were directed to the dining area, which had been set in traditional Japanese style. That called for removal of our shoes and being seated on cushions at low tables. All of this was preceded by the usual rounds of hot saki while we became acquainted with our most gracious hosts.

About the time we were being seated, Group Captain Stephensen, "Joe Steve" to the Air Force, pointed out to F/L Jack Reid and me that our RCMP crew member was suffering from acute embarrassment. There he stood, in all his splendour, in his sock feet with the big toe of his right foot protruding through a large hole, while he tried valiantly to hide the problem with his left foot.

Ah yes, the lesson: Always check your socks before you go to a Japanese dinner.

The C5 and Anthony Eden

In June of 1953, we were dispatched to London to fly Anthony Eden, Britain's Foreign Secretary, to Boston where he was to undergo the third in a series of operations in an attempt to correct a life-threatening gall bladder problem. 412 Squadron was assigned the trip after the President of the United States offered a USAF aircraft - Prime Minister St. Laurent having intervened.

The story, however, concerns our departure from London-Heathrow on the morning of 5 June 1953. The C5 was held under heavy security in the BOAC maintenance area, and promptly at 0900 hours a large limousine escorted by two motorcycles arrived with Mr. and Mrs. Eden. His personal doctor had arrived earlier and our crew nurse, Sister Fardella, had made all necessary preparations in the rear VIP compartment. Although Mr. Eden arrived dressed for the office, it was readily apparent that he was really a stretcher case. Accordingly the bed had been prepared and he was immediately made as comfortable as the facilities of the C5 would allow, and that was pretty comfortable.

No sooner had this been accomplished than another limousine arrived, and out stepped the man with the cane, a large cigar steaming away as he slowly mounted the ramp to say his good-byes to his longtime colleague, whose life was obviously in the balance.

As Sir Winston entered the VIP compartment, Sgt. Mignault (the steward) and I overheard one of those confidential conversations that 412 crews were often privileged to hear. As the door to the compartment closed, we could hear Mr. Eden say to Sir Winston "My God, Winston, why can't we have an airplane like this." We knew then that Prime Minister St. Laurent had made

Crown Prince Akihito of Japan is pictured here in the co-pilot's seat of the R.C.A.F. C5 which flew him from San Francisco to Victoria, B.C., to begin his 10-day tour of Canada prior to attending Queen Elizabeth's coronation. With the prince is F/L Dave Adanson of Calgary.

Anthony Eden

his point; Canada had not only responded in Britain's time of need, but in doing so had responded in a manner that left an indelible impression.

To say that we were proud needs hardly be said; to say such incidents were the heart and soul of life on 412 Squadron is the real story.

And as Sir Winston descended the stairs to return to his car, he stopped momentarily in front of me, cigar still steaming away, casually and slowly surveyed the scene, removed the cigar from his mouth and said, "God bless you all."

COMET DAYS 1952 -54
by S/L Rowly Lloyd

It was a typical Sunday morning in the summer of 1952, with my wife Ruth and I having a late cup of coffee in our apartment at Lachine, Quebec when the 'phone rang. On the other end of the line was W/C Mussels, then Senior Air Staff Officer at Air Transport Command Headquarters, requesting that I drop around to his apartment, which was in the same building. The old wartime hospital at Lachine had been converted to apartments for personnel of ATCHQ and 426 (T) Squadron.

The reason for W/C Mussels' invitation was not for coffee, but to advise me that four crews had been selected from ATC units to be trained on the Comet aircraft which were to be delivered to the RCAF in early 1953. I was advised that I was to be one of the four captains, along with S/L Don Dickson (Now deceased) and fellow Flight lieutenants Stu Olsen and Les Hussey. We were each to have a familiarization flight on a British Overseas Airways Comet training flight from London to Singapore and return. To make *my* flight from London to Singapore, I had to leave on Trans- Canada Air Lines the next day for London to join the BOAC crew on the day after. Needless to say, preparations for that adventure were hurried and hectic, but exciting nevertheless.

Our training program was to consist of a one-week course at the BOAC ground school on the theory of jet propulsion, an eight-week course at the deHavilland ground school in Hatfield, and then back to BOAC at London Airport for the flight phase.

The first-officers selected were F/Ls Dean Broadfoot, Bob Edwards, Herbie Herbert and Mac Hall, with navigators Carl Brown, Don Stewart, Herb Wright and Al Martin. The radio officers were Ken Wark, Art James, Joe Menton and Russ Chalk. The flight engineers were led by Cam Bain, who later became the Comet Detachment Engineering Officer, with Wally Hoehn, Fred Bowman and Horace Easy, and the transportation technicians were Ed Grose, Chuck Fortier, Joe Bergin. In addition to the aircrew training, roughly 30 ground servicing crew under Flight Sergeants Capriano and Sam Martin underwent a thorough program of training, both in the UK and on the long-range training flights.

After an initial check-out at London Airport, each aircraft, with two crews on board, were to fly two enroute training flights, first from London through Rome, Cairo, Khartoum, Entebbe, Livingstone to Johannesburg, and second, from London through Rome, Beirut, Bahrain, Karachi, Calcutta, Rangoon, Singapore, Rangoon, Columbo, Bombay, Karachi, Bahrain, Beirut, Rome to London. Comet 5301 was successful in completing the two trips without incident but our aircraft, 5302, ran into difficulties on the Beirut stop outbound.

The BOAC flight engineer who was with us decided that on our Beirut stopover, the fuel tanks should be calibrated, and proceeded to do so on the following day. However, instead of using external power, the aircraft batteries were used - and *well* used. When the aircraft was being refuelled for the next leg to Bahrain, there was insufficient battery power to operate the fuel tank shut-off valves and as a result, fuel continued to be forced into the wing tanks long after they were full. Finally, several ribs in the wing cracked and rivets were popped. Needless to say, the flight was delayed while deHavilland designed and built a repair kit so we could fly the aircraft back to the UK. In the

April 1953--Crew of the tour of the Prince Akihito of Japan. (L to R): LAW Grace Honkawa, flight attendant; LAC Joe Lanteicne, flight attendant; F/S Gerry Mignault, steward; W/O Benny Benoit, flight engineer; F/O Al Kirk, R.O.; Prince Akihito; F/L Hank Enns, Nav.; F/L Dave Anderson, captain; G/C Joe Stephenson, conducting officer. (Courtesy of Dave Adamson)

L. Col. P.R. Bingham with the Nine Pounder presented to 412 Sqn. by the Royal Canadian Regiment, February 28, 1952.

meantime the crews had a well-deserved (!!!) rest in the hotels and on the beaches of Beirut - then a most beautiful spot. As an aside, on the leg from London to Beirut we had set a record for the longest flight by a Comet to that date. This was front-page news in the London papers as we learned on our return to that city.

The second attempt at our trip to Singapore went well and on our return, we prepared for the trans-Atlantic trip home. On June 16, 1953, we arrived back home in Ottawa to a warm welcome from friends and families. Before I was able to get off the aircraft, W/C Morrison, Officer Commanding 412 Squadron, came on board to advise me that the Comets were to be detached to Station Uplands and that I was to be the OC of the detachment. We subsequently took up temporary residence in the National Aeronautical Establishment (NAE) hangar at Uplands before becoming the first tenants of the newly constructed cantilever hangar, now known as Hangar #11.

The flying that summer was fun, as the aircraft was a novelty everywhere we took it. Several flights were made across Canada to familiarize weather people and controllers with high level flight. W/C Morrison and I flew the first jet transport flight into the United States when we landed at Washington National to show the aircraft to the USAF. As I was taking General White, head of Air Materiel Command, USAF, on a tour of the aircraft, he remarked on the smoothness of the exterior, with no aerials sticking out anywhere, and then he turned to the Colonels with him and barked, "Why in Hell can't *we* build something like this?"

In January of 1954 however, the catastrophes suffered by BOAC Comets caught up to us, and our two aircraft were grounded. It was to be several years before the cause was determined, but eventually the decision was made to rebuild and put the aircraft back in service. Dean Broadfoot headed a new group of aircrew and groundcrew through another training program at deHavilland in the UK and returned the two Comets to 412 Squadron at Uplands.

A productive 10 years of flying passengers on the trans-Atlantic route to Europe and VIPs to other parts of the world followed before the aircraft were finally retired in July, 1965.

The RCAF and 412 Squadron can be justly proud to have been the first military organization in the world to be equipped with jet transport aircraft, and to have pioneered in this aspect of aviation so successfully.

Prime Minister St. Laurent's World Tour
February - March 1954
submitted by Dave Adamson

The ultimate trip in 412 Squadron was to be assigned to a world tour and the ultimate passenger was the Prime Minister. Such was the luck of those crew members picked for Prime Minister St. Laurent's tour of the world in the spring of 1954.

Preparations were long and thorough, including having the crew fly the complete trip on a training exercise in December of 1953. No stone was left unturned and as we departed Rockcliffe with the Prime Minister on February 4, we did so with the certain knowledge that we were prepared for any eventuality, from the logistics of in-flight feeding to the care of those who were bound to suffer from gastro-intestinal problems. We were ready, the C5 was ready, and the passengers were anxious to embark on their world adventure.

And so it went, a routine 412 Squadron trip that departed on schedule, took six weeks, flew 27,000 miles in 106 hours and 45 minutes and arrived back in Rockcliffe precisely on schedule at 2130 hours on 17 March, 1954.

To say that it was a unique and memorable adventure is to understate the wonder and sense of fulfillment for all involved, passengers and crew alike. Of all the incidents encountered on the trip, however, the one that sticks most in my mind was our departure from Rome for Bahrain on Tuesday morning, 16 February at 0915 hours.

During our four-day stay in Rome, the C5 was placed under the security and care of the Italian Air Force and Sgt. Johnny, last name now forgotten, was in charge. Flight Sergeant Benny Benoit and his technical support crew undertook during that four-day period to teach Sgt. Johnny and his crew a working appreciation of English, and Sgt. Johnny and his crew reciprocated by introducing our crew to the Italian language and Rome. A little pasta and some duty free was also, no doubt, involved.

At any rate, as the passengers loaded at Rome there stood Sgt. Johnny, all six feet of him, at rigid attention in his best uniform, saluting smartly as each passenger ascended the ramp. Prime Minister St. Laurent made his diplomatic good-byes, shook Sgt. Johnny's hand and boarded. That left G/C Stephenson and me, and at that point I introduced Sgt. Johnny to the Group Captain, impressing on him the great service that he and his crew had provided during our visit. The Group Captain gripped Sgt. Johnny's hand and thanked him profusely - finally saying good-bye, and as he turned to climb the ramp, Sgt. Johnny, using every English word he had learned during the past few days, said, "Good-bye you crazy son-of-a-bitch Canadian!" The Group Captain, who realized he'd been had, never tired of telling that story.

412 (T) Squadron
As seen through the eyes of Glen Parslow during his first tour April '54 to November '58

Ivan Moreside, Gar Ash and myself, following completion of the North Star (DC-4) OTU at Trenton, were transferred to 412 Squadron on the 29th of April, 1954. Our first priority, of course, was to find out what 412 was all about. However, given the Squadron's resident expertise in the form of training officers, check pilots and highly qualified aircraft commanders and crews, it didn't take long to understand the finesse requirements of VIP flying operations. For example: when taxiing, apply power smoothly and slowly, synchronize the power and use gentle braking action to turn rather than noisy power changes; pay special attention to power changes and synchronization in the air and use shallow smooth turns avoiding any possible G Forces, flight plan to avoid turbulence and on and on and on.

Possibly the greatest challenge facing the pilots and crew was the emphasis placed on VIP ramp times (door opening) at destinations. For example if your ramp time was 1100 hours you were to be on the ramp exactly at 1100, and while the VIP book allowed you plus or minus 1-1/2 minutes, aircraft commanders inevitably caught Base Commanders like Cam Mussels' exasperated but friendly glance at his watch if it wasn't exactly 1100 hours.

To achieve such accuracy one had to know every trick of the trade. For instance, if you started to run early or late, you adjusted your power accordingly. One therefore frequently found himself either at high airspeeds up until just before touchdown at destination or at reduced airspeeds for varying periods of time.

Generally these procedures were easily acquired. Flights, however, where conditions necessitated full instrument approaches required more finesse since you were dependent upon the air traffic controllers. In those instances, by listening to other aircraft reporting their positions, you knew where they were and their altitude. If they were slightly ahead of you and could therefore delay your approach, you'd probably request an early descent in which you'd increase your airspeed to be in the approach position ahead of them. In effect you always had to be a step ahead of the controller, who in most instances pitched in to assist you at meeting your ramp time since guards of honour and government dignitaries were frequently part of the welcoming committee.

Moreover, each member of the flight crew was an integral part of the operation. On all VIP flights in those days, we carried a complete crew that included a co-pilot, a flight engineer or crewman, a radio officer, a loadmaster, and on northern and oceanic flights, a navigator. All played their special role to ensure the success of the flight. To describe the cohesiveness of the 412 crews would require a book in itself, since it was that joint team action and cooperation that made 412 Squadron what it was, and is today.

The fact that flight stewards have not as yet been mentioned is not an oversight. Flight stewards, assisted many times by the loadmasters, made the flight truly a VIP operation. To become a successful flight steward, one had to possess characteristics usually found only in senior members of the Diplomatic Corps. In those days, for example, flight stewards were required to requisition the food and supplies they needed from the combined mess kitchens. Anyone who did this and was able to serve delicacies that one would expect to be served in Ottawa's Rideau Club had to be nothing short of a magician as well as a culinary expert. Diplomacy was indeed their key-note, and the cooperation they received from the messes across the country was ultimate proof of their diplomatic prowess.

On flights from civil airports, the stewards were reimbursed

Departing Rockcliffe for his world tour, Prime Minister St. Laurent speaks to the crowd. (Courtesy of D. Adamson)

Prime Minister and Mrs. St. Laurent departing on his world tour, shown shaking hands with G/C Joe Steven Stephenson. (Courtesy of D. Adamson)

W/C Howard Morrison, CO 412 Squadron, captain for World Tour of Prime Minister St. Laurent, February 4-March 17, 1954. (Courtesy of D. Adamson)

for funds they spent on the purchase of food and supplies. To stay within their budgets and still provide the same class of food to their fellow crew members, they frequently shopped in supermarkets and specialty stores, actually preparing the meals and delicacies in their hotel room or enroute the next day. For those who are acquainted with the restricted space that stewards are obliged to work in, the end product had to be nothing short of a miracle. It was a well-known fact that no matter how well the operational crew performed and how excellent, how smooth, and on time the flight was, if the service in the passenger compartment wasn't up to snuff, the trip could be a disaster. There is more on this aspect further on.

In the meantime, two short anecdotes come to mind during the time W/C Gord Miller was the Squadron CO. Gord was to be in command of the C5 operations on one of the Royal Flights. All members of the crew spent considerable time ensuring impeccable dress and deportment, and that everything was highly polished.

However, Gord always had a weakness for dogs and three or four days before the flight, he was playing with the neighbours' puppy on his front lawn. He and the pup were having a great time with Gord on his hands and knees, butting the pup with his head. Everything was great until Gord made the mistake of lifting up his head too soon. The pup must have taken a shine to Gord's nose since he immediately chomped down on it with his sharp puppy teeth. Over the next few days Gord's nose received special care and attention from the base hospital who put it back in such good shape that the Queen never noticed - or at least she never commented on it.

Another incident that Gord would rather forget involved his chastising the 412 officers at a Friday morning briefing for not attending beer calls and other social mess activities to the same extent as members of the resident fighter squadrons. It's not certain why Gord raised such an issue since 412 members were always "on the road," whereas the fighter boys spent their days in Ottawa simply "boring holes in the sky."

That night, having been away on a flight for a couple of days, we arrived back around 8 p.m. and, since beer call had started at 5 p.m., a contingent of fellow 412'ers were in pretty good shape when we arrived at the mess. They didn't waste any time telling us about Gord's untoward comments and after all, "Where was he tonight?" It was suggested we should call him, purchase a few cases of beer and go over and pay him a visit. When he answered the door, his wife Marg very astutely decided to go to bed and let Gord handle "his boys," which he did. When we left around midnight he undoubtedly regretted his morning's remarks and we're certain Marg felt the same way, given the state in which she found her house the next morning.

At the Monday morning briefing, Gord acknowledged that the 412 spirit was indeed alive and well and he even managed a thanks to those who saw fit to join him at home after beer call. He had with him a rather worn and bedraggled officer's dress cap that one of us had left at his home. His comments were to the effect that the hat didn't meet 412 standards - however, it would be in his office should the owner wish to claim it. No doubt it's still there.

Turning now to a flight in the winter of 1955 that should never be forgotten, since it was one of those that should never have taken place. Bob Hanbidge and I were on standby when a call came in late that cold afternoon to provide an aircraft and crew to fly the Hon. Paul Martin, Canada's representative to the UN, and two passengers down to New York that evening. In their wisdom (or possibly lack thereof) Dispatch arranged for a C-45 despite the status of the VIP. When we arrived to flight plan, we called ATOC to get permission to use the famed Dak 1000 since it was available and ready to go. Apparently in ATOC's opinion three passengers didn't warrant a C-47 and we were to use the C-45.

Duke of Edinburgh looks over the C-5 cockpit.

Princess Elizabeth and the Duke of Edinburgh with C-5 crew during 1951 Tour.

Of course, when Paul arrived he had enough passengers to fill all the seats including the one required for our flight steward. Moreover, there was too much luggage and it would have to be stored in the small toilet in the rear. Being late and in a rush to get to NY, Paul didn't want to take the time to arrange for Dak 1000 so the steward would have to remain in Ottawa. That was alright since they had just come from a cocktail party and wouldn't need the refreshments.

After take-off and reaching cruising altitude we found the aircraft colder than normal, in fact it was *extremely cold*. Possibly because the excess baggage was blocking the heat vents in the rear. Enroute several of the passengers had to use the toilet which required the crewman to move out the baggage and replace it each time it was used. The flight was something like one would expect in a Looney Toons comic. Looking back into the darkened compartment we could make out the forms of the passengers bundled up in their coats attempting to sleep to forget the cold. Paul had one of our winter great coats as well as his own pulled over him.

On our approach into LaGuardia, we normally asked for and received a courtesy Customs clearance for dignitaries. When Customs heard it was a C-45 they must have assumed that it couldn't be a very high-ranking dignitary and despite our protests we were told to report to Customs. Lo and behold, didn't Customs put Paul and his whole entourage through the whole nine yards despite the fact that Paul's aide kept telling them who Paul Martin and the passengers were. By this time, we thought Paul would blow a fuse and I didn't want to be around when the news reached 412.

Apart from our report to the squadron on the illogic of using a C-45 for such passengers, nothing was ever heard. Long after Paul was out of the political arena, the trip was mentioned to him since it had been such an embarrassment to the crew. The only thing he remembered, thank goodness, was the hassle he got from Customs which must have over shadowed his memory of the flight itself.

As I Look Back
by WO John R. Dagg
Aero Engine Tech 1955 - 63

These are a few of the memories of a trip on the best aircraft ever, the C5 10000. This was a visit to Latin America by The Honourable Pierre Sevigny, Associate Minister of National Defence.

Departure time promptness was a big factor for 412 Squadron, so as the trip was to depart at midnight on 2 Aug 61, the number 3 engine was turning at 1159 hours. Our estimated time of arrival at San Juan Airport was 0730, 3 August.

After take-off and everything was settled, the steward, and I helping, started to make up the berths. As we made them up, some passengers went to bed! One of the funny situations began. Funny now as I look back, but embarrassing then. No sooner had The Honourable Mr. MacQuarrie and wife got into bed, when the catches on the seat which made the bed let go, and down went the middle, including Mr and Mrs MacQuarrie. We immediately apologized and made a mad dash for a suitcase or two, which we put under the middle, and everything was back to normal.

The steward was heating water in a hotcup which would only make about four cups of coffee at a time, so he had a tray with milk, sugar, four coffees and water sitting on the metal galley counter. To see the funny side of this, you would have to visualize flying at altitude, all the passengers asleep and a narrow hallway between the curtained-off berths at approximately three or four o'clock in the morning. All of a sudden we hit an air pocket and over went the coffee, milk, sugar, etc. Some of it landed on the front of the steward and the rest on the floor. He looked down with a forlorn look on his face and said, "What am I going to do now?" It seemed so funny, and the way he looked, I sat right down on the floor and laughed. After we came back to our senses, we had a nice mess to clean up, because flying at this altitude and near the door, it had frozen to the floor.

So much for the humorous part. As I mentioned earlier, promptness regarding takeoff time was a BIG factor, and after a number of years in the squadron, it became an all-out effort to maintain the promptness. On the same trip, approximately two hours from landing, I was checking the analyzer when I saw a straight line indicating nine plugs on #2 engine not firing. I tapped the engineer on the shoulder and pointed to the analyzer; he in turn told the captain. His answer was, "It's likely the analyzer." I said, "OK, you check on landing." Which he did and we had a few good "bangs." This is where, being with this squadron, you had to perform. It was now about 2330 hours and take-off was scheduled for 0800 hours. That night, in another country where we couldn't speak the language, the engineer and I fixed the snag, which was a magneto distributor and a set of plugs. We had time enough to go to the hotel, have a shower, pay for a bed which I never slept in and back to the aircraft for the scheduled takeoff. A rough night but worth it to maintain the schedule.

There was another show of teamwork and capability to overcome a situation. On landing, I believe in Rio, #2 and #3 engine cut out, which in turn lost our hydraulic pressure. The engineer and I jumped for the hydraulic hand pump, and if you have ever had to do this you would realize what it is like. Any braking action or nose wheel steering caused a rapid action on the hand pump with very little pressure, then as the pressure builds up, the hand pump becomes very hard to pump. This went back and forth until we were at the ramp, where the guard of honour was waiting. Another situation successfully carried out. A bit of humour on parking, I was asked if this is what we do in Canada, shut down the two inboard engines for taxiing.

The trip had other minor incidents, but all in all was very enjoyable and we all kept up the good name of 412 Squadron and were proud to do it with the Best Aircraft, I feel, the C5 10000.

Just a note, approximately 1966 or 1967, after the C5 was put into storage, I was asked by Captain Eichel if I would put it back in flying condition which we did and he and a man from California flew it there. To sit in the cockpit and run it again and then see it fly was a great joy to me.

Of all the aircraft which should be in Canada's museum, I believe the C5 should be there. It flew Kings and Queens, many Canadian and other country dignitaries, and furthermore it was the only one like it ever built.

FLYING EXPERIENCES
by F/L LJ Halpin - Navigator 1957 - 60

I enjoyed my flying experiences on 412 Squadron as I flew on several flights carrying royalty (Royal Tour 1959), Prime Ministers and VIPs.

One interesting event that I recall was an explosive decompression we had on COMET 5301 on 26 Feb 58, during a compass swing and air test. I was taking a sun heading check with the periscopic sextant at 42,000 feet when we had the pressurization loss. I recall finding myself on the floor and wondering what happened, as we were in a rapid descent after hearing a loud bang.

The cause of the decompression, we later found out, was that the metal cover over the port wing dinghy flew off and perforated the fuselage near the main cabin entrance door. The hole in the fuselage was approximately the size of a basketball. No other aircraft damage resulted, and except for escaping breath and excessive ear-popping to the crew and maintenance staff in the cabin, no injuries resulted.

The fact that the COMET withstood this explosive decompression was a reassuring sign to all aircrew as the previous history of the COMET had been in question.

Some crew members on that flight were F/L W Carss, F/L I Moreside, F/L RT Brown, F/L JAG Thompson and F/L R Mackenzie.

A MEMORY OF INTEREST
by Stan Heath, Pilot 1959

For the 1959 Royal Tour involving the Queen and Prince Phillip, there was a requirement for a four-engine aircraft small enough to get into some smaller airstrips like Mayo Landing, Dawson City and New Glasgow. Ottawa arranged to borrow a Heron aircraft from deHavilland, the same type aircraft that the Royal Flight in England contained and which Prince Phillip was fully qualified on. I was assigned to the Heron and was advised that Phillip may request permission to pilot it. (He is not allowed to fly with the Queen on board). However, on the Whitehorse, Dawson city, Mayo Landing part of the tour, the Queen was too ill to go (she was carrying Prince Andrew at the time) and sure enough the Prince asked me if he could fly the Heron that day; probably the only time that he has ever flown as first officer with the RCAF. He is an excellent pilot. On the Charlottetown, New Glasgow, Sydney, Halifax leg, the Queen was on board so Prince Phillip was a passenger.

Cockpit of DeHavilland Comet MK1A. August 1958.

Transporting Dignitaries and notables

Flight Lieutenant J.S. Shipton has fond memories as flight navigator with 412 Squadron from 1958 to 62 when he flew in squadron Comets, North Stars, and the C5 as crew navigator. He recalls one memorable trip:

"The trip was the AOC's inspection of the RCAF detachment at Resolute Bay in August of 1958. We left the AOC at Resolute and were making a flight to Alert on the northern-most tip of Ellesmere Island at 85 degrees north latitude. One of the passengers was a retired Inspector of the Royal Canadian Mounted Police (RCMP), Henry Larsen, who in the RCMP supply ship sailed from west to east through Bellot Strait in 1941-42 to circumnavigate the Canadian Artic."

"On departure from Resolute Bay to Alert, the aircraft commander invited Mr. Larsen to sit in the co-pilot's seat. He donned the intercom headset and then began running commentary with the names of the islands, capes, points, and lakes that were passing beneath the aircraft. The navigator position in the aircraft is behind the co-pilot's seat, and I quickly stood up with the map of the area in my hands in order to see these places that our passenger was pointing out. I noticed that he did not have a map, but was naming these topographic features from memory. Needless to say, the crew and I were duly impressed."

The years spent at Uplands also proved to be very exciting and intensely active. From 1963 to 1968 the squadron operated two VIP-configured Yukon aircraft which successfully completed a wide variety of tasks, including the annual National Defence College overseas tours, round-the-world trips, as well as innumerable special flights for high-ranking dignitaries. At the same time, the Yukons maintained a weekly flight schedule to Marville, France, and subsequently to Gatwick, England.

Sometimes the squadron faced adversity and schedule changes that always kept the personnel on their toes. One such incident occurred in October 1961 when the Honorable John Diefenbaker made his state visit to Japan. Flight Lieutenant Shipton was flight navigator during that trip:

Flight Lieutenant Shipton remembers, "The flight to Japan started out like it had been arranged by the Keystone Cops of movie fame or Murphy's Law. Anything which could go wrong did, or words to that effect. Back-up aircraft were the order of the day. Everything was arranged originally as follows: the C5 would airlift our crew to Elmendorf AFB, Anchorage, Alaska, and our slip crew would take over from the Comet crew, who were to bring the PM to Alaska, and we would crew the Comet through Shemya in the Aleutians and on to Tokyo for the visit. Well, things began to snowball, as they do when something goes wrong. The first problem occurred after the Comet had refueled at Vancouver and departed for Alaska. The landing gear would not retract, so fuel was dumped to get the aircraft down to its landing weight, and a normal landing was made. In the meantime, a squadron Cosmopolitan aircraft, which just happened to be in Vancouver was thrust into the breach. The baggage from the Comet was removed and loaded onto the Cosmopolitan, and the PM and party boarded for the flight to Alaska. As the Cosmopolitan did not have the range to fly to Japan from Shemya, a quick telephone call was made to Anchorage to alert the C5 crew to be ready to take the PM to Japan. As this had not been part of the C5 crews' task, a quick search was on to obtain the necessary maps, charts and letdown plates for airports enroute and pre-flight planning for the crew. The C5, which had brought our Comet crew to pre-position us for the onward flight in the Comet, was now going to be the prime vehicle for the flight to Japan."

"The squadron Cosmopolitan arrived in Anchorage and another exercise in moving the baggage to the C5 commenced. By now the crews had it down to a science. The original itinerary had now gone by the board as the flight in the 260-knot Cosmopolitan to Anchorage and the planned flight in the 260-knot C5 could not compare to the much faster Comet at 390 knots, so a decision was made to notify the Canadian Embassy in Tokyo to delay the original arrival until further advised." However, the story continued:

"A few hours after the PM had left Anchorage in the C5, the Comet crew had solved the undercarriage problem at Vancouver and arrived in Anchorage. We left them there and proceeded in the Comet to Shemya where we arrived about two hours after the C5."

"Again, the baggage was moved from the C5 to the Comet and we awaited further orders from the Senior Air Force Officer with the PM's party, a Group Captain J.K. MacDonald, a former CO of my old squadron, 426. The decision was made to stay overnight in Shemya and depart in the early a.m. for Japan."

"At 5:30 a.m. we departed for Japan. As everyone was tired, the passengers settled down for the six and-a-half hour flight. Before the sun rose that morning, I was doing my plotting at the navigator desk, when I felt a tap on my shoulder and on turning found myself staring at the PM of Canada. He asked if I could get him a glass of water, to which I replied "Affirmative!"

My Time at 412
by M.H. Brunotte, 1963

When 426 Squadron left Trenton for RCAF Stn. St. Hubert, I moved again and remained with the Squadron until it was disbanded in 1962 (the second unit to shut down while I was a member). Even though we seemed to have done an admirable job during the Congo crisis, someone had decided that the old North Stars had to go. The Squadron personnel were split up between Trenton, Downsview and Uplands, and that was how I came to know what had been called by some the "Royal Ottawa Air Force," also officially known as 412 VIP Squadron. The fact that this unit was indeed a VIP Transport Squadron was made very clear to me when one of the first entries in an L-14 pink sheet I got to read was "Dirty ash trays." This, as a major unserviceability, seemed a bit much, considering the way we had managed at 426 Squadron to keep the North Stars on schedule and in the air, but in time I adjusted to the increased importance placed on shiny aircraft, as Friday became the traditional polish day.

My remaining days in the RCAF were spent with 412 Squadron, still in time to get to know the C5 and our two Comets, and even crewing on two of the last flights of 5302, in July 1963 with F/L Goddard, and in August of that same year aboard 5301, with F/L Billings on the Uplands - Marville - Uplands runs. Before too long however, I became acquainted with the CC-109s, the Cosmopolitans. One particular Cosmo, No 11160, seemed to be hounded by gremlins, because its No 1 inverter kept acting up while the aircraft was airborne, yet checked out OK while on the deck. In order to trace the possible cause, I was sent on a flight. The Captain not being burdened with anything other than keeping the bird aloft, decided to buzz a nearby farm of a recently retired buddy. The manoeuvre he put the machine through kept me off balance and it was all I could do to hang on to my tools and test equipment, not to mention my breakfast, as the blood seemed to drain from my head.

I did not find the cause of the inverter trouble on that flight, and upon landing thanked the Captain somewhat sarcastically for the trip. His reply was, "Whoever said you can't do aerobatics in a Cosmo?" It turned out that he used to fly with the Golden Hawks. I do not recall the inverter trouble ever being rectified.

412 (Transport) Squadron History

by Major General (Ret) Leonard V. Johnson, CD
F/L 1957-62, LCOL & CO, 1968-69

In July, 1957, after more than three years as a pilot instructor No. Four (Transport) Operational Training Unit at Trenton, Ontario, my wife, Shirley, our four-week-old daughter, and I drove to Ottawa on posting to 412 (Transport) Squadron. We left our furniture in storage and moved into the home of a friend who was on the de Havilland Comet course in England preparatory to returning that aircraft to service with 412 Squadron. Three months were to pass before we finally got settled in a home of our own. Early next morning, outfitted with a new summer uniform acquired for duties with the elite VIP squadron, I reported for work and flew a local familiarization training flight in a Dakota with Les Reid. Next day, I went to Montreal, Greenwood, and back. On the 25th, I flew to Fredericton and returned; on the 26th, I went to Centralia and came home, and on the 28th it was to Goose Bay overnight, returning on the 29th. On the 30th, I went to Camp Borden and back in an Expeditor, and August began with a six-day trip to Fredericton, Cold Lake, and Saskatoon with Stan Heath. We flew hard, but we were young and we didn't tire easily.

By the end of August, I had flown 155 hours in 38 days, and each hour in the air had been matched by at least two hours waiting time at such places as Lachine, Goose Bay, Camp Borden, Knob Lake, Great Whale River, Summerside, and Chatham. I had learned that God was THE SQUADRON, Moses the DISPATCHER who rostered the crews and wrote the DAILY FLYING ORDERS which determined our fate, and the ten commandments were a set of unwritten rules that began with "Thou shalt go wherever the dispatcher sendeth thee, without question," and ended with, "Thou shalt complaineth not, lest thy God reject thee."

In addition to our VIP passengers, we also hauled a lot of freight - groceries to Goose Bay, well-drilling equipment to Fort Chimo, an automobile to Victoria, and miscellaneous small cargo of all kinds. North Star crews frequently augmented 426 Squadron on flights to Europe and the Middle East, a two-week round trip. Crew training flights also took us to Europe fairly often. At times our work was no different than that of any other transport flying unit in Air Transport Command.

Ours was a simple code of duty. The squadron wives, with no court of appeal or any thought of redress, banded together in mutual support and took pride in their self-reliance. We husbands, largely relieved of family responsibilities and complaints from our long-suffering wives, were free to serve our first love, the RCAF, a jealous mistress if there ever was one. The arrangement served us well, even by the standards of a more enlightened age. We were mostly blessed with stable, enduring marriages that bring joy to our reunions, where those of us who are left can get there and rejoice together in our shared experience.

North Star 17518 at one of many stop-overs during the 1950 World Tour.

Crew of the last Yukon flight (SF 162 from Gatwick) by 412 (T) Sqn. before the aircraft was transferred to 437 (T) Sqn. **Top to Bottom: (L to R):** *W.O. C. LaGroix, MWO J. Mignualt, Cpl. M. LaRoche, CPL. M. LaRoche, WO A. Anderson, CPL. L. McMillan, CPL. G. Dufresne, CPL. J. Brien, Capt. R.A. Last, Capt. H.W. Jobb, Capt. G. Scott, Maj. B.D. O'Connor, and L/Col. L. V. Johnson.*

We were a carefree band of brothers, but our wives deserve most of the credit we claimed for ourselves.

The end of the summer leave period brought the squadron back to full strength and I got reacquainted with my family and found a place to live. There was still another aspect of life at Uplands to discover, however.

As members of a lodger unit on an Air Defence Command station, we were expected to share the night and weekend duty rosters. The station commander was one Group Captain Campbell H. Mussells, DSO, OBE, DFC, CD, Commanding Officer RCAF Station Uplands, golf course architect, scourge of airmen's battered cars, military entrepreneur, and tyrant. "Muss" won his DSO and DFC in Bomber Command and his OBE for command of 426 (Transport) Squadron during the Korean Airlift, when he was reverently known as "God" Mussels in awestruck U.S.A.F. circles.

Early on a Saturday morning at the end of my first tour of duty as senior duty officer, the telephone rang in the quarters. Moments later, I was standing rigidly at attention with the telephone a foot from my ear, hearing an irate group captain thundering, "YOUNG MAN, WHAT IS YOUR NAME AND WHAT UNIT ARE YOU FROM?" This was the beginning of a chewing out over some minor dereliction of duty he had observed, an event that signalled that the group captain missed nothing and forgave no sins whatever. As hard as I tried after that, he always found fault and I never escaped his wrath. The postwar air force was never big enough for Muss, who shouldered his way through it like the proverbial bull in the china shop. I admired him; we became friends in later years, and his death was a great loss.

I flew the Dakota, Expeditor, North Star, C5 and Cosmopolitan; participated in the Royal Tours of 1958 and 1959, flew the National Defence College to Asia in 1959; and carried John Diefenbaker to the Arctic on the first such trip by a prime minister. The intrepid adventurer, stuffed with Arctic grayling fried in the galley, was asleep when we crossed the Arctic Circle, the precise time of which was logged by the navigator and recorded by the press aboard. In 1961, I got as far as Shemya with Air Force 10,000, the C5, as part of a three-aircraft relay team that took The Chief to Japan. The C5, stripped of her finery, succumbed to a cutting torch in California within 10 years, but she left her memory behind.

My first tour on 412 Squadron was marred by the loss of a B-25 Mitchell and a fine crew at Milwaukee, Wisconsin, in 1960. Two years later, one of our North Star aircraft was lost at Hall Beech, NWT, after multiple engine failures. Fortunately, there were no casualties, but the airplane remains there, another hulk on the barrens.

Although the Napier Eland engine in the original Cosmopolitan sometimes gave us heart attacks, few failed in the air. During a routine flight from Tampa to Uplands, I diverted to Olmstead AFB, Harrisburg, Pennsylvania, after one engine lost oil pressure. The standby crew from Uplands brought parts and took my passengers home with them. Next morning, after repairs were made, I got a favorable weather briefing and filled a flight plan to Ottawa. While awaiting take-off clearance, I looked out and saw a wall of black cloud and heavy rain crossing the airfield. I barely had time to head the airplane into wind before a violent squall line struck. I could not take to the air without learning more about that monster; so I taxied back to the ramp and went to the weather office, where a bewildered forecaster was mourning the loss of his anemometer, blown away by the wind. Disgusted by his inability to tell me what was going on, I called Homer, our forecaster at Uplands, for a briefing. Only then did I learn that the weather was below limits at Uplands and at all the usual alternates. We were out of money and clean clothes, but we were also out of luck, so we cancelled out for another day.

Early next morning, our weather problems over, we took off for home. Just after passing Syracuse, there was a thump in the left engine and a flicker on the gauges, but everything returned to normal and we pressed on without incident. After landing, I wrote up what had happened to the engine and a technician checked it out. After a time, he called me to ask which engine I had been concerned about because he had found both of them unserviceable. Suddenly, I was thankful for the squall that had sent me back to the weather office and the call to Homer.

I was a chief pilot, check pilot, flight commander, and deputy aircrew leader. I maintained currency on three or four types at a time, and I went everywhere the squadron went, but it is the people I served with that I remember best thirty years later. It has been said, and it is partly true, that lieutenants have buddies, colonels have rivals, and generals have only enemies. Although I see them rarely, the best friends of the best days of my life were my squadron mates, when we were young together and flying our asses off.

In February, 1962, I was promoted to squadron leader and posted to the operations staff at Air Transport Command Headquarters, back at Trenton. Everything I had learned at 412 Squadron was relevant there, and my four years were productive and satisfying. In 1966, I attended the U.S. Armed Forces Staff College, at Norfolk, Virginia, and then I was posted to Canadian Forces Headquarters in the rank of wing commander. This miserable two-year experience, the first of two which together confirmed my unsuitability for service in the head-shed had a happy ending. In June, 1968, I went to my career manager and pleaded for a move. "No. 412 Squadron as CO," he replied, as if he had been thinking of it all along. Within a week I had rewritten my instrument rating exams and was on the way to Trenton for a Cosmopolitan refresher course.

My first concern was to reestablish my status as an aircraft commander. Unlike my first tour at 412 Squadron, when I flew for several months as second dickey with pilots I had trained on the Dakota, while I satisfied them that I was literate enough to write a passenger bulletin, smart enough to make a ramp time, and smooth enough on the brakes, I brooked no delay. At the first suitable trip, I scheduled myself for a route check, passed it easily, and declared myself a VIP aircraft commander. This didn't stop the route and proficiency checks, however, and within a few weeks I held three valid instrument ratings issued by three separate authorities in air Transport Command. Every squadron commander should aspire to be the best pilot on his squadron, and nobody else has had as much documentary evidence to support that claim as I had.

I took command with the conviction that flying proficiency and flight safety took precedence over every other consideration. No commanding officer should ever be satisfied on this question, especially at 412 Squadron, where excessive concern for chickenshit sometimes took priority over the quiet, alert cockpit that is the hallmark of a good flying operation. Flying standards were too sloppy for my liking, a judgment soon confirmed by the annual visit of the Aircrew Standard Unit.

Another issue of concern was an operational restriction which prevented the Cosmopolitan from landing and taking off from gravel runways and therefore from flying in the sparsely settled areas of Canada. I first got approval for a northern training flight using hard-surfaced runways at Frobisher Bay, Thule, and Whitehorse, to get people acquainted with the range of the airplane. One of the two pilots with me on that flight had never been north of Val d'Or, Quebec, a few miles northwest of Ottawa.

Convinced that careful handling would minimize damage from flying gravel thrown up by the nosewheels and propellers, I then got grudging approval to conduct gravel-runway trials. With Captain Vic Bantle, then chief Cosmopolitan pilot, I went to Great Whale River (now Poste de la Baleine) where, as it turned out, about four inches of fresh gravel had just been laid. After two or three landings and takeoffs, we taxied to the ramp, shut down, and ran down the stairs past a still-turning propeller to see what, if anything, had happened to the airplane. Except for a dent about the size of a dime on one of the flaps, we couldn't find any damage. The Cosmopolitan had just become a much more useful airplane. Had it not become so useful, it would probably have been retired long ago.

Within a year or so, a permanent Cosmopolitan detachment had been established in Europe, giving valuable experience to crews and getting 412 Squadron back into long-range oceanic flying. The squadron similarly expanded the utility of the Falcon, with trans-Atlantic ferry flights and participation in the 1970 London-Sydney Air Race under the command of Major D.B. "Doc" O'Connor.

By then I was back at Trenton with the operations staff crusading successfully to lift an operational restriction on the CC-106 Yukon and sending surplus check pilots off to more useful work.

STRANDING THE PRIME MINISTER
by Donald F Deeprose, L/Col (Ret), Pilot 1963 - 65

From mid-1963 until end-Aug 1965, I had about the best job in the RCAF — I was Pilot Leader on 412 (T) Squadron and an aircraft captain flying the two VIP Yukon a/c. Having the privilege and honour of flying VVIPs and VIPs to and from various parts of the world was, without doubt, the high point of my 30-year air force life. Queen Elizabeth and Prince Phillip were undoubtedly the highest ranking VVIPs I flew, but also there was the Queen Mother, the Shah and Empress of Iran, Princess Alice, Governor-General George Vanier and Mrs. Vanier, and Prime Minister and Mrs. Pearson; among the VIPs were numerous Cabinet Ministers, military chiefs and many officers and government officials of slightly lesser rank.

Apart from flight safety itself, the comfort of and service to the VIPs were the top priorities; meeting published ramp times probably came next. Even one goof-up in meeting those priorities could jeopardize one's career, thus flying VVIPs and VIPs hither and yon occasionally incurred some quite stressful moments. Needless to say stress was felt by all members of the crew, particularly the cabin crew, who also had to perform in a near faultless and circumspect manner.

I experienced two quite stressful moments on one trip while flying Prime Minister Pearson, the Secretary of State for External Affairs (Paul Martin), their wives, their individual entourages, and about 25 media personnel. The main purpose of the trip was to allow the PM and Mr. Martin to attend the NATO Summit held in Paris in Jan of 1964. Besides a 2-day layover in Paris, the trip's itinerary called for a night stop in Marville, a fly-over of the Vimy Memorial while enroute for a 6-hour stop at the USAF's Evreau AFB, then back to Ottawa. The time in Marville was to allow the PM to "inspect the troops" and attend a Mess Dinner; the few hours in Evreau were to allow him to travel by road to Dieppe and attend a ceremony dedicated to the Canadian dead

The maiden flight of Dehavilland's Dash 7.

buried there. Recalling events, as best I can after 29 years, the stressful moments came about this way:

About seven hours into the flight enroute to the Paris/Orly airfield — the PM would be greeted at a big airport reception — I became a little uneasy when, after being handed-off from Shannon Oceanic control to Paris Area Control, we were unable to contact the Paris Area controller. Actually, I had been worrying all during the flight thinking about the fog that was blanketing all of central Europe and how it might disrupt our arrival plans. We had a scheduled ramp time of 10:00 GMT and Paris/Orly was forecast to be below landing limits until late morning; also our alternate airfield, Marville, was not a solid alternate as it was forecast to COME UP TO alternate limits by late morning. All actual-weather reports we had received enroute disclosed that both Paris and Marville were below landing limits. In anticipation of dense fog upon arrival, I had had sufficient fuel loaded so that we could, if necessary, orbit over Paris for nearly three hours before having to head for an alternate airfield. (Having to land at an alternate airfield when carrying a VVIP is a captain's nightmare: not only does it create havoc with the VVIP's plans and the plans of those at the bypassed airfield; a higher work and stress load is imposed on the crew; it greatly disrupts the alternate airfield's routine and also that of local political establishments; and such an incident could make undesirable international headlines.)

The PM's military aide had occasionally visited the cockpit to keep posted on the flight's progress. I appreciated that as it relieved me of worrying about when the PM might want flight and other information. The aide was up front as we crossed the Channel Islands (Jersey and Guernsey). At that time, about 9:00 GMT, we were only minutes away from the coast of France and still had had no contact with Paris.

I was eager to descend as soon as possible to permit a slow cabin depressurization which would lessen the possibility of passengers experiencing ear discomfort; but, without a Paris Control clearance to do so, I was stymied. With each passing minute and only silence in response to our radio calls, the level of stress increased. By now my unflappable 1st Officer, F/L Tom Wilson (also an experienced Yukon captain) had begun to fret.

After a dozen or so calls to Paris control on several frequencies and just fifteen minutes short of being overhead Paris — still at cruising altitude and airspeed — we got a response: "Canadian Airforce 929, I 'ear you, thiz iz Pariz Control, you will land at LeBourget, contact LeBourget Approach on frequenzy 123.7." The heavily accented voice came through our earphones as welcome as a voice from heaven; the message however was not what we wanted to hear. Dammit!! What's going on in this crazy country?

For a moment Tom and I exchanged startled glances, then he transmitted: "Paris Control, Canadian Air Force 929, we are flight planned into Orly; we have Canada's Prime Minister on board, we request clearance into Orly!"

"CAF 929, thiz iz Pariz, I repeat you will land at LeBourget, change frequency now."

"Paris, 929, I repeat, we have Canada's Prime Minister on board and we must land at Orly!"

"CAF 929, Pariz, I again repeat, land at LeBourget, change to 123.7. OUT." End of conversation!!

LeBourget!!! In our exhaustive preparation for the flight Tom and I had not given a single thought to the possibility of landing at LeBourget, thus we were quite unprepared for such a contingency; while we knew LeBourget was just 20 or 30 miles from Orly on the northern outskirts of Paris, we knew nothing more about it — airport elevation, runway length, approach procedure, nav facilities, weather conditions, overshoot procedure, and a half-dozen other vital things we had a need to know.

There was a mad scramble in the cockpit as I reduced engine power and dug frantically in my briefcase for the LeBourget airfield/approach chart; Tom changed radio frequencies and called LeBourget Approach while rummaging about for his chart. Fortunately, LeBourget Approach came on the air and immediately supplied us with a heading to fly, descent instructions, landing runway, and LeBourget weather, to wit: sky obscured 200', visibility 1/2 mile in fog. Damn, below limits! But wait.....the chart shows GCA available.....with GCA we might get in.....we'll have to go for it; I sure don't want to go anywhere far from Paris.

I advised the PM's aide we would attempt a landing (he had had earphones on and had heard all that was going on) and asked him to inform the VIPs of the unexpected turn of events; I instructed the Navigator to advise the other passenger. Tom and the Flight Engineer hurried through the pre-landing checks while I studied charts and manoeuvred the a/c as per Controller instructions.

After those first few rather hectic moments taken to get our minds and the cockpit in order, we were talked-down to landing by the LeBourget GCA. The GCA radar team was very proficient and the approach and landing went smoothly. Taxiing into the ramp of the unfamiliar airfield in fog necessitated a very slow taxi-speed that gave me time to consider the screwed-up situation we were in and, after shutdown, what the first dozen or so immediate things I would have to do to get things back on track — it also gave me time to wonder about the imminence and locale of my next posting. The only consoling factor in the whole mess was that we would make our ramp time almost to the second — wrong airport maybe.....but one must collect "brownie points" however one can.

While the engines were still winding down, one can imagine the sense of relief I felt when out of the mist strode a welcoming party; in the forefront I was able to discern the uniform of an RCAF Group Captain (G/C Ogilvie, I believe). Hey! Maybe things aren't so bad after all.

The happy ending to this stressful event was attributable to the Canadian Defence Liaison Staff (CDLS) Paris. CDLS had apparently received word earlier in the morning that French air controllers had gone out on strike and CDLS had consequently made arrangements with French Airforce personnel to handle our arrival and landing at LeBourget; obviously CDLS also advised all others having a need to know of the different arrival airport because there was a well-attended reception for the PM and party. All's well that ends well as the old saying goes.

On to Marville and Beyond

The Air Traffic Controllers ended their strike sometime during the night; so, when the fog lifted a bit the next day, we flew the a/c to Orly, thus obviating any change from the previously planned departure arrangements. The following afternoon we flew the entire party to Marville, where fog again necessitated a GCA-assisted instrument approach.

The flight itinerary for the next day had us departing Marville at 0900 GMT, fly over the Vimy Memorial then land at Evreau AFB at 1030 GMT, depart Evreau at 1630 GMT and land in Ottawa at 0230 GMT (2130 EST) — a long, hard day for sure.

In the morning, Marville's weather was sky obscured 200', visibility 1/2 mile in fog. The forecast weather for Vimy was clear sky, visibility 1 to 1 1/2 mile in fog; for our Evreau arrival, ceiling 200' overcast, visibility 1/2 mile in fog. The 0730 Evreau actual weather was ceiling 100', visibility 1/4 mile in fog. Our alternate airport would be Shannon where weather was well above alternate limits. Not very promising for either Vimy or Evreau but worth a try — if unsuccessful, then onto Shannon for refuelling, and home.

There was no problem departing Marville and, in moments we were above the blanket of fog into a clear sky on a heading to Vimy. The Navigator picked up the Vimy Memorial on radar and homed us onto it, visibility was about a mile and, from 1000' AGL, Tom and I got a good view of it. Over the memorial, I commenced a timed manoeuvre that would, hopefully, bring us back in about 4 minutes on a reciprocal heading with the memorial 1/2 mile off to starboard. At that time, Tom surrendered the co-pilot's seat to Mr. Pearson; Mr. Martin stood between my seat and the co-pilot's seat. Tom took a mike and headphone to a seat in the crewrest compartment where he could look out a starboard window; there, should he spot another aircraft in the vicinity, he would warn me if a turn to starboard might create a risk of collision.

Unfortunately, on the run back to the Memorial on a southeasterly heading, we were into sun and, with the glare and all, saw the Memorial only briefly on the starboard side. I held heading 15 seconds then banked to port and went into a racetrack pattern to the northeast; upon completion of this, we were inbound on a southwest heading. With the sun now portside, we spotted the memorial about 1 mile ahead slightly to starboard; this was perfect as I was then able to circle the monument to starboard. Upon circling starboard, I was on the high side of the turn flying by instruments thus I never saw the monument again; the PM and Mr. Martin were able to get a good view of it for only about 30 seconds. To make good our ramp time we could linger no longer and I rolled out of the manoeuvre heading for Evreau AFB. The VIPs went aft and Tom again took possession of the co-pilot's seat.

Prior to Evreau, we entered cloud and I was then on instruments until moments before touchdown. The USAF GCA team did an excellent job in talking us down for a landing under conditions of 300' ceiling and 1/2 mile visibility. A "follow me" jeep met us at the end of the runway and led us through the fog into the ramp.

After welcoming the VIP party, the Base Commander soon had it and all other passengers on the road to Dieppe. Prior to their leaving, the PM had discussed the weather situation with me; he toyed with the idea of cancelling the Dieppe trip but, on my telling him that the Base meteorologist was reasonably sure the existing weather would not worsen until after dark, he decided to carry on as planned. He would cut everything as short as possible and wanted to leave for Ottawa IMMEDIATELY on return from Dieppe. Yes, sir!

We were ready and waiting to go by 1500 — the fog condition had changed little in the intervening hours. Shortly after 1600, the PM with his party returned and were promptly boarded. The media people had not yet arrived. The PM fretted about this as he thought they had been ahead of him on the road. He was most anxious to get airborne and, after another few minutes of questions and fretting, he said; "Don, if they're not here within 10 minutes we'll leave without them; I have scheduled an extremely important announcement in the House tomorrow and I can't risk being stuck here."

I went forward and told Tom of the situation and instructed him to start the starboard engines as soon as the "door open" sign was extinguished; the port engines would be started when I got upfront. I returned to the VIP compartment and briefed the VIP party about the flight back to Ottawa.

What a sense of relief when, a minute or so later, the media gang arrived and were hustled on board. I went back into the VIP compartment and told the PM that everyone was on board and the First Officer was about to start engines. The main door was still open as I left the ViP compartment (extreme rear of the a/c) and I glanced out to see if the boarding stairs had been removed — they hadn't been and I immediately saw why — HOLY SUFFERING SUCCATASH!!! I was unable to see the wingtip — in the few seconds I had been in with the PM, the a/c had become engulfed in a peasoup fog.

I hurried to the cockpit where Tom informed me that, about two minutes before, really dense fog, looking like a line of huge wind-blown tumbleweeds, had just rolled over the a/c. I radioed the Meteorological Officer who advised me that, now the heavy fog had drifted in, it was in for the night; in fact, noon the next day was the earliest to expect conditions suitable for takeoff. A bad nightmare had just become a reality. Walking aft through the passenger compartment to the VIP compartment, I was bombarded with questions whether we were going or not.

"Please stay seated, I'll let you know shortly," was my reply. With the weight of the world on my shoulders, I knocked on the VIP compartment door prior to entering. Mr. Pearson and Mr. Martin were facing each other across the table while Mrs. Pearson and Mrs. Martin were in easy chairs behind.

"Sorry, sir, bad news!" I said, addressing the PM, "A few minutes ago the fog completely closed in on us."

A stunned silence.....broken after a few long seconds by a very upset Mrs. Pearson: "But we must go, there is so much to be done tomorrow!" The PM, also visibly upset, shook his head a couple of times, then said: "This is terrible, simply terrible. This means that the Cabinet reshuffle will have to be put off at least a week, Paul?" They talked for a minute or so, then the PM looked up at me and said: "It's not your fault, Don, it's mine. I just should not have gone to Dieppe. Is Orly still open?"

"Yes, Sir, it is Sir."

"Perhaps we can get an a/c out of there — we just have to get back to Ottawa tonight. Can you hire us an a/c out of Orly?" Geeez!!! The world on my shoulders got much weightier. How could I make such arrangements? Who would pay for it? And if I could make arrangements, what would be the fall-out from the PM being flown into Ottawa by some fly-by-night French charter outfit? What horrible headlines there would be. I can't let it happen!

"I might be able to, sir, but do you think you could get through to Orly? The fog is so thick that driving there would be near impossible; at night, on French backroads in this peasoup fog, your lives would be in danger." The PM looked out his window. "Good Lord! I can't even see the ground!" He pondered the situation briefly. "You're right, Don. What do we do now?"

"I'll go speak with the Base Commander and see what he can do for us, sir."

The Base Commander had known for several minutes we weren't going anywhere; he was at the bottom of the boarding stairs when I hurried down. He had anticipated the contingency and already had his people finding accommodation for us all. Also: "I've ordered the staff cars and bus back, as soon as they arrive we'll all head over to the club; we'll sort things out from there over a good stiff martini." Wheeeeww! I had never expected to meet a White Knight but here was one, not in armour but dressed in the uniform of a USAF Colonel.

Feeling a ton or so lighter, I bounded up the stairs to advise the PM; also to discuss the next day's departure. He wanted to leave just as early as possible. I told him about the forecast — bad until at least noon — but suggested that if he was willing to risk having to sit awhile with engines running on the runway, we might get away earlier if the fog should ease even momentarily. Good! I suggested everyone should be aboard by 0945 for a possible 1000 takeoff. Great! I advised the other passengers of the departure time before everyone was driven to the Officers' Club.

The Base Commander did a terrific job in satisfying our requirements. Maybe too good — at some passengers' request, the bar was left open considerably beyond normal closing hours.

The next morning, everyone was aboard by 0945 — not without incident however. Just before the Pearsons and Martins were to be boarded, a high-profile TV newscaster — a late-night reveller — vomited in the aisle and over a seat immediately for-

The Change of Command Ceremony, June 24, 1966. Wing Commander D.C. MacKenzie takes command of the 412 (T) Squadron from W/C/M.C. Bryan. (Courtesy of D. MacKenzie.

ward of the door. Murder was a thought that entered my mind. A cabin crew member was still cleaning up the mess as the VIPs boarded.

Visibility was less than 1/4 mile when we started engines. I had made arrangements for a "follow me" jeep to lead us out and onto the runway button. There, the jeep driver was to wait until such time as I considered visibility safe for takeoff; then, at my request, he would drive the full length of the runway to ensure nothing but centreline paint was on it. On getting word it was clear, we would go.

On the "button," we could see ahead for what Tom and I considered to be a little better than 1/4 mile before the white centreline paint strips disappeared in the murk. Beyond that one runway light was faintly visible. Upon asking the tower controller for "full-bright," one additional runway light was visible.

There was no doubt in my mind that I could make a safe takeoff under the existing conditions. If an engine failed right after takeoff, we would have only a 1/2 hour flight to London/Gatwick which had fairly good weather, and I could not have a better pilot than Tom in the right seat. Tom and I had flown many times together and I hoped he had as much confidence in me as I had in him.

"It's good enough for me, Tom, what do you say?" I said into my mike. "Let's go, sir," he replied, and then called the tower controller for our airway clearance. Upon receiving that, Tom requested that the jeep driver check the runway and I confirmed with the senior flight attendant that everyone in back was ready for takeoff.

The runway was declared clear and takeoff clearance received. I pushed the Power Levers from GROUND RUN over the gate into the FLIGHT IDLE position, rechecked all engine and flight instruments — particularly the heading indicators — then released brakes and advanced the PLs to the full power stops. My eyes were glued onto the runway, Tom's on the engine instruments and the airspeed (a/s) indicator. Acceleration was rapid and only a couple of minor steering corrections were needed to hold the a/c on the centerline.....the visibility seemingly decreased as speed increased. At a predetermined a/s of 115 kts, Tom called "V1" (the a/s beyond which, if an engine fails, the pilot is committed to takeoff because not enough runway remains to stop); I moved my right and left hands (respectively) from the PLs and nose steering wheel to the control yoke and my eyes from the runway to the flight instruments. About 5 seconds later, when Tom called "VR," I pulled back on the yoke and the a/c reluctantly got airborne. At 122 kts, Tom called "V2" and I eased the yoke further back to maintain that initial climbing speed. Wheels up, flaps to 5 degrees, hold a/s until 500'; then flaps up, allow a/s to build to best climbing speed and we were away on an uneventful flight to Ottawa.

In that I kept my job for another year and a half, I guess my performance was not considered a goof-up by those who monitored such things.

A SHORT TAIL

by Bob Buckles, Pilot

Willis Eichel and I were in Washington National overnight and returned to the airport in mid-morning to prepare for the flight home. It was a fine bright morning and the parade route was lined with flags, etc. The outside speaker at Butler aviation (Tower Frequency) was repeating the message periodically, "Washington National is closed from 1100 to 1145." An honour guard was being reviewed and many dignitaries and their wives were in attendance. Cannon were firing a salute. Just then, some irreverent pilot (probably Eastern) called the tower to say, "What's

Capt. R. Smith is assisted by a nurse and a laboratory technician for the transfer of two kidneys from Portland to Hamilton where two patients, one in Toronto and one in Hamilton, await.

it closed for?" The tower replied, "It's an official send-off for the President of Norway." The pilot responded, "You mean an official hand-out."

"No, No," the tower replied, "Dean Rusk and many other dignitaries are here," to which the pilot replied, "Har de har har!"

All of this was heard by the whole party over the speaker that some one forgot to turn off! No one ever cracked a smile, but carried on in a most serious manner. Eichel and I had to hide behind a building to conceal our laughter.

LT. GENERAL DONALD C. MACKENZIE, CD

Donald C. (Pablo) MacKenzie arrived at 412 Squadron to accept appointment as Operations Officer in July, 1965. During August and September he was in Trenton checking out on Cosmopolitans (Convair 580). On 24 June 1966, he was promoted to Wing Commander and took command of the Squadron from W/C Mel Bryan.

A highlight of his tour with the Squadron was in 1967, Canada's Centennial Year, during which Montreal Expo took place. Many political leaders and Heads of State visited Canada and it was 412 Squadron's mission to fly all Heads of State, as requested, during their sojourn in the country.

On August 15, 1968, then-Lt. Col. MacKenzie handed over command of 412 Squadron to Lt. Col. Len Johnson. All in all, his three years with the Squadron were most challenging and rewarding, and he looks back on his tour as a major highlight of his service career.

RCAF Tour to Colorado Springs November 4-8, 1970.

412 (T) Squadron
Glen Parslow's Second Tour - August '66 to June '68

W/C Pab MacKenzie, who was later to become LGen MacKenzie, was the Commanding Officer. The squadron had lost its Comets, the C5 and the North Stars, and consisted of two VIP Yukons, and a number of Cosmopolitans and C47s. In 1967 the squadron was to acquire several L182s and Army pilots, since no one could decide where these aircraft should be based following integration. Eventually the aircraft were removed from the squadron and their pilots trained on current squadron aircraft, which gave all of them a home and a better outlook on life.

Integration and subsequent unification had indeed changed the 412 organization. In the early 50's, first at Rockcliffe and then at Uplands, the CO had his own maintenance, servicing and movements organizations as well as his aircrew. Given this complex and self-sufficient organization and a sizeable fleet of aircraft, the squadron was large in numbers and high in spirit. Integration had changed all this and left the CO with only the aircrew and the aircraft. That change probably reduced squadron strength by as much as 75%. Ensuing COs hoped for a reinstatement of the former organization, since under the new arrangement they were, like the other resident units, completely dependent upon the new centralized base support organizations to keep their aircraft in the air. Nevertheless, 412 diplomacy and the need to meet VIP commitments always seemed to win out. The system was working well under the new organization primarily because of the very close rapport that existed between the Squadron CO and the hierarchy of the new base support units. Pab MacKenzie certainly set a fine example in this new environment. Likewise, the fact that a number of former 412 Squadron members became Base Commanders at CFB Uplands also helped to ensure that the 412 role was accorded its necessary priorities.

The squadron was therefore functioning well in Aug 1966, with the longer-ranged Yukons being used for global operations in support of the PM, other members of Cabinet and Royalty. Full crews were still required on these aircraft, including the Navigator, since INS and other modern navigation aids had not found a place in the military's inventory. A major improvement however, included the single side band radio (SSB) that, in ideal conditions, allowed you to communicate with ATOC in Trenton when you were halfway around the world. ATOC in turn could patch you through by telephone to anyone you wanted.

Speaking about SSB ideal conditions brings back memories of an around-the-world training flight. We were airborne out of Beirut, Lebanon enroute to Lahr, Germany. The passengers, however, wanted to go to the USAF base in Ramstein since the PX shopping was much better than in Lahr. As Command approval was needed to change our destination the RO was directed to call and see if he could get us a clearance to land there. G/C Sandy Sanford was the Command Duty Officer and ATOC put our call through to him. Apparently it was 3 or 4 in the morning in Trenton when Sandy was awakened to be asked that earth-shattering question. According to the RO it was fortunate that the aircraft commander wasn't on the SSB line. But being Sandy, he authorized the change and wished the passengers, not the crew, good shopping.

On the other hand, ionospheric conditions weren't always ideal, and this always seemed to occur when VVIPs were on board. The best example was a flight to London, England, and return with Lester B. Pearson, the PM, on board. The aircraft and crew were required to spend a full week in London since a request to undertake essential training in the busy European centres had been turned down because of a shortage of flying hours.

Hence, the entire crew was forced to suffer the trauma of living in downtown London and existing on pub grub for a whole week.

On the return flight to Ottawa on 27 November 1967, General Charles de Gaulle of France decided to utter that profound statement to be heard around the world, " VIVE QUEBEC LIBRE." Shortly after that utterance, our SSB was being overworked from the Acting PM's office, Paul Martin, in Ottawa. It must have been de Gaulle's pronouncement that disturbed the ionosphere, but regardless of the cause our contact was sporadic on all frequencies despite the RO, Bill Vradenburg's, valiant efforts. Paul was suggesting that we land in Gander where the PM could appear on national and international TV to comment on de Gaulle's brave but uncalled-for quote. Consequently, our destination remained uncertain until the PM's staff on board told us to have the Acting PM meet the aircraft on arrival in Ottawa, where the matter could be discussed in private. However, the PM would not be making any comments on national or international TV that night. There were a great many flood lights on our aircraft when we ramped in Ottawa and the local press and TV were in full strength - but as the PM had said, there were no formal comments made that night about the infamous quote. There was however, a lot said between National Defence HQ, Air Transport Command and 412 Squadron about the quality of SSB communications.

It was during Pab MacKenzie's tour that the Falcon Fan Jet came on strength and began to compete in international air races. The aircraft did wonders for the squadron in that it provided rapid transportation for military and government VIPs who could now visit distant points in North America in hours rather than days.

For instance, VIPs could undertake flights to the Maritime Provinces and or Manitoba and Saskatchewan and return the same day. Consequently, there was a continuing demand for the use of these aircraft and the crews were very busy. However, the fact that it was a new aircraft and a delight to fly moderated to some degree the heavy commitments.

COSMOPOLITAN IN EUROPE

by A. F. McDonald

The three hi-jacked airliners on the desert at Qa Khana in the fall of 1969 were only of passing interest to the personnel of 412 (T) Squadron. This organization that I toiled for as a Cosmo Captain was tasked with transporting military personnel, government VIPs, Heads of State and others across Canada and the United States. We did not realize that "terrorism" would soon have some of us in Europe.

European and Middle East air carriers at this time were particularly susceptible to air piracy since it was a new kind of crime. Effective security had not been developed to cope with it. Travel in Europe became pregnant with the problems of non-scheduled destination changes and delays, coupled with increased security checks or bomb threats.

A number of international meetings were scheduled in Europe for the fall of 1970, which included a large number of high-ranking Canadians. As a result of the piracy threat the Cabinet became involved in how best to provide safe travel for these VIPs. Prime Minister Trudeau's solution was his directive that wherever possible, members of Parliament were to travel in military aircraft.

Within 24 hours of this directive, a Squadron Cosmo was winging towards Lahr, Germany from Ottawa to provide a feeder

Over Hohenzollern Castle in Germany

by commercial air or on the 437 (T) Squadron Boeings and Yukons. The Commander-of-Forces in Europe, General Laubman, was to control the aircraft and assign priorities to it, which would also include airlift of service passengers. But the aircraft, operating a long way from home in Ottawa, had a number of unknowns about it: would it stay serviceable with only partial maintenance support being provided at Lahr, was the Cosmo reliable enough on its own to meet all departure and arrival times at different European airfields, and was one aircraft enough? We were soon to find out.

Immediate tasking began the day after our arrival. The Minister of Finance, the Honourable E.J. Benson and the Governor of the Bank of Canada, Mr. Rasminsky were to travel between Brussels and Copenhagen for the World Bankers' meeting.

The Cosmo had been positioned at Brussels on the previous evening and my crew and I had found a restaurant within spitting distance of the hotel which was only too happy to slake our thirst with a beer named Stella Artois and provide us with an excellent dinner. A couple of toasts were drunk to our first tour, and many of the restaurant patrons then got into the celebration, providing welcoming toasts for us on behalf of Belgium. On the following morning, feeling a little off-colour, I welcomed on board Mr. and Mrs. Rasminsky and Mrs. Benson, who disapprovingly stated that her husband would be along in a moment. He had enjoyed too much of Brussels last night - their first in Europe. It was comforting to know that our decision-makers on occasions have clay feet - or is it that misery likes company. Both of us were soon drinking gallons of coffee on our way to Copenhagen - albeit in different locations on the aircraft.

Flights to London, Paris, Rome, Cairo and Prague followed for other government officials. The aircraft lived up to every expectation throughout the fall and winter.

My last rotation to Lahr, and final flights on the squadron before transfer to a desk, began on April 18, 1971. For the next three weeks (a typical duty period) the aircraft seemed to be on continuous duty. Our first flight began on the 19th of April when we positioned Cosmo 109151 in Ypenburg, Holland to take the former Governor-General, his wife and their supporting staff to Brussels.

Mr. Michener had flown with us many times and knew each of us. On this flight he asked if we would be able to survey the dyke projects a few miles southwest of Ypenburg. With Amsterdam Radar providing us with complete isolation along the air routes, we were able to carry out a short air tour of the area being reclaimed from the sea. At Brussels, one of the busiest airports in Europe, all traffic was stopped for the arrival of our Regal party. The Governor-General and Mrs. Michener were accorded full state and military honours, but the arrival was a bit tense because of the formal decorum. It relaxed noticeably when many youngsters waving Canadian flags from the outside walkway of the nearby terminal building cheered enthusiastically on the appearance of their Excellencies.

By the way, there's no doubt the wonderful health of the Governor-General affected our sports outlook, since a few days after this flight the sports field at the Lahr Caserne was being circled by sweating, panting crew members who jogged for the 8.5 minute mile. The most demanding day during the tour occurred on 1 May when we left Koln, Germany for Lahr with Gen and Mrs. Laubmann. Shortly after getting airborne the instrument standby system went off the line, shorting all the flight instruments. Fortunately, we were able to correct the malfunctioning system on the way to Lahr, since we were to leave Lahr for Lisbon, Portugal as soon as possible after deplaning our passengers, to pick up General Dextraze and party.

The flight to Lisbon entails overflight clearances for France, Spain and Portugal, and it requires excellent prior planning to be done by the Air Movements staff in Lahr Headquarters. This of course, did not seem to have been done. The Director for overflights was shaken out of any weekend diversions when I informed him the Cosmo wasn't going anywhere until assurances were provided that overflight clearances had been processed for both Spain and Portugal. France was already covered under a blanket military authority.

The Director assured me that everything was properly done except for the paperwork. He convinced me to carry on, with the proviso that he would personally contact the appropriate Embassies and radio the clearance authority to the Cosmo on HF. Knowing Lieutenant Colonels to be honourable men, the Cosmo was soon purring along towards Lisbon.

Communications with the Portuguese evidently broke down, and our arrival at Lisbon was a bit of a surprise. Their military, rather than impounding us, however, assisted us as well as their capabilities allowed on our arrival, and we were able to depart for Lahr with our passengers approximately 1.5 hours later. We eventually landed at 2000 hours - our on-duty time was just over thirteen hours.

During this tour we flew a total of 65 hours. In addition to our Regal passengers and General Dextrase, the Cosmo carried the Honourable Mitchell Sharp, Generals Laubman, Dare, Turcot, Leonard, Doyle, Bell, Adamson, their wives and many more. Everyone admired this aeroplane which proved to be dependable and able to cope with minimum support. It did the tasks demanded of it.

As a parting remark, the aircraft took over most of the flying done by 109 Composite Unit, (disbanded on 1 April 1971) which had three Dakotas and about 35 officers and men toward the final phase of their operation. From a cost-effectiveness viewpoint that's not bad for one Cosmo, five crew members and servicing support at Lahr.

The aircraft continued to operate in Europe with some changes until 1980. A full crew was transferred to Lahr as a detachment rather than continuing crew rotation every three weeks. Eventually the Cosmo was replaced in Europe in 1980 by the two Dash 7's.

NOTES FROM THE FLYING LOG
by Brigadier-General Gord Diamond

412 Squadron, my longest flight and youngest, most fragile passengers. In May, 1971, Jerry Elias and myself flew a 412 Squadron Falcon from Ottawa, completed a couple of other taskings enroute and landed in Fort Smith, NWT, to RON for a mission the next day. The following morning we were to fly Audubon Society personnel, Canadian Wildlife and American Wildlife ornithologists and six Whooping Crane eggs from their nesting area near Fort Smith to Andrews Air Force Base in Maryland for relocation to a protected sanctuary in Maryland. The military executive jet flight was part of the joint government effort to save the Whooping Crane population, which eventually through such efforts, proved successful.

We arrived in Fort Smith in the late afternoon, and after checking into the hotel and changing, went over to the Wildlife office to have a look at their project. It was a good thing that we didn't stop for a cold beer in the hotel before doing so, because when we arrived the first chick had already pecked his way through the shell, and was sitting in a cardboard box kept warm by a light bulb on an extension cord. A second was already threatening to do the same. The scientists were concerned, to say the least, and made an impassioned plea for us to fly immediately and take the whole lot to Andrews Air Force Base before they all hatched. So we ran back to the hotel, checked out, rounded up all the equipment and personnel and launched off for an overnight flight via Winnipeg to Washington D.C.

Naturally, it was one of the worst trips I can recall on the Falcon. We experienced some of the most challenging weather I had yet encountered in flying and the whole route was cluttered with heavy thunderstorms. All the unhatched eggs were individually placed in moulded foam sections in two modified executive brief cases, each with a large thermometer inserted through a hole drilled in the top. For the duration of the six-hour flight, the briefcases remained on the laps of the scientists, more attentively guarded than the crown jewels.

The one hatched VIP travelled extremely well in his cardboard box, secured by a seat belt, with extension cord plugged into the electric razor outlet in the washroom. For our quick turn-around and fuel stop at Winnipeg in the early morning we called ahead to have food delivered because we didn't have time to get any supper in Ft. Smith. As fate would have it, the only place Base Ops could get to deliver at that hour was the Colonel's Fried Chicken, which brought a few laughs from the passengers, but only the unfeathered variety!

Of course, the hardest landing I ever made in the Falcon was on our 6 a.m. arrival in Washington D.C. after a 23 hour day, but I breathed a sigh of relief when it was reported from the back that all our fragile flyers were OK, and there were no further breakages.

BAD CAM IN IRAN

by Ray Paquette

On 19 February 1974, we took off out of Lahr on a nine-day tour through the Middle East countries of Lebanon, Saudi Arabia, Iran and Turkey. Our VIPs were the Honourable Don MacDonald, Minister of Trade and Commerce, Mrs. MacDonald, plus a small entourage. While primarily on a trade mission, the minister would attend the opening ceremonies of our new Embassy in Tehran. The Shah was in power at the time and we all looked forward to this stop as the highlight of the trip.

By the time we arrived in Iran, we had made stopovers in the Middle East cities of Beirut, Ryad and Jeda, and we were getting cautious about the food we ate. We were all heavily into Kaopectate! After settling into the Imperial Hotel in Tehran, I decided I would follow Rod Dionne, our flight steward, to a restaurant for something to eat. He found an American-looking restaurant and we looked over the menu. It was all in Arabic but the waiter spoke a little English. "Just order anything that's been boiled," said Rod as he pointed out the soup to the waiter. I was hungry and I knew that soup wouldn't fill me, so I said to the waiter, "Just bring me a local dish, whatever everybody else eats around here." That should be safe. "You'll be sorry," said Rod, as he stared at his soup.

My order arrived and it looked like breaded veal and it was delicious. Rodney was getting down to the last spoonfuls of his soup and laughing at me, when he noticed a huge eyeball looking up at him from the bottom of his bowl. It was "Goat's Eyeball Soup" and I almost fell off my chair laughing at him. By the time we got back to the hotel, I wasn't feeling so great myself and I wasn't finding Rodney's experience so funny.

The remainder of the crew, Gord Kelso, Kip Powick and Pete "Mad Dog" Davies advised us that we had been invited to the US Embassy and would be leaving in an hour. "You guys go ahead without me," I said, "I'm not feeling too well."

I went to my room, and though I was pretty sick for a while I didn't worry, but about an hour later when my temperature shot up, I did what any well seasoned Senior NCO would do who is sick and alone in a foreign country: "I panicked!" By then the crew had left for the embassy and I frantically tried to get the front desk to get a doctor. Finally they put me through to the US Embassy and they sent an English-speaking Iranian doctor.

The doctor checked me over, suspected food poisoning, and asked what I had eaten for my last meal. I didn't know, so he called the restaurant where Rod and I had eaten our supper. There was a bunch of Arabic spoken which I didn't understand and the doctor came back to my bed and said, "I don't know why you should be so sick. You didn't eat anything abnormal. Everybody around here eats Camel nuts. The problem may be that you ate BAD camel nuts!"

I was then, not only physically sick, but also psychologically ill, and the rest of the crew got the last laugh, so I thought I would include it in this publication, since I will never live it down anyway.

GLEN PARSLOW'S THIRD TOUR
July 1971 To January 1974

On 17 July 1971, Bob Hallowell, whose aircraft inventory included Cosmopolitans and Falcons, turned control of the Squadron over to yours truly. The two VIP Yukons had been transferred to Trenton in an effort to consolidate all Yukon operations. It was undoubtedly a dollar and cent issue that prompted the move, but it literally eliminated 412's VIP global role. Apart from the one 412 Cosmo based at Lahr, it in fact limited the Sqn to North American operations.

Fortunately, however, 412 crews were rotated every few weeks to fly the Lahr-based aircraft, and since maintenance of the aircraft remained vested at CFB Ottawa, Cosmo crews, by

Their Royal Highnesses, Queen Elizabeth and Prince Phillip board a 412 (T) Sqn. CC-109 Cosmopolitan during their 1973 Canadian Tour.

way of ferry flights, remained qualified in Oceanic and European rules and procedures. Eventually however, the development and move to Lahr of the Dash 7 allowed a permanent crew to be established in Europe and the Cosmos returned to Ottawa. Hence there was a period when the Squadron no longer operated on a global basis.

A courtesy call on Gen. Chester Hull, the Commander of ATC, disclosed that any time he requested a Falcon aircraft, our crews should expect him to fly in the left-hand seat, with the aircraft commander occupying the right-hand seat. If he had work to do, or was tired and didn't want to fly, he would advise the aircraft commander, and would sit in the rear cabin.

Apparently, going into Winnipeg one day, he was in the left-hand seat and the First Officer was in the rear compartment along with the two Mrs. Hulls, Chester's wife and his mother. It seems the landing was heavier than normal (whatever 'normal' is for a General's landing), and his mother exclaimed to the First Officer, "It's a good thing that his dad wasn't on board or Chester would certainly have heard about that landing!" Needless to say, that story was used when CFB Ottawa honored Chester on his departure from Command HQ.

Returning to the earlier comments about the importance of flight stewards, you'll recall that if their performance wasn't letter-perfect the flight could be a disaster, despite how well the flight itself was flown. Fortunately such disasters were few and far between and generally only occurred when new stewards, who hadn't fully learned the ropes, were pressed into service because of shortages of qualified people. However, even with the head steward on board, if the ingredients are just right, disasters can occur.

It was 11 February 1973, on a flight from Ramey AFB in Puerto Rico with a full complement of senior generals enroute to Ottawa. Five minutes after take-off the steward came up front and said, "Sir, I'm sorry, but I left the filet mignons in the mess." Having been seen off by the U.S. brass, there was no way we could return, so we looked at our routing home. Lo and behold, we would pass directly over Charleston AFB. The decision was simple. Crank up the SSB and ask Charleston Base Ops to order the required number of partially cooked filets, and have them ready to go on our arrival. Fortunately, no untoward pronouncements had been made by any heads of state that day, and the SSB was loud and clear. We advised the passengers that we would be making a ten-minute stop in Charleston and that hopefully, it wouldn't change our ramp time in Ottawa. In the meantime, it was suggested that the steward should open up the bar and serve our distinguished guests the delightful finger snacks that he had prepared.

Lady Luck was on our side. Charleston had the filets ready and waiting. The bill was paid and we departed in very short order, arriving in Ottawa on our original ramp time. Undoubtedly most of the passengers weren't taken in by the unscheduled stop, but you can well imagine what would have happened if Charleston hadn't responded so admirably to our rather strange request, or for that matter, if the SSB had been out of sorts that day.

While the steward didn't fit the novice category, it only proves that the best can err. However, at the end of the flight, it was the steward who was getting the accolades in the rear of the aircraft and, quite frankly, they were well-deserved.

The last flight worthy of mention was Royal Flight 876. Fortunately, it was customary that these flights were flown by Squadron COs. The remainder of the crew was comprised of Major Pearson, MCpl St. George, Sgt White, Sgt Turner, MCpl Jackson and Captain Bailey. Previous Royal Flights on the C5 and the Yukons normally involved a flight to London to pick up the Royal entourage and remain with group for the entire itinerary, returning, in the end, to England. Unfortunately PM Trudeau, possibly since he may have been criticized for doing pirouettes in the company of the Queen on one of his London visits, had decided that Canada's civil carriers should jointly handle the Royal Tours, with one small portion being allocated to the Military. It would appear that the Military's voice on the tour committee must have been rather weak, since the portion that was to be done by 412 Sqn was a 45-minute chock-to-chock flight from CFB Summerside to Charlottetown on Cosmo 151.

Despite the shortness of the flight, it was indeed a great

Commanding officers and wives at the 1972 reunion.

ITINERARY
PRIME MINISTER'S TOUR

FROM	DEPARTURE DATE	DAY	LOCAL	TO	ARRIVAL DATE	DAY	LOCAL	N. MILES DISTANCE	FLYING TIME
ROCKCLIFFE	FEB 4	THU	1445	GOOSE BAY	FEB 4	THU	1900	761	3:15
GOOSE BAY	5	FRI	0700	LONDON	5	FRI	2000	2218	9:00
LONDON	7	SUN	1515	PARIS	7	SUN	1730	185	1:15
PARIS (ORLY)	10	WED	1030	BONN	10	WED	1145	260	1:15
BONN	12	FRI	1030	GROS TENQUIN	12	FRI	1115	105	:45
GROS TENQUIN	12	FRI	1400	ZWEIBRUCKEN	12	FRI	1430	50	:30
ZWEIBRUCKEN	12	FRI	1530	ROME	12	FRI	1930	690	4:00
ROME (CIMPIANO)	16	TUE	0915	BAHREIN	16	TUE	2000	2075	8:45
BAHREIN	17	WED	1015	KARACHI	17	WED	1530	862	3:45
KARACHI	19	FRI	1415	PESHAWAR	19	FRI	1715	605	3:00
PESHAWAR	20	SAT	1600	LAHORE	20	SAT	1700	206	1:00
LAHORE	21	SUN	1515	NEW DELHI	21	SUN	1730	300	1:15
NEW DELHI (PALAM)	25	THU	0900	AGRA	25	THU	0930	100	:30
AGRA	26	FRI	0900	BOMBAY	26	FRI	1200	550	3:00
BOMBAY	27	SAT	0930	MADRAS	27	SAT	1230	552	3:00
MADRAS	28	SUN	1500	COLOMBO	28	SUN	1700	380	2:00
COLOMBO	MAR 4	THU	0800	DJAKARTA	MAR 4	THU	1900	2000	9:00
DJAKARTA	6	SAT	0930	MANILA	6	SAT	1630	1400	6:30
MANILA	7	SUN	0900	SEOUL	7	SUN	1730	1500	7:30
SEOUL	10	WED	1000	TOKYO	10	WED	1300	500	3:00
TOKYO	13	SAT	0900	MIDWAY	12	FRI	2200	2250	10:00 Date Line
MIDWAY	13	SAT	1000	HONOLULU	13	SAT	1630	1150	5:30
HONOLULU	15	MON	2359	SAN FRANCISCO	16	TUE	1145	2190	9:45
SAN FRANCISCO	17	WED	0915	OTTAWA	17	WED	2130	2200	9:15
								23,089	106:45

DEPARTURE TIMES ARE THE TIMES AT WHICH THE AIRCRAFT SHOULD BE AIRBORNE AND IN CONSEQUENCE THE MEMBERS OF THE PARTY SHOULD PROVISION TO EMPLANE 15 MINUTES PRIOR TO THE INDICATED DEPARTURE TIMES.

THE ARRIVAL TIMES INDICATED ABOVE ARE RAMP TIMES, I.E., THE TIME AT WHICH THE PRIME MINISTER WILL DEPLANE.

ALL TIMES SHOWN ARE LOCAL TIMES.

honour having the Royal Party on board, and in keeping with 412 Sqn tradition, the doors opened in Charlottetown exactly on the designated ramp time. On arrival, the Queen's pilot advised me that I was expected, along with a large number of others who were involved in her Maritime tour, to be presented to the Queen the next morning. Those being presented would be properly briefed before being ushered into the room set aside for this purpose. Our briefing was indeed short and we were told that our meeting with the Queen would be brief. We were then lined up down a long hall in the order of our supposed appearance. Waiting in line, it was evident that each presentation took anywhere from one to three minutes, and given the size of the line-up, this was understandable. Entering when instructed, I expected to do a quick turn about after being presented with a signed portrait from the Royal Couple. However, Prince Philip, being a pilot, engaged me in what turned out to be a longer conversation than normal. He asked about aircraft on the Military's inventory and was surprised to learn that the Yukons had been replaced by Boeing 707s. He had understood that we no longer had the long range capability since Canada's commercial carriers had been pressed into service. The Prince may have used that information to get the Military back into the Royal Tours, since mixed airline Royal Tours were very short-lived.

During this tour, my last with the Sqn, the first 412 Squadron Reunion was held in September 1972. It was the first time that former members of 12 Communications Flight, formed on the 10th September 1939; members of 412 Fighter Squadron, formed on 30th June 1941; and members of the current 412 Transport Squadron joined together on the 33rd anniversary of the Squadron founding. It was evident from the success of that event that the spirit that existed at the time of its founding and during wartime fighter operations, was the same that exists on the current Squadron. A/V/M John Plant, who gave the formal address on this occasion, emphasized that very point and in his concluding remarks said, "I wish you were 412 Squadron, Royal Canadian Air Force, and not whatever it is." He was alluding to the fact that the impact of unification had been anything but positive, and he didn't like what unification was doing to what, at one time, was famed around the world as the RCAF. He concluded, however, on the optimistic note that, "In less than 20 years, the pendulum will swing back, and the RCAF will return again." Unfortunately, it was an optimistic expectation that could never materialize.

On 13 January, 1974 the reins were turned over to Mike Zrymiak.

THE DECLINING YEARS
1966 TO PRESENT
anonymous

Going back over thirty years of service, one cannot help but reminisce about the good times that were encountered and enjoyed. There was a camaraderie throughout that can not be duplicated or replaced.

The RCAF differed from the other two services. Discipline was not the keynote in the RCAF as it was in the Army and Navy. "Responsibility" was the magic that motivated and drove the RCAF, and it was extended from the Air Marshalls down to the AC1s and AC2s. For instance, LAC crewmen at 412 were fully responsible for the aircraft away from base, and no matter how extreme the weather, the aircraft was always ready well in advance of the departure time. In short, the RCAF rank structure didn't carry the rigidity that it did in the other services. However, it would take a book to do the subject of responsibility vs. discipline in the RCAF complete justice.

Integration, followed shortly thereafter by Unification, completed Paul Hellyer's dream to unify the three services. After all, why couldn't a pilot fly his airplane in the morning, command his destroyer in the afternoon, and undertake army maneuvers in the evening?! Paul's dream of establishing a precedent that would be followed by all NATO nations never materialized. In fact it was ignored by most other member nations, but the damage it did to the esprit-de-corps of Canada's three services lives on. In retrospect, it is easy to see that the integration of common support elements is where the process should have stopped.

Shortly after unification, Air Transport Command promulgated an order that precluded pilots from attempting an approach in weather conditions that were reported as being below the IFR limits. Since the reporting of weather conditions at airports was the responsibility of personnel in the control tower, pilots were allowed by flying regulations to attempt an approach, since the weather conditions as viewed by the pilot might be quite different. However, when the pilot reached his minimum descent altitude of 200 feet and didn't have the runway in sight to land safely during the prescribed time interval, he was obliged to overshoot, and in keeping with his fuel requirements, proceed to his alternate airport. Apparently, an ATC pilot had landed his aircraft at one of the Canadian Air Bases in Europe in unsafe weather conditions and proceeded to run off the runway into the muddy infield. Instead of coming down hard on the pilot for his unprofessional approach to safety standards, ATCHQ drafted the order taking away the responsibility accorded pilots in the flying regulations. As the order only applied to Transport Command, 412 Sqn pilots were continually overflying their destinations and proceeding to their alternates despite the fact that other military aircraft and commercial carriers were landing and taking off at the airport that 412 was obliged to overfly. Given the expertise resident in 412 Sqn crews, it was indeed difficult for aircraft commanders to tell their VIP passengers that they would have to proceed to their alternate, especially when the passengers could see other aircraft landing and taking off at the destination airport. As a result, the new pilots joining our ranks were indecisive and concerned about the support they could expect to receive from the hierarchy. This was a complete about-face from the self assurance exuded by those who were on the Squadron in the 50s and 60s.

It was also during this same period that the order came down for aircrew to remove their former RCAF cloth wings and pin on the new metal CF wings. Aircrew had won their wings as members of the RCAF and were extremely proud to wear them, since they were part and parcel of the famed RCAF WWII heritage. In defiance, a number of the old timers simply sewed their RCAF wings on the back of their left lapel and pinned up the new wings in keeping with the order. At the time, it seemed that a simple order allowing those who joined before unification to wear the wings of their choice until retirement, and those who joined afterward to wear the new wing, would have been a much more realistic and human approach. However, once an order is promulgated, it is difficult to rescind.

It is apparent from discussions with serving Air Element members that the esprit-de-corps of the old RCAF no longer exists. For example, if a pilot whose spouse is working is transferred, he or she frequently opt for release rather than be moved. Also, officers who are earmarked for rapid promotion frequently turn down the promotion and leave for greener pastures. Even the former CO of 412 Sqn, who started the wheels in motion for the 50th reunion, decided to leave the military early to work with Bombardier.

Notwithstanding these setbacks that started with the 500 cut, the assignment of the total VIP role to 412 Sqn has certainly done wonders for the morale of the Squadron, as did the re-equipping with Challenger aircraft. The latter completely restored its former global role. But why does 412 Sqn remain so great? Why was it so much better than its counterpart, the former Transport Canada Executive Flight? Simply because the constant turn-over of 412 personnel provides a continual flow of fresh new ideas - better ways of doing the job. This was not the case in the Transport Canada VIP Flight, and this is why 412 Sqn remains fresh, alive and great.

Lastly, an example of 412 Sqn's impact upon its members. F/L Russ Bagnell, a wartime pilot who came back to instruct NATO students, was transferred to 412. Russ was one of the 500 cut. With a wife and five young children to raise, he, like the others, was devastated. However, having learned the basics of VIP flying at 412, he moved his family to the U.S.A. where he entered the field of corporate aviation. In a relatively short period he moved up to the exalted position of Chief Pilot on Cox Enterprises' Gulfstream Jet operation. He retired from flying, having designed and supervised the building of Cox's executive hangar in Atlanta, Georgia. Over his years with that organization, he was held in especially high regard by the Company's CEO. Russ quite candidly claims that his success was a result of what he learned about VIP flying from his days at 412. While he is currently living in Florida, he has attended all 412 Sqn reunions, and like the rest of us, he is looking forward to meeting his old friends at the next one.

Hopefully, the recent move to distinctive uniforms for the three operational elements of the Canadian Forces is a prelude to the re-establishment of the Canadian Air Force, the Canadian Army and the Canadian Navy. And while most of us would like to see the re-instatement of the term "Royal" as expressed by A/V/M Plant at the 1972 reunion, we agree that, given the current politics of the country, this will never happen. But, like the A/V/M, most of us agree that the restoration of the three distinct services could again restore the 'responsibility' that former RCAF members enjoyed, and which in turn, created such a great organization.

THE RECENT YEARS

In 1983, two Canadair Challenger aircraft were taken on inventory by 412 Squadron. The acquisition of these aircraft re-oriented the Squadron to its former global VIP role.

The year 1985 saw the retirement of the Falcon aircraft after 17 years of service with the Squadron. As well, 1985 marked the silver anniversary of the Cosmopolitan until its retirement in 1994. Moreover the acquisition of the former Transport Canada VIP mandate by the Squadron expanded the challenger fleet to eight aircraft.

The consolidation of responsibility under DND for VIP administrative flight service substantially increased Squadron manning levels. Total Squadron personnel strength reached almost 100. In addition, changes to the Challenger fleet continued with substitution of four 600 Series Challengers with four 601 Series aircraft. Royal visitors continued to utilize the service of 412 Squadron. Their Royal Highnesses, the Duke and Duchess of York and His Royal Highness, the Prince Edward were flown on Challenger transatlantic missions during 1987. During their visit to Canada in 1991, the Duke and Duchess of York were airlifted aboard a 412 Squadron Cosmopolitan.

Challenge, change and achievement are the hallmarks of 412 (Transport) Squadron: In May, 1987, the deHavilland Dash 7 aircraft were replaced by two Dash 8s in Lahr. These in turn were replaced in May, 1990 by the Cosmopolitan aircraft from the 412 Squadron Detachment in Winnipeg. As well, 412 Squadron celebrated its milestone 50th Anniversary in August, 1989.

Throughout 1990 and 1991, members of 412 Squadron once again led the way by pioneering VIP aircraft missions into the Persian Gulf area during Operation Desert Storm, and throughout the former Soviet Union and Eastern Bloc countries.

Given the severe military reductions in 1994 the Squadron was downsized to 4 challenger aircraft and with the closure of CFB Ottawa the Squadron was relocated to the MOT hangar at 58 Service Road, McDonald Cartier Airport, Gloucester, Ontario. (To avoid any confusion the reader should be aware that the McDonald Cartier Airport is the new name for what was known as the Ottawa International Airport. The good news is that the Squadron continues its prestigious role of providing airlift for the Prime Minister, the Governor General and foreign dignitaries and heads of state-accordingly, the Squadron members face the future with confidence, optimisim and enthusiam, based on more than 50 years of service and tradition.

INVESTURE OF 412 SQUADRON
HONORARY COLONEL

On August 26, 1993, Lieutenant General W.K. Carr, CMM., DFC., OSt J., CD., CMJL, was invested as the Honorary Colonel of 412 (transport) Squadron. The following is the parade order for the investiture issued by the Commanding Officer, Lt Col Wayne Thompson.

NOTES ON THE INVESTITURE
Lt Gen Bill Carr's long association with
412 SQN and uplands

Bill Carr was presented with his wings by the late Air Marshall Billy Bishop, Canada's greatest fighter pilot and WW1

LCol W.C. Thompson, CO 412 Sqn on left, and Lt. Gen. W.K. Carr holding the scroll investing Bill Carr as the Honorary Colonel of 412 (Transport) Squadron.

VC, DSO, DFC holder, fifty-one and one half years ago outside old hangar 2. Iron Bill MacBrien was the Stn Commander, and no one, not even God, was held in greater fear by the young sprog pilots of Bill's class. However, the awe and admiration in which Billy Bishop was clothed, was something none were to forget. To each member of the class, even including Bishop's son Arthur, the occasion, very special in its own right, was made an historic moment not to be forgotten by any lucky enough to have his wings pinned on by the hero, unmatched in fame or fortune.

Thirty six years ago, almost to the day, Bill was appointed as Commanding Officer of 412 Sqn. Until that time, his career had been exciting, and in peace and war, he had heard much about this elite unit. That he should be chosen for this job, made him aware that the maintenance, and indeed even the enhancement, of 412's reputation would be some kind of challenge. Would he measure up? At the outset, events made it doubtful.

AN ELITE UNIT

During his first week in the chair, three events made him wonder how elite the Sqn. really was. First, one of the Comet aircraft on flight test, loaded with 'erks', had the inflatable raft stored in the wing, break loose. The dinghy cover cut an eight foot gash in the pressure hull, and being at 41,000 feet, an explosive decompression occurred. However, owing to superb airmanship by the pilot, F/L Bill Carss, no one was hurt and the aircraft landed safely. (This was the world's first such event where the aircraft and personnel survived. Needless to say, engineers and writers from all over the place came to have a look!)

The second event, much less life-threatening, but career-threatening none-the-less, arose when it was determined that members on the Comet conversion course in the UK had inflated their expense accounts, to offset some of the discretionary costs they had generated in serving their own welfare. This was greatly frowned upon and not the kind of behavior expected of the elite members of 412 Sqn. When this was passed to Bill for resolution, he was heard to remark, "How come, if they are so elite and smart, this bunch could be so stupid as to get caught?"

The third event in this fun-filled week, was the failure of the Unit Instrument Check Pilot to pass his annual Instrument Check Ride. Such an occurrence could be likened to landing the C5 with royalty on board, in front of an admiring crowd, with 'the wheels in the well.' Unforgivable!

"On Friday, feeling very perplexed at this sequence, the AOC, Fred Carpenter, affectionately known as 'Flat-top' (Because of his crew-cut) called me and said he was not very favourably impressed with my record as a CO. He then proceeded to tell me, in some of the well-chosen words he was famous for, what would happen (to me) if things didn't improve immediately."

"Things did get better, and 412's honour was soon restored, despite other events which occasionally marred the record. I guess I am the only Royal Pilot, who, with the Royal Passenger and entourage on board, succeeded in scaring hell out of all and sundry when I blew two tires on landing at Prince Albert. The moral of this story is - if you're going to screw up, make sure you do it in front of the Prime Minister, The Minister of Defence and Royalty!"

1994 is the 50th anniversary of "D" Day and the 53rd anniversary of 412 Sqn. Time flies, and the Hon Colonel is convinced that despite its ups and downs, experiencing its passage is better than the alternative.

Traditionally, Honorary Colonels raised and endowed fighting military units. An admirable role, but hopefully not the course-of-action expected today. Bill Carr noted that while he was sympathetic, and most strongly endorsed, the Squadron's desire to acquire Regional jets and Global Express Challengers for their VIP role, at $20 million a pop, the powers that be should be aware that if this was a condition of his appointment, the Honour should be immediately withdrawn!

He noted seriously that there might still be some useful purpose Honorary Colonels might serve. From where he sat, Bill observed, lobbying could on occasion serve a purpose even if it violated the chain of Command. For example, his experience in researching Newfie jokes might be of help in digging up information about some political masters which, if exposed, could embarrass them, but which discreetly used, could influence decisions favourably.

General Carr commented that he had to retire to be demoted. In jest, he remarked that the reason he had progressed might have been the result of luck, and perhaps not being caught. Regardless of the past, to now be chosen to represent and help 412 Sqn, was an honour he would never have anticipated.

412 Sqn. has an unparalleled record among Air Force units. Not all thought its choice of motto to be appropriate. The late Governor General Massey once remarked to Bill Carr that "Promptus Ad Vindictum", which he translated to mean "Swift To Kill", failed to send a message of comfort to its VIP clients! Its history shows what an impact a small unit like a Squadron can have on the image of an Air Force, and indeed a country. Excellence and professionalism are the hallmarks of the Squadron.

Bill Carr thanked the Commander of ATG, General Jeff Brace, and Lt Colonel Wayne Thompson for the great honour which had been bestowed on him. He appreciated that approval had come down the chain, but its origin had come from the sharp end, where the action really is, and where the future success will flow.

He dedicated himself to help 412 Sqn. in any way he could, but never to overlook the aims and loyalties of the personnel, which made its success what it was, and was destined to continue to be.

Annex A

To: 1011-1 (CO 412 Sqn)
Dated: 20 Aug 93

NUMBER ONE FLIGHT

Flight Commander	- 370		Maj Fowlie
Flight WO	- 222		WO Donker
Flight Markers	- 811		Sgt Gilbert
	- 031		Sgt Mendonca
	- 682		Sgt Hokke
764 MCpl Evans		683	Cpl Trops
990 MCpl Polson		635	Cpl Perron
666 MCpl Basque		542	Cpl Campbell
364 MCpl Whelan		059	Cpl Despres
452 MCpl Blight		446	Cpl May
630 MCpl MacDonald		101	Cpl Velss
436 MCpl Douglas		567	Cpl Dauphinais
893 MCpl Goudreault		242	Cpl Mercier
926 MCpl Desjardins		966	Cpl Rau
469 Cpl Cloutier		233	Cpl Shanks
984 Cpl Hartley		666	Cpl Lopez
778 Cpl Hartley		853	Cpl Hicks
778 Cpl Machabee		433	Cpl Toutant
937 Cpl Provan		459	Pte Gagnon

Annex B

To: 1011-1 (CO 412 Sqn)
Dated: 20 Aug 93

NUMBER TWO FLIGHT

Flight Commander	484		Maj Harrod
Flight WO	333		WO Caldwell
Flight Markers	872		Sgt Frignon
	261		Sgt Lahaie
	857		Sgt Schlegel
711 MCpl Croteau		798	Cpl Dubois
291 MCpl Gaumond		712	Cpl Fraser
812 MCpl Wharry		798	Cpl Gavin
226 MCpl Christensen		748	Cpl Harriet
960 MCpl Daigle		123	Cpl Harrity
479 Cpl Charbonneau		881	Cpl Labreche
656 Cpl Lamontagne		539	Cpl Lemon
780 Cpl Leblanc		911	Cpl McGrath
880 Cpl Brown		102	Cpl McLaughlin
658 Cpl Laprise		242	Cpl Ridsdale
702 Cpl Cassivi		819	Cpl Stahn
217 Cpl Belanger		064	Pte Gigvere
977 Cpl Birkin		587	Pte Inman
072 Cpl Distefano			

Annex C

To: 1011-1 (CO 412 Sqn)
Dated: 20 Aug 93

OFFICERS ON PARADE

The following 412 Sqn Officers will assemble on parade:

Capt Abbott	Capt Lessard
Capt Dumont	Capt McCarthy
Capt Guerette	Capt Waters
Capt Hartzell	Lt Menard
Capt Kennedy	Lt Nicholson
Capt Kupecz	2Lt Mills

Memorandum

1011-1 (CO 412 Sqn)
20 Aug 93

Parade Order 412 Sqn Parade

1. <u>Purpose:</u> 412 Sqn will assemble on parade to invest LGen Carr (Ret) as the Sqn's Honorary Colonel on 26 Aug 93.
2. <u>Place:</u> The Sqn parade will be held in 13 Hgr, 7 Wing Ottawa.
3. <u>Time & Date:</u> 1030 hrs on 26 Aug 93.
4. <u>Dress:</u> No 1A order of dress (Medals, name tags, shoes or ankle boots; navy cap/hat service, army beret, airforce wedge).
5. <u>Parade Rehearsal:</u> A parade rehearsal will be held on 25 Aug 93, 1300 hrs in 13 Hgr. Dress will be dress of the day.
6. <u>Parade Details:</u>
   1030 hrs - Parade markers report to parade MWO;
   1035 hrs - Parade fall in;
   1045 hrs - Arrival of Comd ATG.
   1050 hrs - Arrival of Honorary Col and Wing Comd; and 1130 hrs - Reception in 13 Hgr.
7. <u>Format:</u>
   - 7 Wing Piper Band in position in hgr;
   - Sqn fall in;
   - Arrival of BGen J.C. Brace, Comd ATG;
   - Comd ATG proceeds to dais - Air Salute;
   - Arrival of Honorary Col and Wing Comd;
   - Honorary Col proceeds to dais - Air Salute;
   - Parade inspected by Honorary Col;
   - Introduction and presentation of scroll to Honorary Col by Comd ATG;
   - Address by Honorary Col;
   - Medal presentations by Honorary Col;
   - Honorary Col returns to dais - advance in review order, Gen Salute; and
   - Honorary Col departs escorted by Comd ATG and Wing Comd.
8. <u>Composition:</u>
   Parade Commander- LCol Thompson
   Deputy Parade Commander- Maj Tidy
   Parade SWO- MWO Bouchard

(Signed)
W. C. Thompson LCol
CO 412 Sqn
998-3412

Annex
Annex A - No. 1 Flight
Annex B - No. 2 Flight

Cosmo Flight (8392C)

by D.S. MacIntosh

I see from my window
on the starboard side
the blur of the prop.
like a plastic disc
before the nacelle
that houses the mighty
power plant, as ever
westward the Cosmo
pressed.

the starboard wing,
and the aileron that
is trimmed and true;
The static lines are
black and lean as they stretch
from the trailing edge
of the wing.

Above, the sky is
an eggshell blue,
Below, like a sea of cotton
waste the cloud banks
boil and rise in columns
that overflow, to spill
in a void of measureless
space.

And further below
to a greater depth
where the clouds for
a time are rent in twain,
I view the scene,
(as an eagle must)
of the Rocky Mountain
ridge terrain.

The naked splendor
before my eyes
is interrupted for a spell
as an orange,
fresh from the Steward's tray
is peeled,
and my eyes are directed
by sense of smell.

We have the sun
at twelve o'clock
as we gently roll
from side to side,
yet ever steady on
a course that's true;
The sky above now
disappears and the vapor
by my window floats
as the cotton sea
we're descending through.

'Til now on the
final approach I see
the patchwork quilt
like fields below,
and strapped to my
seat in steady descent,
I think of the man
in command of the ship,
as I feel her roll
and the port wing dip.

With a gentle bump
he sets her down and then
on a sudden, a mighty roar
of the engine's thrust,
for without a hitch the pilot
has reversed the propeller's
pitch; she shudders and
trembles from stem to stern
as we clear the active
with a left hand turn;

And I share in the whistle
of the turbo-prop,
as this 412 Cosmo
grinds to a stop,
for we've taxied in
to the A.M.U. where we'll
all deplane and thank the
crew for a job well done,
that has made our flight
a successful one.

Ode to 412

Anonymous

There they sit, Our mighty fleet,
Cosmos, Falcons, My God they're sleek,
With tops so white and bottoms that gleam,
A fine clean sight from a well trained team.

A team of techs doing a job superb,
To ensure we'll have the right type bird,
To carry our Rolly or maybe Pierre,
From eleven "A" to God knows where.

They freeze their hands in 20 below,
In summer they sweat in streams that flow,
They slosh through rain, get feet soaked wet,
While tightening bolts or changing a set.

The panics on, a delayed departure,
What are the probs? You say it won't start Sir
The switches are right, we have proper power,
And we only have ten until the hour.

Come on you guys, let's have a look,
Ah, here it is. It's in the book,
The pump gets changed, the engines primed,
And away it goes, another flight on time.

Canadian skies crisscrossed with white.
It fills our hearts, that glorious sight,
To say they're proud is only fair,
Cause they filled our skies with bubbly air.

Promtus Ad Vindictam

412 Transport Squadron
Commanding officers

Wing Commander W.H. Swetman, DSO, DFC	1 Apr 1949 - 12 Aug 1949
Wing Commander B.H. Moffitt, DGFC, AFC	13 Aug 1949 - 26 Aug 1950
Wing Commander R.I. Trickett, DFC	6 Sep 1950 - 11 Feb 1952
Wing Commander H.A. Morrison, DSC, DFC, AFC, CD	12 Feb 1952 - 7 Jan 1955
Wing Commander W.G. Miller, CD	8 Jan 1955 - 2 Mar 1958
Wing Commander W.K. Carr, DFC, CD	3 Mar 1958 - 3 Aug 1960
Wing Commander J.W. Borden, DFC, CD	4 Aug 1960 - 8 Aug 1963
Wing Commander M.G. Bryan, CD	9 Aug 1963 - 15 Jun 1966
Wing Commander D.C. MacKenzie, CE, CD	15 Jun 1966 - 16 Aug
Lieutenant Colonel L.V. Johnson, CD	16 Aug 1968 - 25 Jul 1969
Lieutenant Colonel C.R. Hallowell, CD	25 Jul 1969 - 17 Jul 1971
Lieutenant Colonel G.S. Parslow, CD	17 Jul 1971 - 15 Jan 1974
Lieutenant Colonel M.M. Zrymiak, CD	15 Jan 1974 - 23 Jul 1977
Lieutenant Colonel G.G. Parent, CD	23 Jul 1976 - 6 Jul 1978
Lieutenant Colonel J.E. McGee, CD	6 Jul 1978 - 20 Jul 1981
Lieutenant Colonel R.C. Landry, OMM, CD	20 Jul 1981 - 6 Dec 1983
Lieutenant Colonel W.F. Buckham, CD	6 Dec 1983 - 6 Jun 1986
Lieutenant Colonel R.L. Gage, CD	6 Jun 1986 - 22 July 1988
Lieutenant Colonel P.A. Corry, CD	22 July 1988 - 26 July 1990
Lieutenant Colonel S.A. Browarski, CD	26 July 1990 - 27 July 1992
Lieutenant Colonel W.C. Thompson, MVO, CD	27 July 1992 - 25 May 1994
Lieutenant Colonel W. F. Burke, CD, CDS	25 May 1994 - Present

NOTE: Rank shown is that worn at time of appointment

Bases

RCAF Station Rockcliffe	1 Apr 1947 - Jun 1955
CFB Ottawa (Uplands)	June 1955 - Oct 1994
Ottawa INTL Airport	Oct 1994 - Present

Aircraft
1 April 1949 - 1 July 1994

Canadair North Star	Apr 1949 - Apr 1962
Canadair C5*	Aug 1950 - Apr 1966
Comet 1A	May 1953 - Jul 1965
North American Mitchell	Sep 1956 - Nov 1960
Canadair Yukon	Nov 1962 - Feb 1968
Cessna L18	2 Apr 1965 - Aug 1967
Canadair Cosmopolitan	Jul 1959 - Jun 1994
Dassault Fan Jet Falcon	Aug 1967 - Dec 1985
de Havilland Dash 7	Jan 1980 - May 1987
Canadair Challenger	May 1983 - June 1994
de Havilland Dash 8	May 1987 - Apr 1990

* Indicates one only of type in service

412 Squadron History Book
Committee Members

Dean Broadfoot	Capt. Dale Hackett (412 Sqn.)	Joe Menton	Bobby Ray
George Broadley	Don Heaslip	John O'Callaghan	Garry Scott
LCol Stefan Browarski	Les Hussey	Maj Glen Palmer	Jim Shipton
Des Callaghan	Art James (deceased)	Ray Paquette	Harry Smith
Bob Cameron	Carl Lagroix (deceased)	Glen Parslow	Gord Webb
Russ Chalk	Paul Lemieux	Paul Pawliuk	LCol Wayne Thompson (CO 412 Sqn)
Chuck Cowie	Rowly Lloyd	Bill Penfold	Maj Ron Tidy (DCO 412 Sqn)
Dewy Dewan	Chuck Lockwood	Midge Pennington	LCol Frank Burke (CO 412 Sqn)
Ed Grose	Terry Martin (civilian)	Vern Peppard	Capt. Tony Jones (412 Sqn)

D.R. ADAMSON, LIEUTENANT GENERAL, CD CMM, joined the Royal Canadian Air Force in 1941. He flew on operations over Europe with 180 Squadron RAF, 2nd Tactical Air Force on B-25 aircraft during World War II.

Following the war he was engaged in experimental and research duties with the Defence Research Board flying B-25 and A-20 type aircraft.

In 1951 he was transferred to 412 Squadron and flew on domestic and international operations until 1954 when he was moved to AFHQ to the Directorate of Transport Operations.

He served with the United Nations Emergency Force in Gaza as the Air Staff Officer in 1960, following which he became Staff Officer Operations at Air Transport Command Headquarters, Trenton.

In 1963 he attended the Joint Services Staff College in England, and on completion of that course in 1964, he commanded 437 Squadron at Canadian Forces Base, Trenton. He later became Base Commander at Trenton, and Chief of Staff Operations, Air Transport Command.

In 1968 General Adamson was appointed Director General Operations (Air), at Canadian Forces Headquarters, Ottawa, and in 1971 was promoted to Major General and became Deputy Chief of Staff (Operations) at NORAD and later Deputy Commander in Chief, NORAD, at which time he was promoted to Lieutenant General.

Following retirement in 1978, General Adamson took up a career in Aerospace Marketing, during which he held positions with DeHavilland and Boeing, retiring in 1986 from the position of Vice President Marketing and Sales at the Boeing DeHavilland Division.

General Adamson remains active as a private consultant in industrial, aerospace, and government relations marketing activities.

EMIL M. ALBOTA, SGT., born in Ottawa, Ontario in 1919. After graduating from Ottawa Technical High School in 1938, he began his military career. He served one year with the Canadian Navy then re-enlisted to the Royal Canadian Air Force in 1939 as an Air-Frame Technician.

During the war years of 1940 to 1943, Sgt. Albota flew Catalina Flying Boats for the Eastern Air Command. After the completion of this term, he was transferred to the 168th (Heavy Transport) Squadron to repair and maintain Liberators and flying Fortresses.

After the war ended in 1946, Sgt. Albota and a small group of men were selected to reconstruct aircraft. This four-engined Liberator (number 554), was to be Canada's first V.I.P. aircraft. Seats were removed, the aircraft rewired, and a bed was set up in the compartment to accommodate Canada's first V.I.P. - Prime Minister MacKenzie King. The maiden flight of this VIP aircraft was to transport MacKenzie King to a conference in San Francisco, California.

Upon completion of this task in 1946, Sergeant Albota was transferred to the 412th (Transport) Squadron in Ottawa, Ontario where he continued to maintain the V.I.P. Liberator.

Then, in 1951, Emil was again re-assigned, this time to the 426th Squadron to repair and maintain North Stars for the Korean War. Another transfer for Sgt. Albota in 1952, this time overseas to Baden for a one-year tour throughout Europe. Over the next 14 years, he served in several locations, to include Dorval, Quebec; numerous locations overseas; Trenton, Ontario; then back home to Ottawa, Ontario, where he retired from the Air Force in 1968 to join the private work force.

Sergeant Albota passed away on October 26, 1993 and is survived by his wife, Dorothy, seven children and seven grandchildren.

EUGENE L. ARNOLD, MAJOR, born in Wetaskiwin, Alta. in 1928. He completed his secondary education at Chilliwack, British Columbia and U.B.C., joining the RCAF in 1948. He was one of 14 pilots who graduated from #1 FTS Centralia on Course 4 in December 1948 and considered himself fortunate to be posted to 435 (T) Squadron, Edmonton, on air transport operations flying C-47 Dakotas. Three years of intensive northern and arctic flying followed, during which time he married Dollie Benham. In 1952 he was posted to the newly formed 4 (Transport) Operational Training Unit at Lachine, P.Q., as a flying instructor. Here he became chief pilot on the C-119 Boxcar and assisted in the move of the OTU to Trenton. The family moved back to Montreal in 1955 where F/L Arnold served as Operations Officer at Air Transport Command HQ in Lachine. In 1959-1960 he attended Course 24 at the RCAF Staff College.

A four-year Sabre tour at Zweibrucken, Germany, and Maryville, France, followed: Deputy C.O. 434 (F) Squadron, C.O. 441 (F) Squadron, and C.O. 5 Air Movements Unit. Service back in Canada at NDHQ rounded out the remainder of his military career, except for a shining two-year interlude at 412 (T) Squadron. Posted to the squadron in November 1970, he served as Deputy C.O., flew the Falcon, organized the move of the Squadron into Hangar 12 and managed the first 412 Squadron Reunion in September 1972.

Major Arnold retired from the Canadian Forces in 1975. He and his wife now reside near Chilliwack in a large log home they built for themselves at Cultus Lake, British Columbia

A.L. AULD, (AL) MAJOR, born in Nova Scotia in 1928 and educated at Verdun High School ("Buzz" Beurling's old school) Verdun, Quebec. His military flying career began in March 1953 as a student on the first course at newly re-opened RCAF Station Penhold. Advanced flying to wings standard was completed on B-25 Mitchell's at RCAF Station Saskatoon. Then on to RCAF Station Winnipeg Flying Expeditors and Dakotas for the Air Navigation School and Air Radio officers school until 1956 when he was transferred to 408 Squadron at RCAF Station Rockliffe, flying Dakotas and others (on wheels, skis and floats) mostly in northern Canada.

Major Auld was next transferred to 412 Squadron at RCAF Station uplands in 1957 where he flew Comets, Dakotas and B-25s until 1962 when he was transferred back to Rockcliffe to Air Force Headquarters practice flight where he was appointed personal pilot to the Commander Air Material Command. In 1963 he was temporarily reassigned to 412 Squadron to complete the last flights of the Comets prior to their retirement. When Rockcliffe closed in the spring of 1964, Major Auld was transferred back to Uplands where he continued to fly the commander's aircraft.

In 1965 Major Auld transferred to Air Force H.Q. in a flying position in the Directorate of Flying Regulations and Air Traffic Services (DARTS). While there, he modernized and redesigned CFP100 and served as the Air Force Observer to ICAO Headquarters

Next came a three-year tour in Europe with 109 Communications flight at LAHR, West Germany. In 1971, he returned to Canada as the Chief Standards Officer at 426 Squadron (OTU) in Trenton. Major Auld retired in 1974 and immediately began civilian life as an instructor in the Flight Operations Training Department of Air Canada, where he is still employed as the Ground Training Manager (L-1011/DC8) in Toronto.

Major Auld and his wife Marilyn (Lynn) now live in Brampton, Ontario. They have two sons and two grandchildren.

WILLIAM J. BARRETT (JIM), born in Wetaskiwin, Alberta in June of 1941. After completion of Senior High School, he joined the Royal Canadian Air Force in July of 1960 as a Direct Entry Pilot, completing his pilot training at Centralia, Ontario; Penhold, Alberta; and, Gimli, Manitoba.

His Wings and Commission were received in December of 1961 and the first assignment was to the 423 AW (F) Squadron, based at 2 (F) Wing, Grostequin, France flying the CF100 Canuck.

Tours of duty that followed included Air Training Command, instructing on the Harvard at Penhold, Alberta and the Tutor at Gimli, Manitoba.

Then, in 1968, he moved on to Air Transport

Command and a flying tour on the DeHavilland Buffalo with 429 Squadron Detachment at Namao, Alberta. Administration caught up and he next served in the Personnel Branch of NDHQ in Ottawa from July, 1971 until September, 1973. Then an assignment came to join 412 (T) Squadron, on the Cosmopolitan.

The tour with 412 Squadron started on 3 September 1973 with the Initial Cosmo Course, followed by the Advanced Cosmo Course in August/September, 1974.

From 1973 to 1977, he served in such roles as line pilot, training officer and check pilot. On 17 May 1976 he was promoted to the rank of Major, and on 17 June 1976 was assigned the position of flight commander (Cosmopolitan). Significant flights that he participated in were the visit to the North West Arctic by Governor General G. Leger in May of 1976 and the visit to Canada of HRM, Queen Elizabeth, in July of 1976.

In 1977 he was posted to Colorado Springs, CO and a brief tour with the "Smoky Two" Cosmo of NORAD when Lt. Gen. D. Adamsom and Lt. Gen K. Lewis were the senior Canadian Military Officers at NORAD.

Then in May 1979, he retired from the Canadian Armed Forces and became involved with Corporate Aviation in Vancouver, British Columbia.

At present, Major Barrett, his wife, Linda, and their two children, Robert and Tracy, reside in Richmond, British Columbia. He is currently employed with Canadian Forest Products Limited and is flying a Cessna Citation Three.

BILL BARRY, WING COMMANDER, born near Russell, Manitoba, in 1916. He attended schools at Endcliffe and Russell, then worked as a printer/reporter and a surveyor. He joined the RCAF in 1941 and after training as a navigator, he proceeded overseas where he completed his operational training in time to fly on the 1000-Bomber raids of July 1942.

He was then assigned to 1474 Flight RAF for airborne intelligence work. On one occasion, December 2, 1942, he took part in the intelligence "Decoy" flight in which the crew was to secure knowledge of the frequency used and other characteristics of the Junkers 88 Radar Night Fighter. It was successful, enabling the Allied Forces to use countermeasures thus saving many bomber aircraft and crews.

Following his return to Canada, Bill remained in the RCAF and was dispatcher and navigator with 12 Communications or 412 Transport Squadron in 1945-1946. He was for many years one of the three trained flight dispatchers in the RCAF. He later worked in Public Relations and in 408 Photo Squadron.

Following Staff College in 1953-1954, he was Organization Staff Officer at Air Force Headquarters and at Air Defence Command.

He retired in 1964, and then in Edmonton, managed a Personal Finance Counselling firm, and Alberta Government Personnel Directorate, the Alberta Rent Regulation Program and the Alberta 75th Anniversary Commission.

He is married to the former Eva Morden, of Morden, Manitoba, and they live in Delta, British Columbia with four children and four grandchildren near them in the Greater Vancouver area.

DAVID BENTLEY, MAJOR, born in Charlottetown, P.E.I. in 1927. He attended Prince of Wales College and then served with MOT from 1946 to 1951 as a licensed radio operator stationed in Montreal, Ottawa, and the Arctic.

He joined the RCAF in 1951 and after graduation as a radio officer was assigned to 426 (T) Squadron in Dorval, serving there from 1952 to 1954 during the time when operations were concentrated on the Korean airlift. In 1954 he was transferred to 412 (T) Squadron, remaining there until 1957. He was a member of the crew that flew Lester Pearson to Moscow and Asia in 1955. From 1957 to 1962 he was an instructor with 4 (T) Operational Training Unit in Trenton and also flew Yukons with 437 Squadron at that base. In 1962 he was transferred to the Aerospace systems Course in Winnipeg and on graduation remained with CNS and subsequently ANS until 1968, during which time he was promoted to Squadron Leader. In 1968 he was transferred to Defence Headquarters in Ottawa to the Directorate of Air Requirements, remaining there until his retirement in 1973.

Major Bentley and his wife Rita have two children and one grandchild, and now reside in Victoria, British Columbia.

LLOYD F. BERRYMAN, FLIGHT LIEUTENANT, born in Hamilton, Ontario in 1921. Upon graduation from Westdale High School he joined the RCAF and received his wings at No. 14 S.F.T.S. Aylmer, Ontario. Following posting overseas, he joined 412 Squadron (Spitfires) at Biggin Hill, Kent, in October 1943 and served with the Falcons prior to and following the invasion of Europe to completion of his tour in October of 1944 in Holland. Awarded the Distinguished Flying Cross in September of that year for operations against the Luftwaffe in the Nijmegen bridge area, he returned to Canada for further hospital treatment following a crash landing in the U.K. After the war he served with 411 (Reserve) Squadron in Toronto, flying Vampire Jets.

Following a successful business career he served as Mayor of Burlington, Ontario, where he has resided for 30 years and remains active in the business community upon retirement. Married to the former Brenda Price of Sault Ste. Marie, Ontario, Lloyd has two sons - David and Timothy - both University graduates and former professional athletes.

PETER BOYER, MAJOR, born in North Bay, Ontario in 1948. Following completion of his secondary education, he enrolled in the Canadian Forces in 1968 and received training at CFB Esquimalt, CFB Borden and culminated with his wings graduation at CFB Moose Jaw in 1969. He went on to become an instructor at PFS on De Havilland Chipmunks in 1970 followed by three years as a jet instructor at CFB Moose Jaw.

In 1974 he was transferred to CFB Trenton and served for two years as a Twin Otter SAR Pilot in 424 Squadron. He converted to helicopters in 1976 and served an additional year with 424 before being transferred to CFS Gander to reinaugurate 103 Rescue Unit, on the island of Newfoundland.

Following two years as a Lababrador Aircraft Commander he was posted to DFRC Vancouver to serve a three year ground tour in recruiting.

In 1982 he resumed flying duties at 412 Squadron Ottawa as a Falcon VIP Pilot. In 1983 he became one of the cadre of six pilots to fly the new Canadair Challenger. Following four years of VIP flying, he was selected as a Challenger instructor at the 426 OTU at CFB Trenton where he served for three years prior to assuming his position as Challenger Standards Officer at Air Transport Group Headquarters.

He retired from the Air Force in March 1990 and currently flies Boeing 757s with Canada 3000 in Toronto. He is married to Edie and together have two children, Michelle, 16, and David, 14.

D.J. BRIGGS, CD 1 MAJOR, (RETIRED), born in Cleethorpes, United Kingdom, Briggs considers Scarborough, Ontario to be his home town. While serving with 631 Air Cadet Squadron, he received a flying scholarship. January, 1962, he enrolled in the Royal Canadian Air Force and received his wings in July 1963. Following a short period flying Dakotas in Winnipeg, Manitoba, he joined 405 (Maritime Patrol) Squadron where he flew the Argus aircraft.

In 1967 he assumed duties as an operations officer in Canadian Forces Base Greenwood Operations. In 1969 he was transferred to Primary Flying School at Borden, Ontario and subsequently moved with the school to Portage la Prairie, Manitoba becoming a flight commander. During 1972 he moved to Training Command Headquarters,
Winnipeg where he served as a staff officer for air training matters.

In 1976 Major Briggs became Chief Pilot at 414 (Electronic Warfare) Squadron at North Bay flying CF100 and T-33 aircraft. Major Briggs was posted as a student to the Canadian Forces Command and Staff College, Toronto in 1979. He was posted to National Defence Headquarters, Ottawa during 1980 where he served first as a staff officer in a NATO plans section and later as a staff officer for air training and air display matters. In August 1984 he was posted to 412 (Transport) Squadron Ottawa, flying the Cosmopolitan aircraft where he was later appointed Deputy Commanding Officer.

Taking retirement from the Air Force in 1988, Briggs is currently a training/check pilot with the Ministry of Transport in Ottawa where he resides with his wife, Heather. They have two daughters, Stephanie and Shelley.

ROBERT BRINKHURST, SQUADRON LEADER (RETIRED). Born at Cutknife, Sask on Oct 28, 1929. Joined the RCAF, Oct 1954. Posted to 428 AW (F) Squadron, RCAF Station Uplands on CF 100's from Aug, 1956 to Dec, 1959. Married Ann Doreen Gravel from Ottawa in 1957. Instructed on T33's at RCAF Station Portage La Prairie until Feb, 1963. Instructed on Canberra T4's and B2's at RAF Bomber Command Station Bassingbourn Herts, UK, until Aug, 1965.

Had the dubious distinction of being inadvertantly ejected from a Canberra T4 during a training flight. Endured a tour at CFHQ in Ottawa until
Jan, 1969 during the early years of integration of the three services. Joined 412 (T) Squadron, June, 1969, with Flight lieutenant (Captain) rank. The highlight of the Squadron tour was participating in the London to Australia Air Race in a Falcon 20, Dec, 1969 - Jan, 1970. Finished the Squadron tour as Falcon Chief Pilot, Sep, 1973. Remained actively flying with 412 (T) Squadron as Base Flight Safety Officer until retiring from the military, Aug, 1975, with the rank of Squadron Leader (Major). Continued flying on corporate jets until Oct, 1989 at Age 60. Recommenced flying, June, 1991 and still flying as of Sep, 1993. Also still married to the same beautiful girl.

M.H. BRUNOTTE, was with 426 Squadron until it was disbanded; (the second unit he had been with). Even though they seemed to have done an admirable job during the Congo crisis, someone had decided that the old North Stars had to go. The squadron personnel was split up between Trenton, Downsview and Uplands, and that is how he came to know the Royal Ottawa Air Force at 412 VIP Squadron.

That fact was made very clear when one of the first entries in a L-14 pink sheet read, "Dirty ashtrays." It seemed a bit much after the way they had managed at 426 to keep the North Stars on schedule and in the air, but in time he adjusted to the increased importance placed on shiny aircraft.

His remaining days in the RCAF were spent with 412 Squadron, still in time to get to know the C-5 and the two Comets, but mainly working on the Cosmos. One particular Cosmo, No. 11160 seemed to be hounded by gremlins, because its No. 1 inverter kept acting up while the A/C was airborne, yet checked out OK while on the deck. In order to trace the possible cause, he was sent on a flight. The captain, not being burdened with anything other than keeping the aircraft aloft, decided to buzz a nearby farm of a recently retired buddy. The maneuver he put the machine through kept Brunotte off balance and it was all he could do to hang onto his tools and test equipment, as the blood seemed to drain from his head.

He did not find any cause of the inverter trouble on that flight, and upon landing thanked the captain somewhat sarcastically for the trip; the captain replied, "Whoever said you can't do aerobatics in a Cosmo?" It turned out that he used to fly with the Golden Hawks.

MELVILLE G. BRYAN (MEL), WING COMMANDER, born 25 July 1923 in Fort William, Ontario, enlisted in the Royal Canadian Air Force in 1941. Graduating as a pilot in 1943, he served as a flying instructor until posted overseas in 1944. Completion of operational training as a heavy bomber pilot was coincident with "VE Day" and operations with the "Tiger Force" were terminated by "VJ Day."

Returning to Canada in 1945 he served with: No 124 Ferry Squadron, Rockcliffe 1945-1946; No 435 Transport Squadron, Edmonton 1946-1949; 122 Photo Wing and No 9 Transport Group Headquarters, Rockcliffe 1949 - 50; No 412 Transport Squadron, Rockcliffe 1951-1952; and No 105 Communications and
Rescue Flight, Edmonton 1952-1954 as the personal pilot for the Air Officer Commanding Tactical Air Command. Promoted to Squadron Leader in 1953 he was appointed Commanding Officer of 105 C & R Flight.

From 1954 to 1958 he served at Air Force Headquarters, Ottawa in the Directorate of Personnel Manning; attended Staff College, Toronto 1958-1959; and was Commanding Officer of the RCAF Unit, Fort Churchill, where he was promoted to Wing Commander in 1962. From 1962-1963 he served as Commanding Officer No 115 Air Transport Unit, El Arish, Egypt with further service with the United Nations in the Yemen; Commanding Officer No 412 Transport Squadron, Ottawa, 1963-1966; Commanding Officer No 4 Transport Operational Training Unit, Trenton 1966-1969; Senior Staff Officer Operational Requirements at Mobile Command Headquarters, St. Hubert 1969-1970; and Deputy Commander, Northern Region Headquarters, Yellowknife from 1974 until retirement from the Canadian Armed Forces in July 1974.

In 1974 he joined Transport Canada, Western Region, Edmonton and is currently the Superintendent Pilot Training flying Douglas DC3, DHC6 Twin Otter, and Beechcraft B55 and King Air A100 aircraft.

Married in 1944 to Arlene Jonasson, they have three children: Beverly, Douglas and Donald, a pilot killed in a mid-air collision in 1978, and seven grandsons.

BILL BUCKHAM, BRIGADIER GENERAL, was born in Vancouver, British Columbia in 1938. His military orientation started in 1954 when he joined the Air Cadets. This portion of his career was highlighted when he received an Air Cadet flying scholarship in August 1956. In April 1960 he received his pilots wings and flew as a member of 443 Squadron (Auxiliary) in Vancouver until graduation from the University of British Columbia in 1963. Following graduation he enrolled in the Royal Canadian Air Force (Regular) and enjoyed successive
tours as a multi-engine instructor and standards officer on the Expeditor, Dakota and Chipmunk at No. 1 Advanced Flying School, Rivers, Manitoba; No. 3 Flying Training School and Flight Instructors School, Portage la Prairie, Manitoba; and Central Flying School, Winnipeg, Manitoba.

In February 1970, Bill joined 412 (Transport) Squadron, Ottawa and flew Falcons until his promotion to Major in October 1973, when he was posted to the Directorate of Air Requirements at National Defence Headquarters. In 1975-1976 he attended Canadian Forces Staff College in Toronto. Bill was then posted to 436 (Transport) Squadron, Trenton, Ontario as Deputy Commanding Officer and flew the CC130 Hercules from 1976 to 1980.

Promoted to Lieutenant-Colonel in January 1980, he was posted to the Directorate of Air Plans as head of Continental Plans. In February 1982 he was appointed to the Directorate of Postings and Careers, responsible for pilot postings and careers.

In December 1983, Lieutenant Colonel Buckham assumed command of 412 (Transport) Squadron and served as Commanding Officer until June 1986.

In June 1986 he was transferred to the Directorate of Air Capabilities Review of National Defence Headquarters until his promotion to Colonel in August 1986. From August 1986 to July 1989, Colonel Buckham served as Base Commander of Canadian Forces Base Edmonton.

Colonel Buckham was appointed to the position of Deputy Commander of Air Transport Group, Trenton, Ontario in August 1989. The Deputy Commander is responsible to the Commander for the conduct of Canadian Forces Air Transport Operations, Training, Standards and Evaluation, and Search and Rescue. Brigadier General Buckham continues to fly and has accumulated approximately 8,000 hours flying time throughout his military career.

He is married to the former Keatha Jean Davis of Vancouver, BC and they have two sons, Christopher and James.

LAWRENCE F. BURT, MWO, upon graduation from No. 2 T.T.S. Station Camp Borden (entry 16) in late June 1952 (at age 21), along with AC1's Juan (Joe) Erickson, George Gebauer and Fred Ditchfield, was transferred to 412 Squadron RCAF Station Rockcliffe. Having originated from a primarily bachelor homestead community out of Big River Saskatchewan, some 90 miles northwest of Prince Albert, the required cultural and social adjustments that confronted him were to say the least quite noticeable and interesting. To use a word out of today's lingo to describe those dances in the drill hall where actual bus loads of gals came out from the city (Ottawa) to meet the fellas, they were simply "awesome."

With the V.I.P. transport squadron of the RCAF and having such a diversification of aircraft it was an instant and very interesting challenge for a budding airframe technician. In fact he believed it provided the greatest opportunity for overall experience for the technicians that were available in the entire RCAF at the time and perhaps for all time.

Early in 1954 he met Doris McLaughlin, a photo tech working in the white house, and on 30th of October they were married. They have four daughters and now seven grandchildren.

His military experience includes the following: 412 Transport Squadron Rockcliffe three years plus.—Bameo CFB Uplands, working on all 412 Squadron aircraft.—Number 2 T.T.S. Camp Bordan airframe maintenance instructor, three years plus.—426 Transport Squadron Trenton, two months.—426 Transport Squadron St. Hubert, eight months plus.—Number 4 O.T.U. Trenton, 20 months. Out of this time January, February and March of 1963 were spent on North Star detachment at Marville, France.—Number 102 KU Detachment UNMOGIP Kashmir, India, June 1, 1964 to June 15, 1965. They were the first crew for this Caribou Detachment. For six months they operated out of Srinagar Kashmir, India and for six months they operated out of Rowalpindi, Pakistan.—Bameo CFB Uplands working on 412 Squadron Cosmo aircraft. During this time they re-engined the fleet from the very unreliable Napier Eland engines to the very reliable Allisons, four years plus.—429 Tactical Squadron St. Hubert, six months. Buffalo aircraft.—442 Transport and Rescue Squadron Comox, four years. Buffalo and Labrador Helicopters.—Air Transport Command Headquarters, Trenton. Technical support staff, one year.—Air Command Headquarters, Winnipeg. Technical support staff, six years.—Bameo CFB Edmonton. Senior non-commissioned member CC130 Herc maintenance, two years.—440 Transport and Rescue Squadron CFB Edmonton. D/Sameo twin otter aircraft and squadron SWO.

He was honored with the CD2, the Centennial Medal, the Jubilee Medal and the UNMOGIP Medal recognizing two tours (back to back) of duty. After 35 years and 12 days of very interesting and certainly challenging service, he retired January 8, 1987. Thanks to 412 Squadron for providing him with a good start which helped to make it a pleasantly memorable life.

R.E. CAMERON, (BOB) W.O., born 1931 in Abbotsford British Columbia. He joined the RCAF in February 1951, and in June 1955 was assigned to 412 Squadron as a Flight Engineer on North Stars C-5 and the Comet.

During his time with 412 Squadron, he flew with many distinguished passengers including Princess Margaret, Governors General Massey, and Vanier and also Prime Minister  Diefenbaker. He also served with 426 Squadron, 436 Squadron and 437 Squadron.

After retirement from the Canadian forces in 1974, he has flown as a Flight Engineer with Quebec Air, Ontario World Air, Swift Air Cargo and currently with Air Charter Systems Mirabel.

WILLIAM CARLTON, R-148702 RCAF, born 24 August 1918 at Magnetawan, Ontario. At the age of two the family moved to Sask. He went to public elementary and high school in Carnduff, Sask.

In 1938 moved to Ontario and got a job with T. Eaton Co. in Toronto. He joined the Queens York Rangers in 1938. He joined the Air Force in 1942, then went overseas in 1943.

He went to France, Belgium and Holland with 412 Squadron. He was operated on in London, England, in 1945 and came home May 1945. He was discharged July 1945 and went back to work for Eatons until 1953. Then worked for General Fire Extinguisher for 20 years.

He lost his wife in 1972 then remarried and moved to Parry Sound where he resides.

N.E. CARR, (BUD) CAPTAIN, born 1924 in Hamilton, Ontario. He enlisted in the RCAF in November 1942, graduated as an Airframe Mechanic, St. Thomas, Ontario, 1943. Served with 11 BR Squadron and was discharged October 1945. He re-enlisted in Royal Canadian Army Service Corps, August 1950 and served in Korea 1951-1952. After serving as an Instructor with the Soldier Apprentice Program, Camp Borden, was commissioned from the rank of Sergeant in 1955. In 1958 he was accepted into the Canadian Army Aviation program and was trained by the U.S. Army, Camp Wolters, Texas and Fort Rucker, Alabama where he graduated as Aviator-Rotary Wing in May 1959. Posted to the 90th U.S. Army Med. Helicopter Company at Fort Knox, Kentucky, he flew H34 and H37 helicopters and qualified captain status with an instrument rating in both.

He returned to Canada in June 1960 and later that year undertook fixed wing conversion on Cessna L19 at Rivers, Manitoba, graduating in January 1961. In June 1963 was posted to Army Headquarters Training and Liaison flight, Rockcliffe as staff pilot flying Cessna 182L aircraft. In 1964 he was posted to ICSC Vientiane, Laos where he maintained flying proficiency on H34 helicopters. In 1965 he returned to his previous position at T & L Flight, now at Uplands. On integration of the Armed Forces in January 1967, the flight was absorbed by 412 Squadron where Bud continued to fly as VIP Captain and Chief Cessna Pilot until his posting to D. Mov., CFHQ in 1969 as Tasking Officer for Transport Command passenger aircraft and until retirement in 1971. Bud married the former Jane Badgley in November 1958 and has two daughters and two grandchildren. He is now retired and living in Calabogie, Ontario.

W.K. (BILL) CARR, LIEUTENANT GENERAL (RET'D), CMM, DFC, CD, OStJ, BA, BSC. LGen Carr's military career totalled 39 years and commenced with his joining the NPAM COTC (RCE) in 1939 at age 16 while attending Mount Allison University. Upon graduation in 1941 (at age 18), he joined the RCAF and flew spitfires with Photo Reconnaissance Squadrons in Great Britain, Italy and Malta. He returned to Canada in May 1945 and for the next 33 years served his country with distinction at home and abroad.

During his career, LGen Carr was privileged

to be selected to serve in many different areas. In the late 1940s he was part of a unique group of airmen who photographed the Arctic and, in fact, had a lake named after him - Carr Lake - in the Northwest Territories just north of the 62nd parallel. He was Commander of 412 (T) Squadron (VIP) in Ottawa for three years and piloted many of the world's dignitaries including Queen Elizabeth, Princess Margaret and Charles deGaulle during their visits to Canada. He flew the Right Honourable John Diefenbaker during his round-the-world trip in 1959.

LGen Carr flew over 100 different types of aircraft throughout his career and remained active in flying until his retirement having accumulated nearly 16,000 flying hours. Some of the aircraft he flew were the Spitfire, Lancaster, DC3, Comet, North Star, C130, Cosmopolitan, Norseman, Canso, Mitchell, 707, Falcon, Jetstar, CF5, F104 and CL44. He was the first pilot of Colonel rank in the world to obtain 1,000 hours on the C130. He obtained over 1,000 hours on the one and only C5.

He was chosen to go to the Congo and command the first multi-nation Air Force Organization in the United Nations' history; he served as Commanding Officer of RCAF Station Namao; he served on the planning staff for the new Mobile Command Headquarters (a primarily Army organization); he was Commander of the Canadian Forces Training Command; Deputy Chief of Staff for Operations, Colorado Springs, USA (NORAD Headquarters); Chief of Air Operations at National Defence Headquarters; Deputy Chief of the Defence Staff. He was chosen to plan and bring into being - and to be the first Commander of - Air Command in 1975 at Winnipeg, Manitoba.

LGen Carr also devoted much of his time and energy to organizations outside the military. He has had a life-long interest in Boy Scouts and served as National Commissioner of the Boy Scouts of Canada from 1972 to 1977. On relinquishment of this appointment he was asked to stay on as a special advisor and Honourary Vice President. He served in an executive capacity for many different organizations such as Honourary President Royal Canadian Flying Club Association; Honourary Life President of 700 Wing, Royal Canadian Air Force Association; Board of Directors of the RCAF Memorial Fund, Honourary Governor Corps of Commissionaires; Honourary Director of Canada's Aviation Hall of Fame.

LGen Carr was honoured many times throughout his military career. He was awarded: the Distinguished Flying Cross in 1944 for his contributions in Malta and Italy; he was made a Commander of the Order of Military Merit; awarded the Queen's Coronation Medal; the Queen's Jubilee Medal; the Canadian Centennial Medal; admitted to the Order of St. John in the rank of Officer; and to the Companionate of Merit in the rank of Commander with the Military and Hospitaller Order of Saint Lazarus of Jerusalem.

On August 26, 1993, LGen Carr was invested as the Honorary Colonel of 412 Squadron.

Civilian organizations have also recognized LGen Carr as an outstanding Canadian. In 1976, he was honoured by the Canadian Aerospace Institute and presented the CD Howe Award for achievement in the field of planning and policy-making and leadership in aeronautics and space. In 1977, he was awarded the Gordon R McGregor Trophy for his contribution to aviation, particularly transport aviation. He also received scouting's highest award, the Silver Wolf, for his outstanding contribution to the Boy Scouts of Canada. In 1978, he was awarded the Paris-based Federation Aeronautique Internationale's Paul Tissandrier Diploma for outstanding service to the course of general aviation.

LGen Carr attended the Royal Canadian Air Force Staff College and National Defence College. He obtained his BA from Mount Allison University, Sackville, New Brunswick and his BSC from the Rochester Institute of Technology, New York.

On retirement from the Canadian Forces in 1978, he went to work for Canadair. He returned to Canada from Connecticut in 1983 where he held the appointment as Senior Vice President, Government Sales, for Canadair Inc. He retired in March, 1988 as Vice President, Government and Military Sales at Canadair Limited, Montreal, and in April became President of Carr Associates, an aircraft marketing consulting firm. He continued as a consultant with Canadair and its parent Bombardier Inc, until 1992.

He is married to the former Elaine Mulligan of Ottawa and they have three grown children, two boys and a girl. He was born in Grand Banks, Newfoundland on 17 March 1923.

L.R. CARSON (KIT), FLIGHT LIEUTENANT,
born in 1923 (the same year as the RCAF's birth) in Carsonby, Ontario, a rural community on the southern outskirts of Ottawa.

As autumn followed the hot summer of 1942, enlistment in the RCAF followed graduation from the Ottawa Teachers' College.

Pilot training routed through well-known channels of elementary and service flying schools where a slow roll in a Fleet Finch over Cap de la Madeleine, Quebec, could be done as well in French as in English. Graduation and commission happened together on a cold November afternoon at St. Hubert, Quebec, where the distant cross over Mount Royal stood out as a stark reminder of the many nights it had been used as a guide for aerobatic loops at night. One more move to the fighter operational unit at Bagotville, Quebec was made before going overseas.

Little time was wasted in England before posting to 290 R.A.F. fighter squadron, 2nd Tactical Air Force, where they flew Spitfires in support of the army in Europe until the end of the war.

Repatriation to Canada had scarcely begun before being recalled back to Europe for the occupation of Germany and a posting to 412 Fighter Squadron based at Utersen, Hamburg, Germany. It would be impossible to ever forget the jeep rides on a Saturday evening from the air base through the rubble, devastation, and ruin into what had once been a major city. Memorable on a more recreational level were the multi-national gatherings of military at the "Atlanta," the only standing hotel, where communication at times was reduced to sign language. As the Spitfires of 412 Squadron, along with the sister squadrons of 126 Wing, swept low over the green German countryside one sensed in a nostalgic but gratifying way the the era of these famous planes and their role was ending. March 1946, Spitfire 412 Squadron's work was finished.

Peacetime service included desk positions at headquarters and NATO, Paris, while the most memorable flying duties began with the introduction of jet aircraft into the RCAF, where, on 3 September 1949, he was in the right location at Trenton, Ontario, to fly the first jet airshow in Vampire jets over the CNE in Toronto.

With only a handful of jet pilots it was not surprising that the small group came together at Chatham, N.B. to form the first jet operational training unit. Psychologists at that time could have found few better locations to study the behavior of humans under stressful conditions than to observe young pilots converting from propeller to jet flying without the help of flying instruction.

Two peacetime flying incidents though far apart in nature remain vivid: one, the disintegration of a Vampire canopy through explosive decompression at 30+ thousand feet, being momentarily blinded, and having to be led down by the closest wingman, and second, the stillness and utter aloneness almost bordering on earthly detachment while flying at such a height that most of the Great Lakes were visible. By 1958, the University of Toronto and new areas beckoned to be explored.

Married, with four children who grew up in Don Mills, Ontario, eventually spreading to Alberta and Idaho and adding 11 grandchildren, life for him has evolved in a pleasant pattern of varied activities. Writing, teaching, film-making, raising purebred Arabian horses, land development, real estate, and flying, have all had their time and place.

Now, on a warm summer afternoon, with one of his visiting granddaughters sitting beside him in the cockpit and the other in the seat behind he lifts off in his CG-KIT Skyhawk from the north Toronto Buttonville Airport and heads south over the Don Valley Parkway toward the 2,000-foot CN Tower. From the back seat he hears, "It's like magic up here floating over everything. . . . but we're sort of alone and it's a little scary."

But then from Stephanie in the seat beside him, "You're OK Tammy, Grandpa Kit is with us."

Not just wings get a lift.

BILL CARSS, FLIGHT LIEUTENANT,
born in Kamsack, Sask., in 1924. He joined the RCAF in 1943, and received his pilot's wings in March 1945. He spent six months with the Royal Naval Fleet Air Arm, and was discharged in January 1946.

He spent most of the next five years flying in Flin Flon, Manitoba, where he met and married his wife, Rae Schamehorn. Bill rejoined the RCAF in 1951, and spent the first two years as a Staff Pilot at the Air Navigation School in Winnipeg.

In the Fall of 1953, F/O Carss was sent to

the Transport OTU in Lachine, on North Star Aircraft. After three years on 426 Squadron, he was transferred to 412 (T) in January 1957. He was one of the pilots chosen to crew the Comets, which were re-introduced that year. Many firsts were accomplished by 412 Squadron and the Comets, including the first Trans-Atlantic Jet Service. Flight Lieutenant Carss was the Captain of the Comet Crew that flew HRH, The Queen and Prince Philip on their tour of Canada in 1959. He was a Check Pilot at 412, and was sent to Canadair to become qualified on the new Yukon Aircraft. In 1963 he was sent to the OTU as Chief Pilot on Yukons.

He had several Staff positions in the operational side of Transport Command, including ATOC, before joining 437 Squadron and flying the latest Air Force acquisition, the Boeing 707. Major Carss retired from the Armed Forces in July 1977 from Base Operations, his last position.

Bill and Rae have four children including a daughter Jacqueline, an RMC Graduate and a Captain in the Armed Forces. They now reside in Kamsack, Saskatchewan in the family home.

GARRY CHANDLER, MCPL, born in FR of Germany, in 1958. He began a military career in 1975, joining Communications Reserves, Borden as a RT OP 214/LMN 052. Upon completion of Field Orientation Training; Petawawa served for six months at Ismailia, Egypt as a peacekeeper. Promoted to Corporal January 1977 and released later that year.

Joining the regular force in 1979 as a Steward 862 after completing TQ-3 and Sea/Environmental, served as CO's Steward on HMCS Ottawa until the end of 1981. Transferring to Shearwater to work accommodations at Warrior Block until 1983. Upon qualifying as Flight Steward to serve on Boeing 707's at 437 (Transport) Squadron, Trenton where he exceeded 2,000 flying hours; completing TQ-5 and promoted to Corporal, October 1983. The summer of 1986 found him again as CO's Steward but west coast on HMCS Qu'appelle. Completing JLC, posted to Training Division One-Minesweepers, on board HMCS Thunder until her hull changed to HMCS Chignecto, as Senior Steward until present posting to 412 (Transport) Squadron, January 1989.

He received his Canadian Forces Decoration June, 1989 and was promoted to Master Corporal in August. He is flying on Cosmopolitan and Challenger aircraft as a Flight Steward.

MCPL Chandler has two children: daughter Samantha and son Benjamin.

ALAN T.R. CHAPMAN MAJOR, was born in Oxford, England in 1931. He joined the RAF, on a Short-Service Commission in 1951. He did his flight training in the southern United States before returning to Europe to fly Sabre jets on No. 3 (F) fighter squadron in Germany. After a couple of years on squadron, he rounded off his RAF tour target towing, in Meteors, at Sylt in Northern Germany.

He joined the RCAF in 1956 and after the usual indoctrination training at London, Ontario, instructed at Macdonald and Gimli, Manitoba, on T33 aircraft until late 1961 when he was posted to fly CF 100s with 445 Squadron in Marville, France. During this tour he married the former Gwyn Baker, from his home town in England, and following a later tour at Metz, returned to Canada in summer of 1965.

A short tour at practice flight in Ottawa preceded his first tour on 412 Squadron during which he flew the last of the squadron Dakotas and the first of the squadron Falcons. After a short stint in CFHQ as a brand new Squadron Leader, he returned to 412 Squadron in 1971, once again flying the Falcon and performing the duties of Cabin Crew Leader. In 1974 further CFHQ postings to DAOT and DFS completed his Air Force career.

In 1977 he joined the Department of Transport as an Air Carrier Inspector and is the Lead Inspector on the L1011 and Airbus A320 aircraft.

DONALD A. CHILD, BRIG. GEN, born in Wadena Sask, in 1924. Joined the RCAF in 1943 and trained as a Navigator "W" on night fighters until September 1945. Rejoined the RCAF in 1948 and joined 412 Squadron as a Radio Navigator in October 1949.

Flying duties with 412 ranged from "Sked" flights to Goose Bay and Churchill, to pushing the Royal 22nd Regt. out of the back door of a Dak to VIP flights throughout North America and Europe. One flight in the C5 (Canadian 10,000) to Paris and Rome in November 1951, was particularly memorable. The UN was meeting in Paris at the same time as NATO Defence Ministers were meeting in Rome, and the passenger list included L.B. Pearson, Brooke Claxton, Douglas Abbott and Jimmy Gardner. Over 12 days, seven shuttle flights between Paris and Rome were flown.

After leaving 412, he spent approximately 16 years in air defense in Canada, the USA, France and Germany. He flew CF 100s with 419 Squadron in North Bay and 440 Squadron in Zweibrucken, Germany. In addition to air defense staff appointments in Metz, France and Ottawa,

he was Commanding Officer of RCAF Stn Holberg and Commander of the NORAD/BUIC facility at St Margarets, N.B.

From 1972 to 1975, Brig. Gen. Child served with the ADM Policy Staff in NDHQ. His last two assignments before retirement in 1979 were as Military Counsellor to the Canadian Ambassador to NATO and Secretary of the Staff, SHAPE Belgium.

Brig. Gen. Child served on the Directing Staff of the Canadian Forces Staff College in Toronto and holds an undergraduate degree from the University of Saskatchewan and a post-graduate degree from Queen's University, Kingston. He is now retired and resides in White Rock, B.C.

PETER A. CORRY, LIEUTENANT COLONEL, CD, was born in Montreal, Quebec, in 1941. Following completion of his secondary education, he began his military career in 1959 by enrolling in the RCAF Primary Reserve as an Air-frame Technician. In 1961 he was accepted into the RCAF regular force as a Direct Entry Officer candidate and commenced pilot training. He successfully completed his training at RCAF Stations Centralia, Penhold and Gimli, received his wings and commission  in 1962 and was assigned to the multi-engine conversion course in Rivers, Manitoba. On graduation he was assigned to his first flying tour as a staff pilot at the Air Navigation School in Winnipeg flying Expeditors and Dakotas.

In 1963, Lieutenant-Colonel Corry was assigned to the Maritime Operational Air Training Unit Summerside, PEI and trained on the P2V7 Neptune. The Argus Conversion Course completed his anti-submarine warfare training prior to his assignment to 405 Maritime Patrol Squadron in Greenwood, Nova Scotia. Three years as an Argus crew commander prepared him for his 1968 transfer to 449 Squadron, Greenwood, where he served as an instructor and later as the Standards and Operations Officer. In 1971, he was transferred to CFB Greenwood as the Base Flight Safety Officer. Late in 1972, Lieutenant-Colonel Corry was selected for a foreign exchange position with VP49, a P3C Orion anti-submarine squadron in Jacksonville, Florida. The tour lasted two-and-half years and included a six-month deployment to Keflavik, Iceland.

On returning to Canada in 1975, Lieutenant-Colonel Corry was posted to Maritime Command Headquarters in Halifax and later to Maritime Air Group Headquarters as the Staff Officer Flight Safety. In 1977 he attended Course 4 at the Canadian Forces Command and Staff College.

This was followed by a tour as a Pilot Career Manager in National Defence Headquarters, Ottawa until 1981. He returned to flying with a posting to 436 Squadron, Trenton, where he flew the CC130 Hercules until 1985. A year of language training in Trenton and St-Jean, Quebec, preceded his assignment to Air Transport Group Headquarters where he served as the Senior Staff Officer Standards and Evaluations until his appointment to Commanding Officer of 412 (Transport) Squadron on July 22, 1988. He currently flies the CC-144 Canadair Challenger.

Lieutenant-Colonel Corry is married to the former Patricia Gottfried of Camp Morton, Manitoba. They have two sons, Michael, 19, and Steven, 18.

CHARLES ALEXANDER COWIE,

was born August 26, 1920 in Winnipeg, Manitoba. He is married with two grown children. He currently holds a valid Airline Transport Pilot licence with a Class I instrument rating. He has more than 13,000 hours flight time on jets, turboprops and piston engine aircraft.

Military service: Cowie enlisted in the RCAF on May 1, 1940. He was a member of the Tiger Force. He was in an air operations crash on Dec. 30, 1942 while returning to the U.K. He was hospitalized for 10 months. Service in Canada and overseas: War Service: 1940-1946, RCAF Reserve: 1947-1949, RCAF Regular: 1950-1964. He retired from the RCAF.

From 1955-1962 he served with the 412 in the following capacities: 412 Transport (VIP) Squadron Operations Officer, 4 Engine Flight Commander, VIP Aircraft Commander, World Wide VIP Air Transport Operations. During seven years made flights as pilot-in-command all over the world. Many flights in the Arctic, and to the North Pole, Continental U.S.A. including Alaska, many scheduled and random trans-Atlantic flights to the U.K. and France, and other flights to Germany, Norway, Sweden, Italy, Yugoslavia, Greece, Turkey, Pakistan, India, Iran, Malaya, Saudia Arabia, Egypt, Lebanon, Central Africa, Brazil, Uruguay, Argentina and Central America, and Flight Commander and pilot instructor to RCAF Air Council members for continuation instrument flying on specially equipped B-25 aircraft reserved for senior officer pilot training.

He was personal pilot to General E.L.M. Burns, Commander U.N. Emergency Force Middle East (Egypt-Israel) 1958. And from 1962-1964 the personal pilot to Air Officer Commanding Air Defence Command.

From 1966-1972 he was Civil Aviation Inspector-in-Charge of the Aircraft Licensing and Certification Section. 1973-1976 Head Regulatory Procedures Section (Air Law) at DOT Headquarters. 1976-1978 (Transport Canada) Superintendent, Personnel Licensing Standards. 1978-1985 he retired fromthe Department of Transport, Transport Canada after working as the Executive Officer, Contingency Plans and Operations (Air). He dealt directly with the senior aviation authorities of 34 nations.

From 1985 he has been the Chairman, NATO Civil Aviation Planning Committee (CAPC). Duties included civil aviation support of NATO military. Chairman of CAPC is also Chairman of NATO Civil Aviation Agency (NCAA), which is a NATO Civil Wartime Agency. Responsible to NATO Council through the Senior Civil Emergency Planning Committee. Reports to NATO Assistant Secretary General. Responsible for direction and control of NATO's Crisis Element (AIR) the Bureau of Coordination for Civil Aviation (BOCCA). He retired from NATO in 1989.

Cowie was educated in Winnipeg and is a graduate of the Investment Dealers Association (Canadian Securities Commission) (1965), and Business Law, Algonquin College (1973). Cowie also received additional education with DOT Civil Aviation Inspectors Workshop.

HUGH R. CRAM, WING COMMANDER,

born in Harris, Saskatchewan in 1919. After completing two years of Engineering at the University of Saskatchewan he joined the RCAF in early 1941 and received his pilots wings in December of that year. He was posted to the United Kingdom early in 1942.

During the war he flew as a bomber pilot over Europe as well as in the Middle East and Mediterranean areas of operations. He completed a tour of operations with 178 (RAF) Squadron in the Middle East, returned to the U.K. and joined 419 Squadron (RCAF) in six group for a second tour. He flew the Hampdon, Stirling, Liberator, Wellington and Lancaster aircraft at various times in both theaters. He was reported missing in April 1945 during a series of raids on Hamburg. The entire crew parachuted safely and returned to the U.K. three days later. He returned to Canada in June 1945 for service with the RCAF "Tiger Force", which never materialized.

Post war service includes flying with 412 Squadron from 1950 to 1955 as a Captain on Expeditors, Dakotas, North Stars and the Canadair 5 Aircraft. While with 412 he was appointed in 1951 as Squadron Check pilot.

During his time with 412 Squadron, he flew many international flights and carried such distinguished passengers as the Prime Minister of Canada, Governor General Massey, HRH Prince Philip, HRH Queen Mother Elizabeth, Sir Anthony Eden as well as many Commonwealth and foreign dignitaries and heads of state.

After being with 412 Squadron, he was appointed staff officer Pilot Training in Air Transport Command HQs and Staff Officer Training in 1959. In 1960 he joined 435 (T) Squadron and served as Aircrew leader and Squadron Check Pilot on the newly acquired C130 Aircraft.

In 1964 he was appointed as Air Staff Officer to Western Army Command HQs in Edmonton. In 1965,he was appointed for one year as Staff Officer Air Advisor to the Commander with the United Nations Emergency Force in Gaza. In 1966 he returned to Trenton with ATCHQ as Staff Officer Operations until his retirement in 1969.

In 1970 he joined the Executive branch of the Government of the North West Territories in Yellowknife and was responsible to the Commissioner for all Settlement Development in the Kewatin and Franklin regions of the Northwest Territories.

He lived in Eskimo Point, Rankin Inlet and Cambridge Bay. Today he lives in Sidney, B.C. fully retired with his wife Edith. He has one married daughter, Marcia Fenn, who is living with her husband in Port Alberni , B.C.

J.E. CURRIE (BUZZ) CAPTAIN,

born in Maple, Ontario. He joined the RCAF in 1952 at Hamilton, Ontario as an Armament Systems Technician and then was posted to 410 Squadron in North Luffenham, England. In 1955, he remustered to pilot.

After completing flying training in Clareshome, Alberta and Portage la Prairie, Manitoba, he instructed on T-33 Silver Stars for four years in Portage AFTS.

In January of 1961, it was off to 1 (F) OTU to train on the F-86 Sabres in Chatham, New Brunswick followed by two years with 444 (F) Squadron in Baden-Sollingen. When Sabres were replaced in 1963, he remained in Germany as a Base Instrument Flight Instructor. In 1965, he returned to Canada and spent three years with the Charlottetown Recruiting Unit. He served as Detachment Commander and initiated unified recruiting of the three services.

Currie, in 1968, began a long affiliation with 412 (T) Squadron in Ottawa. During four years with the unit, he was Cosmopolitan Training Officer for one year and Chief Pilot for two. In 1972 he was posted to 426 (T) Squadron in Trenton as Chief Cosmo Instructor. Buzz changed to Hercules in 1975, flying with 436 (T) Squadron in Trenton. In 1978, he returned to 426 Squadron for a further two years as Chief Cosmo Instructor.

In 1980 Buzz left the Airforce after 28 years of service. He is presently employed as a DC-8 Captain with Worldways Canada, based in Toronto. Buzz and his wife, Jo, presently reside in Georgetown, Ontario. Their son, Major Patrick

Currie, is a CELE Officer at NDHQ and their daughter Pamela is a special education teacher.

PETER DAVIES, WARRANT OFFICER, born 1936 in Liverpool, England, emigrated to Canada in 1953 after Merchant Deck Officer Training on H.M.S. *Conway* in North Wales. He joined the RCAF in April 1953 and after training at St. John's and Camp Borden he was posted to 400-411 Squadron's Toronto as an Airframe Technician working on Vampire Fighters. In 1954 he attended the CF-100 Airframe Course before transferring to the CF-100 Pilots O.T.U., Cold Lake. From 1954 to 1958 he was employed at the Weapons Practice Unit, 433 Squadron, C.E.P.E. and 121 K.U., Sea Island. Flying training commenced at 121 K.U. Search and Rescue in 1958.

Initially flying DC-3s and Canso flying boats until the Unit received CSR. 110 Albatross in 1961. This Unit was moved to Comox in 1963 and was designated 442 Squadron. As a Flight Engineer in 1970 Davies was transferred to 412 Squadron, Ottawa, to fly C.C. 109 Cosmos. In 1974 he was posted to 426 Squadron, as the Cosmo Flight Engineer Instructor and A.T.G. Standards Check Engineer. In 1978 he was transferred to 436 Squadron flying C. 130 E and Hs. In January 1979 he took part in Op's "Batten," the evacuation of Teheran after the downfall of the Shah. His next posting was to Yellowknife in 1983 for one year as the Chief Cadet Instructor for the Air Cadets in the Arctic. Returning to fly with 436 Squadron till his retirement in January 1987. Total flying hours 13,337. Warrant Officer Davies married Mavis Bertram in 1959 and has a daughter and a grandson.

RALPH C. DAVIS, born in Medicine Hat, Alberta in 1911. After graduating from the University of Alberta in 1934 with a B.Sc. in Civil Engineering he joined the RCAF in 1935. Following flying training in Camp Borden he was posted to RCAF Station Rockliffe in 1936 for float plane and flying boat training after which he was transferred to number 7 General Purpose Squadron for flying duties in the Communication Flight. In January, 1938 he was transferred to number 8 General Purpose Squadron to fly on aerial photographic duties in connection with the mapping of Canada. He flew Northrop Delta aircraft fitted with wheels or floats on photographic assignments in central and western Canada and in the North West Territories.

He was transferred back to 7 G.P. Squadron in the spring of 1939 and was appointed Officer Commanding the Communications Flight and promoted to Flight Lieutenant. His position as Flight Commander was retained when the unit was renamed 12 Communications flight.

In June, 1940, Flight Lieutenant Davis after four years at Rockliffe, was posted to Trenton, Rivers and Regina to participate in the British Commonwealth Air Training Plan. In 1943 he was moved to the East Coast for various duties in the anti-submarine campaign including a year as Base Commander RCAF Station Yarmouth.

Following the war, Group Captain Davis held various staff and command positions in the U.K. and Canada including five years as Director of Flight Safety at Air Force Headquarters. He concluded his Air Force career as Commanding Officer RCAF Station Saskatoon for five years. He was retired in 1963.

He retired a second time in 1976 after 13 years as Director of Accident Prevention with the Alberta Workmens Compensation Board and Director of Inspection in the Alberta Department of Labour.

RONALD D. DAY, FLIGHT LIEUTENANT, joined the Air Force in February 1952 as an Aircraftsman second class (Reserve) and retired as a Major in 1978. In the meantime, he flew B-25s (Mitchell), Harvards, C-45s, DC-3s, Yukons, (CL-44), Falcons, Otters, Lancasters and finally ending his Air Force career with, what he considered the best flying job in the military, that of Chief Pilot Instructor on 707s (Boeings) at 426 Squadron, Trenton. He married Jean Wright of Owen Sound, Ont. in 1955. They have three sons and three grandchildren. After leaving the Air Force, Major Day flew with Wardair Canada on the 707, 747, DC-10 and A310. He was a DC-10 Instructor and Check Pilot for seven years

While at 412 Squadron from 1962 to 1967 (with a six-month tour in Saudia Arabia and Yemen flying Otters and Caribou with the United Nations) F/L Day had, as most 412 members did, many memorable experiences. Long periods of absence on very short notice tested the family bonds to their limits. One of those trips (and most memorable) for F/L Day, was when he was given the job of going to New Delhi, via Beirut, to pick up the newly appointed Governor General, Roland Michener, and his wife, and fly them to London for a meeting with the Queen and then standby, just in case the GG decided to take the CL-44 back to Ottawa instead of Air Canada.

He was so impressed with 412 Squadron service, he decided to continue home with us. The problems encountered during that trip were all overcome by the teamwork of the crew, a trait that is sure to exist to this day in the present 412 Squadron. As of October 1989, Ron is flying with Canadian Airlines International on the A310 and hopes to retire in five years time.

WILLIAM H. DeYOUNG (BILL), FLIGHT LIEUTENANT, born in Brighton, England in 1921. He was educated in England and joined the Royal Air Force in June 1941. After initial training in England he was sent to Canada under the British Commonwealth Air Training Plan and graduated as a Pilot in Calgary, in October 1942. He was assigned to 31 Bombing and Gunnery School, Picton, Ontario as a Staff Pilot and returned to the United Kingdom in March 1944.

He served with several units until his release from the R.A.F. in February 1947. He returned to Canada and joined the Royal Canadian Air Force in January 1951 and after retraining in Calgary was assigned as a Staff Pilot to the Air Navigation School in Summerside and transferred to Winnipeg when the unit moved in 1954. He was assigned to 115 Comm. Flt, in Egypt with the United Nations Emergency forces in January 1957, and upon return to Canada in August 1957, took up duties as a Line Pilot with 412 Transport Squadron in Uplands. During his term with the Squadron he flew as Captain on Expeditors, Dakotas, Mitchell and the Cosmopolitan Aircraft. He was transferred to 1 AFTS Rivers in 1963 and retired from the Air Force in June 1964.

He joined the staff of Sears Canada Ltd and received assignments in management in the merchandising field in Kingston, Saint John, N.B. and Toronto retiring once again in August 1982.

He married Isabelle in Picton, Ontario, in June 1943 and they have two sons, Derek and Garry, both living in Kingston, Ontario.

He now resides in Glen Ross, Ontario and is actively engaged with Lions Clubs International helping the underprivileged.

C.G. DIAMOND, BRIGADIER-GENERAL, CD was born in Victoria, BC, into an RCAF family and was educated in various locations across Canada, the United States and Europe. He graduated from Royal Military College in 1965 with a BSc., and received his wings in 1966.

His first assignment was as a Tutor Instructor at No. 1 Flying Training School Gimli, Manitoba, followed by CF-5s and CF-104s at CFB Cold Lake, Alberta, and Fan Jet Falcons on 412 (VIP) Squadron, Ottawa. As a major, he commanded DEW Line Site Cape Dyer then attended the RAF Staff College in England. He served in National Defence Headquarters from 1975 to 1978 in the Directorate of Air Requirements and as Staff Officer to the Chief of Air Doctrine and Operations.

In 1978 he was transferred to 442 Search and

Rescue Squadron Comox, BC, to fly the Buffalo aircraft and later the Labrador helicopter, and in 1979 was appointed Commanding Officer of 442 Squadron. After Comox, he was posted to Air Command HQ, Winnipeg, on staff and in 1985 was selected to attend the National Defence College in Kingston.

He became BComd CFB Trenton in 1986 and was promoted to his present rank and appointed Commander of Air Transport Group in July 1989. Brigadier-General Diamond and his wife, Irene, are parents of twin daughters, Kim and Lisa. He recently retired from Air Command HQ, Winnipeg.

HORACE H. EASY, born in Ebor, Manitoba on 16 May 1920.

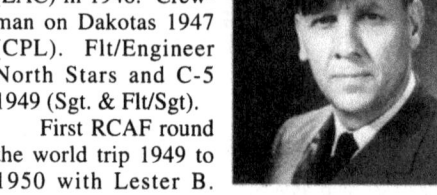

Joined March, 1941. Transferred to 412 (T) Squadron (LAC) in 1946. Crewman on Dakotas 1947 (CPL). Flt/Engineer North Stars and C-5 1949 (Sgt. & Flt/Sgt).

First RCAF round the world trip 1949 to 1950 with Lester B. Pearson on North Star 518. One of the original Flt/Engineers on Comets. Transferred overseas (France) 1954 to 1960. Transferred to 412 (T) 1960 to 1966. Retired Warrant Officer First Class, Central Maintenance at Namao 1972.

R.M. EDWARDS, BRIGADIER-GENERAL, AFC, CD, born in Saskatchewan in 1928, went to school in Saskatchewan and Winnipeg and joined the RCAF in November 1947. Following wings graduation, joined 426 Squadron in Montreal in 1948 and flew the North Star for 3-1/2 years, most notably over the Pacific to Japan during the Korean War. Was awarded the Air Force Cross. Joined 412 Squadron in 1952 and was one of the original crews on the DH 106 Comet. Also flew the C-5, Dakota, Expeditor and North Star carrying many world leaders including the Queen and Sir Winston Churchill. Left 412 in 1956 and was assigned as Executive Assistant to the AOC Air Transport Command.

Attended the RCAF Staff College in 1959-1960 and following training on the CF100 was posted to 440 Squadron at 3 (F) Wing, Zweibruecken. Trained on the F104 in 1963 and was designated CO 441 Squadron at 1 (F) Wing 64-65. Was Base Operations Officer for 1 Wing in Marville and Lahr 1965-1967 and attended the RAF College of Air Warfare in 1968 prior to assignment as Base Commander at Uplands. Attended National Defence College, 1971-1972 and served as DCOS Ops at Transport Command until retirement in 1976. Since that time, has been managing an air charter company in Calgary operating small jet and turboprop aircraft. Holds an airline transport pilot license and flies regularly in Learjet aircraft.

Aside from the tremendous satisfaction gained from being among the very first in the world to fly a four-engine jet transport aircraft, the Comet, his most memorable experience was an assignment as captain of the C-5 which took Robert Winters as the representative of the government of Canada to the inauguration of President Kubitschek of Brazil in 1956. The trip lasted three weeks and was an eventful and enjoyable tour of the Caribbean and South America.

ROBERT W. FASSOLD, M GEN., born in London, Ontario in 1933. With a B.Sc. in Biology (UWO) and a private pilot license, he joined the RCAF as a pilot on a Short Short Service Commission sponsored by 420 Reserve Squadron, London. After basic flying on the Harvard at Moose Jaw (Course 5602) he elected advanced flying school on the B-25 at Saskatoon. He received his wings in May 1957—top in his class (of one) with a school recommendation for assignment as a VIP pilot.

Preferring flying over biology, he transferred to the regular force and was posted to the navigation school in Winnipeg to accumulate the flying hours required for assignment to 412 (VIP) Transport Squadron. He was posted to 412 in 1959, initially flying both the Dakota and the VIP B-25s. On acquiring his "VIP Captain" category he was selected to fly the Comet, which he did to the end of his tour in 1963.

Comet pilots were the elite of RCAF pilots (so designated by Comet pilots) and it appeared to F/O Fassold that after 412 there was no place to go in the flying hierarchy but down! With considerable difficulty he convinced CFHQ that he should be sponsored to become a doctor and after his 412 tour he entered medicine at Western. After medical training he became Flight Surgeon and Base Surgeon at CFB Trenton. Subsequently he did postgraduate training in Public Health (U of T), followed in 1973 by postgraduate training in Aerospace Medicine in San Antonio, Texas. Promoted to BGen and Deputy Surgeon General in 1980, and to MGen and Surgeon General in 1985. In 1988 he left the Forces in favour of private consultant work in the civilian sector.

Despite his good fortune as a medical officer, General Fassold regarded himself primarily as an "RCAF" Pilot and maintained his pilot qualifications throughout medical school and his subsequent medical career. (Even while on postgraduate medical training in Texas he obtained a USAF pilot conversion to the T-37.) He departed the position of Surgeon General at the rank of Major General with the appointment of Queen's Honorary Physician, but more important to him, with a valid "green ticket" on the CH135 Twin Huey helicopter.

CHARLES W. FOX, FLIGHT LIEUTENANT, born February, 1921 in Guelph, Ontario. He volunteered in the spring of 1940 and reported for active service on October 16, 1940 in Hamilton. Following posting to Brandon Manning Depot, Rivers, Manitoba for guard duty and I.T.S. at Regina he began flying on the Fleet Finch at #10 S.F.T.S. at Mt. Hope, Ontario. He graduated second in his course at #6 S.F.T.S., Dunville in July 1941.

Attended instructor's school then posted back to Dunville in October 1941 until May 1943. Next posted to Bagotville, Quebec for O.T.U. Went overseas in August 1943 and took a Spitfire O.T.U. course at Eshatt, north of Newcastle, England. He began his tour with the 412 Squadron at Biggin Hill on January 1944. Served with 412 Squadron until January 1945 including escort duties, daylight sweeps, dive bombing, "D" Day coverage from Tangmere. He followed the front lines through France, Belgium and finished his tour at Heesch in Holland in January 1945.

After serving with the 412, Fox next served with the #410 R & SU, next posted to 126 Wing as an intelligence officer.

He returned to Canada in August and retired from the RCAF in October 1945. He started a career in retailing. He joined the RCAF Reserve 420 Squadron in January 1945. He served with the Reserve until it was phased out in 1957.

He changed from retailing to manufacturing in 1956 and is still active with Tender Tootsies, a boot, shoe, and slipper manufacturer.

He has attended the annual reunions at #6 SFTS, Dunnville, starting in 1946. His love of flying is still being pursued with his involvement as president for two years, 1988-1989 for the Canadian Harvard Aircraft Association based in Woodstock and Tillonsburg, Ontario.

JERRY FREWEN, CAPTAIN, born in Galway, Ireland in 1931. After attending University College Dublin, he joined the RAF and was sent to Canada to undergo training as part of the NATO Training Agreement that the RCAF was participating in. He graduated as a navigator from Number Two Air Navigation School, Winnipeg and returned to England in 1956. A short time later he returned to Canada and joined the RCAF as a navigator and was assigned to the Air Navigation School as an instructor.

In 1958 he completed the CF-100 Conversion Course at Number Three O.T.U., Cold Lake and was posted to 409 AW (F) Squadron at Comox. This posting was followed by a tour as an Air Traffic Controller at RCAF Station Cold Lake, 1961 to 1964. Between 1964 and 1968, he flew with 416 and 414 Squadrons. In 1968 he was posted to 437 Squadron, Trenton and flew on the Yukon and the Boeing 707 aircraft engaged in world-wide operations.

Following a tour with the Canadian forces

Airborne Sensing Unit (1971-1975) he was posted to CFB Uplands as Senior Operations Officer, where he continued to fly with 412 Squadron. A posting to 412 Squadron as Operations Officer (1980-1984) was to be his last military assignment. He is currently employed as an Air Navigation Specialist by the Department of Transport in Ottawa.

Jerry is married to the former Catherine Logan of Weyburn, Saskatchewan.

H. FUJIMURA, W.O., born in Vancouver B.C. in 1926. Joined the RCAF in 1952. After graduating from Camp Borden as an Airframe technician in 1953, he was posted to RCAF Stn. St. Hubert P.Q. There he worked at his trade and was also trained as a Dakota Crewman. In 1956 he was posted to 121 Communications and Rescue flight in Stn Sea Island, Vancouver B.C. There he was also trained to be a crewman on Canso, H21A Piaseki, and Otters.

November 1958, he was posted to 30 AMB Langar, Nottingham and was employed as a quality control inspector. January 1961 he was posted to 109 Comm. Flight at 2 (F) Wing in France, where he was in charge of the crewmen. November 1962, he was posted back to RCAF Stn. St. Hubert for the second time. In March 1965 he began his training as Cl30 Hercules Flight Engineer at RCAF Stn. Trenton. After completion of the course, he was posted to 436 Squadron Uplands, Ottawa. In 1970 he was posted to 412 Squadron which was also at Uplands, and was in charge of the Cosmopolitan CC109 Flight Engineers and the Falcon Crewmen. He flew on both aircraft until 1972 when he was posted back to 436 Squadron., which had now moved to RCAF Stn. Trenton. He retired from the service in 1977. Fujimura and his wife have two children and two grandchildren.

KENNETH R. FULTON, (F/O), J27575, born 10 May 1923, in Bible Hill, Nova Scotia. Grew up on a farm near Windsor, Nova Scotia, in the Annapolis Valley and graduated with Senior Matric in 1941.

Served in the Merchant Navy in the North Atlantic for one year. Joined the RCAF as Aircrew in May, 1942. Stationed at Lachine Manning Depot, Quebec; Victoriaville ITS, Quebec; Portage la Prairie AOS, Manitoba.

Awarded Navigators Wing and Commissioned in May 1943. Proceeded overseas to England in June, 1943. Stationed at Bournemouth; Millom, Cumberland AFU; Ossington, Nottinghamshire, OTU; Topcliffe, Yorkshire, HCU; and arrived at Linton-on-Ouse, Yorkshire, with 426 Squadron, 6 Group Bomber Command, in March 1944.

Flew 37 Operational flights to major German targets and to targets in support of the Normandy invasion. Completed a Tour of Operations in October, 1944, was awarded a Distinguished Flying Cross, and was posted to Honeybourne OTU in the Cotswolds as an Instructor.

Returned to Canada in July, 1945. Attended the University of New Brunswick, graduating with a Degree in Civil Engineering in May 1948. Two days after graduation, married Oota Greene from Fredericton, N.B., and they were subsequently blessed with a son and daughter.

Was a Charter Member of the RCAFA in Fredericton and a Navigation Instructor in the Fredericton Air Cadet Squadron for several years. From 1948 to 1972, was involved in Management in the Construction Industry all across Canada, rising to the level of General Manager.

In May 1972, he joined Public Works Canada as a Senior Project Manager. Since that time, has been involved in the planning and construction of water and sewer projects, schools and medical facilities on remote fly-in Indian Reserves throughout North Western Ontario, flying in excess of 125,000 miles each year, with approximately 50% being in small bush planes.

Have attended several 426 Squadron reunions, both in Canada and in England. Rejoined the RCAFA in 1980 with 444 Wing in Scarborough, Ontario. Have been a member of the United Church of Canada for over 50 years, and have served as a Steward and Elder. Now residing in Thornhill, just North of Toronto, with his wife. Their two children both work and live in Toronto.

NOEL FUNGE, MAJOR, born in Melbourne, Australia. He joined the RCAF in December 1953, graduating as a navigator in 1955. Posted to 408 Squadron, Rockcliffe, he flew in Dakota and Lancaster aircraft on photo-reconnaissance of the high Arctic.

He joined 412 Squadron in 1958 as a navigator on the Comet, C5 and North Star aircraft engaged in VIP transport duties. He served for three years as an exchange navigator on Canberra reconnaissance aircraft of 58 Squadron, RAF Wyton, England.

In 1965, after a short tour as a tactical reconnaissance instructor of CF-104 pilots and photo-interpreters at Marville, France, he was posted to 408 Squadron, CJATC Rivers, as a photo-navigator instructor on C-130B aircraft.

After graduation from the Aerospace Systems Course in 1967, he served as an aerospace instructor at Central Navigation School until 1970. Major Funge then served two years as Staff Officer Navigation Training at TCHQ, Winnipeg; was Navigation Leader, 436 Squadron, Trenton until 1975; and Chief Air Training at 426 Operational Training Squadron. After serving four years as Commander of the Aerospace Squadron at CFANS, then as Staff Officer Navigation and Aerospace Training at ACHQ, he retired from the Canadian Forces in October, 1985.

ROBERT W. GLOVER 38637, F/L, born in Red Deer Alta 30 November 1931. Attended Red Deer schools and Carleton University 1957 to 1961. Played basketball on Red Deer High School Varsity team. Cadet Major in Royal Can. Army Cadets. 2nd Lt. in 78th Battery of 41st Anti-tank Regiment. Joined RCAF 2 July 1951 Pilot Class No. 28 Fts Claresholm, received wings May 1952. Awarded JD Siddley Trophy for best pilot in class.

Flew North Stars on 426 (T) Squadron during Korean War flying to Japan, Korea and Europe in 1953 and 1955. Officer Commanding RCAF STN Resolute Bay June 1955 - February 1956. Served on 412 (T) Squadron 1956 to 1961. Flew DeHavilland Comet Aircraft and served as Chief Pilot Comet Aircraft, Squadron Flight Safety Officer and Assistant Squadron Operations Officer.

Left RCAF in 1961 to become Civil Aviation Inspector with Dept. of Transport and VIP Executive Pilot until 1966. Joined American Airlines 1966 and has flown L188 Electra, BAC111, B727, B707, B747, DC9, DC10 aircraft. Currently captain on B727 and DC10 doing international flying.

Married Bertha King, RN, former Trans-Canada Airlines Stewardess in 1956. Three children Barbara Lynn Glover-Fitzpatrick, Economist with Dept of Finance Ottawa, Deborah Elaine Glover, Phd, University of California and Robert Campbell Glover, Accountant in New York City. One granddaughter, Rebecca Glover Fitzpatrick.

W.P. GODIN, (BILL), F/O (RET.), born Trenton, Ontario 5 August 1923. Joined the RCAF in 1942 and trained in Vancouver-Calgary and Jarvis, graduating as a Wireless Air gunner, Sgt.

Overseas for more training at Bournemouth, then Ireland, O.T.U. Rear Newark and finally to Tholthorpe, Yorkshire, with the famous "allouette", 425 Squadron, flying Halifaxes in 6 Group Bomber Command.

His first 5 "Ops" were as a volunteer belly-gunner, very exciting. On 15 October 1944 they flew a night raid on Kiel. On the way back a crew from 420 Snowy Owls, their sister squadron was shot down, but were pin-pointed. He volunteered as a belly-gunner and flew with the O/C of 420 along with two other "Halies" and were able to locate the survivors in their dinghy about 40 miles off the Dutch coast. Signals were sent and they circled until an Air-Sea Rescue ship picked them up. Godin heard from one of the survivors about five years ago. Very satisfying. The rest of his 29 trips were with his regular crew. He was screened on March 29, 1945 when their "tour of Ops" was reduced to 30 trips from 36.

He has been 30 years with 444 Wing RCAF Assoc., and has served as president three times. He is retired now at 65 and still talks about the RCAF years. Married 47 years with three sons, two daughters-in-law, and three grandchildren. He lives in Scarborough, Ontario.

EDGAR C. GROSE, SQUADRON LEADER (RETIRED), born in South River Ont. in 1927 and raised in Thorold Ont. Grose enlisted in 1946.

Posted from Manning Depot to 426 Squadron, as one of the first post war members of 426 for contact training in Air Movements. Moved to Dorval with 426 in March 1947. Following a year in Goose Bay started flying as an Air Traffic Asst. on 426 North Stars. Flew 600  hours on the Korean Airlift out of McChord AFB Washington and was awarded "Queens Commendation for valuable service in the air." He, with Irish Ellison, started the first AMU training courses with 4 OTU.

Posted in 1957 to 412 Squadron, 3 AMU, as Flight Sergeant, Ed was NCO I/C section and served as crew member on four Royal Tours. Commissioned in 1960 he was posted to ATC HQ and later served as Cargo Officer 2 AMU, Supply Officer RCAF Stn Whitehorse, Air Div HQ where he was promoted to Major. Final posting was CO 2 AMU Trenton. Retired as S/L in Ottawa in 1974. Ed married Gwen Dickie of Kingsport N.S. in 1949, they have three sons, Douglas, Donald, and Derrick.

BEN GRUENWALD, S/L, born and educated at Warner, Alberta. He joined the RCAF in 1941 and received his Wings at Macleod on Ansons. After taking a navigation course at Charletown he did an OTU at Debert N.S. on Hudsons and then flew one across the Atlantic. After another OTU and Torpedo dropping course on Wellington in N. Ireland, he flew to Malta via West Africa and the Middle East. In 1943 he finished a tour on Torpedo Bombers then returned to the U.K. where he spent a short time instructing before being posted to Debert as a Hudson instructor.

From 1944 he spent six years at 412 Squadron and Transport Command HQ where he was current on the Lodestar, DC3, Lockheeds 10 and 12, Norseman, Goose, Expeditor, and the North Star, and became the first Squadron and Command Instrument Check Pilot. From 1950 he spent two years at Officer Selection Unit at Toronto and London, then two years as CO of Fort Nelson, then two years as CADO at Station Sea Island, two years as Sr. Support Officer with 19 Wing Aux., then one year on the Mid-Canada Line. He returned to Vancouver where he spent his remaining two years as SPSO at 5 Air Div., retiring in 1961.

Ben has lived in Vancouver ever since, with his wife Dory (deceased 1985) and his two children.

C.R. HALLOWELL (BOB), COMMANDING OFFICER 1969 - 1971, born in southern Ontario in 1930. He joined the RCAF following the outbreak of the Korean War in 1950, and received his wings at Gimli, Manitoba, in 1951. Following jet conversion on Vampires, he joined 421 Fighter Squadron to transition on F86 Sabres, and went to France with his squadron in 1952. This was followed by another Sabre tour, ferrying new aircraft to Europe until the fall of 1955.

A tour as a flight commander instructing on T-33 aircraft followed, then a posting to Central Flying School in Trenton and Saskatoon where he did a tour on the Red Knight low level aerobatic display.

In early 1961, he was posted to Germany as deputy OC 422 Fighter Sqn. and was promoted to Squadron Leader (Major.) Following the demise of the F86, he worked on mission planning for F104 operations, then returned to Canada to attend the RCAF Staff College in 1965-1966. Bob was one of the last officers promoted to Wing Commander in the RCAF in January 1968. He then did a tour in Air Operations on the tactical side until his posting as Commanding Officer, 412 (Transport) Squadron in July, 1969. This was followed by a three year posting as Commanding Officer, Canadian Forces Station Sioux Lookout, a radar station on the Pinetree Line.

Next was a spell in the "Hole" as a staff officer in Air Defence Command at North Bay. He broke this up with a posting to Egypt with the United Nations Emergency Force as Chief Air Staff Officer in 1976-1977. Upon his return he was rewarded with a move to Comox, B.C. as Base Operations Officer, the position which he held until his retirement in 1980. He then accomplished another ambition, and went bush flying along the west coast on float aircraft.

Bob was married to former Nursing Sister Jean Rowan until her death in 1982. He subsequently married an RCAF widow, Joyce Mohan. Between them they have three sons, one daughter, and so far two grandchildren. High points - first flying the T-33 in 1951 and last flight on the same bird in 1979. Getting 412 back overseas, first with the Falcons on air races, then establishing the Squadron detachment in Germany with the Convair 580 (Cosmopolitan) aircraft.

JOSEPH J. HAMILTON, FLIGHT LIEUTENANT, born 1921 at Portage la Prairie Manitoba, joined the RCAF in October 1940 after completing high school in Regina. Graduated from flying training as a pilot at Dunsville Ontario in July 1941 and arrived in Britain in November 1941. Continued advanced training at AFU and OTU and posted to 411 Squadron Digby Lincolnshire in April 1942. The Digby Wing in 12 Group Fighter Command consisted of 401, 411, 412 Squadrons.

Posted overseas in June 1942 and flew a Spitfire off the Carrier HMS Eagle to Malta. Joined 1435 RAF Squadron in Luga (LUGA) Aerodrome and was involved in air combat over "the George Cross Island" and Sicily during the siege until December 1942.

Returned to Britain and instructed at 560 OTU Dundee Scotland until October 1943. Returned to Canada on leave. Arrived back in Britain and was posted to 412 Squadron at Biggin Hill in January 1944. The Biggin Hill Wing consisted of the original 401, 411, 412 Squadron as 126 Wing 2 TAF (Second Tactical Airforce) moved to Tangmere Aerodrome prior to the invasion of Normandy. Following a mid-air collision baled out into the English Channel, after a period of convalescence was posted to 410 Repair and Salvage unit as test pilot. Proceeded to France in June 1944. Returned to Canada in May 1945 and was discharged from the RCAF at Vancouver in June 1945. Re-entered in the RCAF Regular in April 1951 and instructed NATO students at AFU on Harvard and T33 aircraft at Gimli, MacDonald and Portage La Prairie Aerodromes until September 1955. Posted to Training Command Headquarters at Trenton Ontario as Deputy Flight Safety Officer until September 1959. Following OTU conversion at Summerside was posted to 407 Maritime Patrol Squadron at Comox BC. Was discharged from the RCAF in November 1964.

Joined the Department of Veterans Affairs in Vancouver and was a Veteran Service Counsellor until retirement in March 1985.

During RCAF service the major aircraft flown were the Harvard, Spitfire, Hurricane, T33 and P2V7 Neptune.

Since retirement has resided in Vancouver enjoying travelling, motorhoming and fishing.

W.C. HASKER, F/L, born 1937 in Manitoba. Joined the RCAF in October 1955. After wings graduation, he was posted to Flying Training School Penhold instructing on Harvards, Air Observer School Winnipeg as a staff pilot flying DC3s was next, and in October 1960 was taken on strength of 412 Squadron.

During his stay at 412 Squadron he flew the DC-3 and Cosmopolitan carrying foreign heads of state and high-ranking government and military personnel. These years also included the development of medical Evacuation by Cosmo, Golden Hawk Support, air shows as well as service flights. This was also the time of Napier Eland powered Cosmos and personal experience was one engine failure every two hours.

After leaving 412 Squadron immediately following the presentation of the Squadron Colours, in which he played a major role, he was taken on strength of 111 Ku Winnipeg to fly as the staff pilot for the Air Officer Commanding Training Command. It was during this time, when the Napier Eland engine had a catastrophic engine failure with Air Marshall Slemon on board, that the RCAF finally re-engined the Cosmos.

After leaving the service in 1965 to join Air Canada, he has spent many years serving the Canadian Airline Pilots Association and presently flies B767s out of Vancouver while living in Victoria B.C.

ALBERT C. HINCKE (AL), MAJOR, born in 1932 in Vancouver, joined the RCAF in February, 1952. Following Pilot training at Gimli, Manitoba, he was presented his wings in December of 1952 at the last course to receive wings at the F.T.S. level. Following tours with Maritime Patrol Squadrons, a Flying Training School and Radar Squadrons as a Fighter Controller, he was posted to the Directorate of Flight Safety as an Aircraft Accident Investigator.

In 1976 he was assigned to 412 Squadron and in 1977 became the Cosmopolitan Flight Commander. During 1977, he flew the Minister of Urban Affairs throughout Eastern Europe.

While on 412 Squadron, Hincke flew the Governor General, the Prime Minister, many Cabinet Ministers and visiting foreign dignitaries throughout North America.

In 1978 Maj. Hincke flew the Royal Family on their tour of Canada during the Commonwealth Games. In 1980 he was posted to National Defence Headquarters in the Directorate of Air Operations and Training where he was responsible for airlift tasking. In 1981 Major Hincke was awarded the Order of Military Merit.

Following retirement in 1987 with 11,000 flying hours, he continued his employment with D.N.D. as a Senior Analyst in the Directorate of Establishment Requirements Evaluation.

Major Hincke has four children and nine grandchildren. One highlight in the family was presenting his second son with his military pilot's wings 27 years to the day from when he had received his own.

ROBERT G. HUSCH, MAJOR GENERAL (RETD) CD (PSC, PCSC, NDC), was born in June 1932, at Rutland, British Columbia. He entered the RCAF at the age of 18. Following training as a pilot, during which he was awarded the Junior Pilot Siddley Trophy for top honors in flying ability, he was transferred to 426 Transport Squadron at Montreal. While on 426 Squadron, Major General Husch flew North Star aircraft throughout the world, including numerous flights to Japan during the Korean Airlift. He became an aircraft captain at the age of 20.

In 1955 Major General Husch commenced a four-year tour on 412 (VIP) Transport Squadron during which he flew high-ranking dignitaries of the Canadian Government to all corners of the world, as well as flying foreign VIPS, including the Queen, the Queen Mother and Prince Philip, during their visits to Canada. He served as an instructor and check pilot on the Squadron's Expeditor, Dakota, North Star and C-5 aircraft.

In 1959 Major General Husch was posted to Trenton and appointed the Air Transport Command Project Officer responsible for the flight testing and introduction to operational service of the Yukon aircraft. After graduating from the RCAF Staff College in Toronto in 1963, Major General Husch commenced a two-year tour as Officer Commanding the Aircrew Standards Unit based at Trenton. In July 1966, he was appointed the Commanding Officer of 437 Squadron, which operated Yukon aircraft on world-wide routes. Three years later he was posted to Canadian Forces Headquarters in Ottawa as Director of Force Structure, in which capacity, he was responsible for the detailed planning of equipment, personnel and support requirements for air, maritime and land force elements extending over a 15-year period.

Major General Husch attended National Defence College in 1972 and was subsequently appointed the Base Commander of CFB Trenton.

He was promoted to the rank of Brigadier General in May 1974, and appointed Chief of Staff, Air Transport Command.

In August 1975, Major General Husch became the first Commander of the Air Transport group at Trenton. The Group was comprised of 10 squadrons, had a total of 65 aircraft and was responsible for passenger and cargo airlift on a world-wide basis and for search and rescue operations throughout Canada. Major General Husch was appointed Commandant of the Canadian Forces College in Toronto in August of 1976. In July of 1978 he was promoted to the rank of Major General and appointed Chief of Air Doctrine and Operations at National Defence Headquarters.

He retired from the Canadian Forces in July of 1979 to assume the position of Executive Vice-President of CUC Limited, and international corporation consisting of several companies engaged in cable television, micro-wave transmission and magazine publishing, and Executive Vice-President of Scarboro Cable TV/FM Ltd., in Toronto.

In 1981 he became a member of Century 21 Black Mountain Realty in his home town of Kelowna, BC. At present, he is the owner and manager of the company.

LESLIE W. HUSSEY, WING COMMANDER, born and educated in Ottawa, joined the Royal Canadian Air Force in May 1942. He graduated as a pilot, was posted overseas and attached to the Royal Air Force. He completed a tour of operations on Lancaster aircraft with 550 Squadron, Royal Air Force, Bomber Command. On his return to Canada he was posted to 12 Communications Squadron, RCAF Station Rockliffe for the first time in February 1945. This was followed by duty with 165 Transport Squadron, Edmonton, conversion to B24 Liberator aircraft and a posting to 168 Heavy Transport Squadron, Rockliffe. After several months of flying supplies to Europe, he was released in 1946. He was then employed by the Air Transport Board and later worked as an Airport Traffic Controller at Sydney Airport, Nova Scotia. He was recalled by the RCAF in 1948 and was posted to 412 K Squadron, Rockliffe.

During the next seven years he was current as a Captain on the C5, Expeditor, Dakota and North Star aircraft and flew many distinguished Canadian and foreign dignitaries including Her Royal Highness Princess Elizabeth and the Duke of Edinburgh, Queen Juliana of the Netherlands, Sir Winston Churchill, and a number of Prime Ministers and Governors - General. A major operational experience during 1953 was participation in BOACs DeHavilland Comet aircraft proving flight program and subsequent training and conversion to captain on the Comet jet transport aircraft.

In 1955 he was moved to Air Transport Command Headquarters as Staff Officer, Postings and Careers returning to 412 Squadron as Deputy Commanding Officer in 1959. Graduating from RCAF Staff College in 1963, he served as Staff Officer, Operations, Transport Command and in 1966 was appointed Commanding Officer 436 Transport Squadron flying C130 Hercules aircraft. At the time of the Biafran conflict in Nigeria, during 1968 through 1969, he was seconded to the Canadian Red Cross Society and served on the International Commission of the Red Cross (ICRC), organizing a Nigerian relief supply airlift. A Red Cross Citation commended him for playing "a major role with the ICRC in Geneva in the original planning of the operations and later served as a liaison officer in Nigeria and Equatorial Guinea, where he worked with ICRC and national authorities on operational and administrative arrangements."

In 1970 he assumed the position of Commanding Officer of a second squadron, 442 Transport and Rescue Squadron, CFB Comox, B.C. and later retired from the military in 1973. He was then employed in the Department of Transport, Civil Aviation Branch as the Superintendent, Standards and Legislation developing safety and operating standards applicable to the operators of all Canadian registered aircraft. He retired from this position in 1988 after 46 years association with aviation.

Wing Commander Hussey married Wilma Hall of Ottawa in 1949. They have two sons, William and John, and a daughter, Lesleigh.

PATRICK B. IVEY, born 19 June 1915 at Saskatchewan. Emigrated to U.S. in 1925. Learned to fly at Oakland Airport in 1937 and married Natalie Becker, Berkeley, June 29, 1940.

Recruited into RCAF by Clayton-Knight Committee in Oakland, California, as direct entry pilot June 9, 1941. First posted as F/O service pilot to #3 B & G School, MacDonald, Manitoba, August, 1941.

Posted to #12 Communications Flight, Rockcliffe, May 1942. Detached on temporary duty to Northwest Staging Route, Edmonton, 3 August 1942. With F/L Carl Crossley, flew two float equipped Norsemen from Rockcliffe to Whitehorse, Y.T. to construct emergency fields at Snag, Aishik, and Smith River. Temporary duty was extended through the winter of 1942-1943 to supply these installations by ski equipped Norsemen. The following summer, 1943, flew aerial surveys for DOT in the Northwest Territories from Norman Wells to the arctic coast to locate airport sites for proposed "third line of defense" into Alaska.

Spring, 1944, officially posted from #12 Communications flight, Rockcliffe, to #6 Communications Flight, NWAC, Edmonton. Detached on temporary duty to Jasper on skis to fly aerial support for Lovat Scouts, Scottish commando regiment training for invasion of Norway. Summer, 1944, qualified first pilot on Lockheeds and Expediters on Yukon and NWT flights. Posted in July to heavy transport instrument course, Pennfield Ridge, N.B. In October, appointed personal pilot to AVM T.A. (Tommy) Lawrence, AOC NWAC.

Spring, 1945, promoted to Flight Lieutenant. Appointed OC of Transportation Section of #6 Communication Flight. In November, 1945, appointed OC #6 Communications Flight.

April, 1946, applied for discharge from RCAF to form with S/L E.S. (Ted) Holmes, former O.C. #6 Comm. Flight, the Westland Dusting Service at Edmonton, flying dust and spray equipped Lysanders. Retired from agricultural flying in California 1972.

LESLIE A. JACKSON, PETTY OFFICER FIRST CLASS, was born in Iroquois Ontario in 1939 where he attended Iroquois High School. In 1958 he joined the Royal Canadian Navy as a Steward and completed his formal trade training at HMCS Hochelaga in Montreal, Quebec. On completion of trade training, he served on HMCS Swansea, Buckingham, Cap de Madelaine and Margaree before joining 412 (T) as a M Cpl on 13 July 1970 as a Flight Steward where he remained until January 1974, returning to sea with a posting to HMCS *Perserver,* where he was promoted to Petty Officer Second Class and remained there until June 1976.

He was then posted to CFB Ottawa as Mess Manager of the Warrant Officers and Sergeants Mess until July 1979. While serving in Ottawa he *did a six-month tour in CFS Alert, Canada's most northerly military station, operating the Station's* Exchange. He then proceeded back to sea posted to HMCS *Provider* and was promoted to Petty Officer First Class.

In July 1981, he was posted to CFB Borden as Base Senior Steward and remained in that capacity until July 1984 when he was posted to HMCS *Iroquois.*

In January 1985, he retired from the CAF after 27 years, but not for long, as he joined the Supplementary Class "C" Reserve in June 1986 as an instructor at Steward Training Company, CFB Borden. After 18 months of instructing, he moved to the Standards Cell to become the Standards Writer for the Steward trade at CFSAL in Borden and retains that position today.

He is married to the former Joyce Young of Springfield Nova Scotia and resides in Angus, Ontario where they have their retirement home. PO Jackson and wife Joyce have a daughter, Michele, who resides in Barrie, Ontario and a son, Leslie Scott, who is in the CAF and stationed in CFB Montreal.

PO Jackson's highlight while serving with 412 (T) was his trip to Moscow in 1973 November, taking the Minister of External Affairs to that country. This trip was just prior to leaving the Squadron and it was Col Parslow's parting gesture and will always be remembered and appreciated.

LEONARD V. JOHNSON, MAJOR-GENERAL (RET.), born in Saskatchewan in 1929. He served in the Canadian Army Reserve from 1944-1948, flew forestry patrol from La Ronge, Sask., and joined the RCAF in September, 1950. After graduation from 2FTS, Gimli, in 1951, he flew Dakotas and C-119 aircraft at 435 Squadron Edmonton for two years and then joined 4 (T) OTU Trenton as a pilot instructor. In 1957, he was posted to 412 Squadron where he flew Dakota, North Star, the Canadair C-5, and Cosmopolitan aircraft.

Promoted to squadron leader, he served on the operations staff at Air Transport Command Headquarters until 1966, when he was posted to the five-month course at the U.S. Armed Forces Staff College, Norfolk, Virginia. After two years at Canadian Forces Headquarters, Ottawa, he returned to 412 Squadron as commanding officer in July 1968. This tour ended with promotion to colonel and posting to Air Transport Command Headquarters as deputy chief of staff for operations.

After graduation from the National Defence College in Kingston, he commanded Canadian Forces Base Edmonton for one year. Promoted to brigadier general in 1974, he served as Chief of Staff, Training Command and then moved back to Trenton as commander of the Canadian Forces Training System. In 1978, he was posted to National Defence Headquarters, and, in 1980, to the National Defence College as commandant. He retired to the country north of Kingston in 1984.

Married since 1954 to Shirley Hutcherson, of Sydney, Australia, he is the father of four and grandfather of two. Since retirement, he has been fully employed as a peace worker, lecturer, and author of numerous articles, essays and "A General for Peace," his autobiography.

W.DAVID E. KELLOWAY, SGT., was born in Newfoundland and joined the RCAF at St. John's in 1956. He graduated from Movement Controller (Air) School at 4 O.T.U. Trenton, Ontario in 1956 and was posted to 3 A.M.U., 412 Squadron where his duties included passenger handling as well as flying duties.

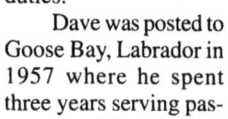

Dave was posted to Goose Bay, Labrador in 1957 where he spent three years serving passenger and freight needs and flying duties on the C47.

Sgt. Kelloway was posted back to 3 A.M.U., 412 Squadron in 1960 for flying duties on Comet aircraft. He was also trained on the North Star, C119, C130, Yukon and Cosmo CC109. He became a member of The Winged Order of Neptunus Rex on 18 March 1964. Sgt. Kelloway spent many hours of flying duties on 412 VIP C5 aircraft #10,000.

He was posted to C.F.S. Gander in 1969 as NCO i/c Base Traffic and Air Terminal duties. In 1973 he transferred to CFB Penhold, Alberta and then to his last posting to 1 AMU Namao, Alberta as a member of the 9 MAMS team.

He retired in 1977 to Red Deer, Alberta. Sgt. Kelloway and his wife, former Barbara Liebeck of Ottawa, Ont. have two children and four grandchildren.

GORD KELSO, MAJOR, was born at Brockville, Ontario in 1934, graduated from Prescott High School in 1952, and joined the RCAF in 1954 on course 5408. Training was at Centralia, Moose Jaw and Gimli, followed immediately by Flying Instructors School. He married Jean Morton in September 1955.

Prior to 412, which he joined in May 1973, postings included Portage, 6RD Trenton, Lincoln Park, Calgary and Sault Ste Marie recruiting units, 436 Squadron, and Carleton University. He flew CC109 Cosmopolitan with 412 and was deputy flight commander from July 1974 to August 1975. Memorable trips included the Middle East, Saudi Arabia and Iran in 1974 and the Canadian Arctic with HRH the Prince of Wales in 1975. Posted to ATGHQ, he continued to monitor Cosmo and Falcon standards and frequent the squadron until posted to 437 Squadron in March 1978.

In September 1978, he accepted a position with Mobil Oil Canada Ltd in Calgary where he remained as Training Captain and later Chief Pilot until moving to Shell Canada Limited as Chief Pilot in January 1988, where he now flies HS125 and Citation 11 aircraft.

Retirement is not in Gord and Jean's immediate plans. They have three children (including one military pilot) and three grandsons.

P. KOCH, (PETER), CD, was born on May 10, 1920 in Hodgeville, Saskatchewan. He enlisted in the Army in 1939, transferring to the RCAF soon after. Served initially with the RAF (1940) and joined 405 Sqdn. in 1941 as Aero Engine Tech, remaining on strength until repatriation in 1945. Opted for release but was held for "Tiger Force" for several weeks, and released to 'Active Reserve.' Served continously at various Western bases reverting to Administrative duties as flying was curtailed. Retired in 1965 with the closure of Saskatoon.

Continues as a hard working advocate of the RCAFA since its inception. Joined 500 (Regina) Wing in November 1948. Active in its membership recruitment, and held a senior administrative position with its Air Cadet Squadrons. On moving to Winnipeg and joining 600 Wing, was appointed the Cadet Wings Training Officer and subsequently its Chief Administrative Officer over seven Air Cadet Squadrons. On transfer to Saskatoon and membership in 602 (Lynx) Wing he became active in that wing's affairs.

An employment opportunity in 1970 meant a move to Kelowna, B.C. where the incumbant reverted to MAL status in the Association. He did however actively pursue the idea of a wing for the area, and in 1983 was successful in achieving this aim. He served as its charter secretary and also president in its formative years. Subsequently he initiated and promoted the formation of 886 (Overlander) Wing in Kamloops, and was named "Member of the Year" by the Pacific Group. More recently as a result of his efforts at membership recruitment he was instrumental in the formation of 889 (North Okangan) Wing in Vernon.

ALFRED J. LAIDLER, WING COMMANDER, born in Weston, Ontario, in 1921, attended Weston Collegiate & Vocational School, and was first employed by Canada Cycle & Motors (C.C.M.) Weston.

Enlisted in the RCAF (Permanent Force #10609) 21 September 1939, and was taken on staff at 1 Manning Depot, Toronto; October 1940 moved to Aeronautical Inspection Directorate (A.I.D.) School, as Sgt i/c Orderly Room; May 1942 transferred to Directorate of Signals, A.F.H.Q.; commissioned from the rank of W.O.1 in December 1943 and on graduation from OTC January 1944, transferred to 164 (T) Squadron Moncton to train as Traffic Officer (Air Movements today), then on to 165 (T) Squadron, Sea Island in April 1944. Transfer to India September 1944 cancelled and attached to 12 (Com) Squadron under W/C Gordon Diamond for duties related to the Quebec Conference. January 1945 posted to 168 (HT) Squadron, served in Rabat, Morroco, and Prestwick, Scotland. Ordered to Ottawa July 1945 to join Tiger Force in India. Japan surrendered before departure, so interim stop was as CADO Station Uplands.

In November 1945, as transferred to 120 (T) Wing, Odiham, England, commanded by G/C Reg Lane; July 1946 returned to Canada and 165 (T) Squadron Edmonton. 1 October 1946 reverted from Flight Lieutenant to Flight Sergeant and TOS Stn Toronto as Orderly Room Clerk. January 1950 transferred to Stn Rockcliffe, then in July 1950 to RCAF Records Office.

Commissioned from the ranks again in January 1951 in Air force Security Branch, served at AFHQ until January 1953, then 1 Air Div Paris and Metz; Maritime Air Command, Halifax, from January 1956 to July 1962; and returned to DAFS/ AFHQ until retirement 30 September 1970. Joined the Public Service and was employed in Department of Energy, Mines and Resources, DOT and CIDA, retiring in February 1980.

W/C Laidler and wife, Joan Nevins of Ottawa, have five children and five grandchildren.

ROGER O. LANDRY, LCOL OMM, CD, born in the small Northern Ontario town of Smooth Rock Falls where he completed High School before enrolling for the pilot training as a Flight Cadet in the RCAF in May 1953.

Following successful flying training courses on Harvards at Claresholm, on T-33 at Portage la Prairie, he was awarded his wings in June 1954. Once Gunnery School on T-33 aircraft was completed at MacDonald, he then attended the F-86 OTU at Chatham, NB, before receiving his transfer to 413 (F) Squadron at Zweibrucken, Germany in January 1955. A restructuring of Air Division squadrons found Roger and his new bride, Dolly Damery, back in Canada in May 1957 to attend the Advanced Flying Instructor School in Trenton.

Instructed at MacDonald and Portage la Prairie before a transfer to Advanced Flying Instructor School where he eventually became Chief of Standardization.

In September 1964, he became Course Director for Officer Cadets at Central Officer School in Centralia, followed in 1966 by a Pilot Exchange posting to Cognac France with the French Air Force, where he trained instructor pilots from Algeria, Morocco, Libya, Lebanon and Sudan. In all, counting NATO allied countries LCol Landry instructed pilots of 16 different nationalities.

Promoted to Major upon his return to Canada in July 1969 and posted to 412 (T) VIP squadron he flew the Falcon aircraft for over four years. He participated in the London-to-Sydney, Australia air race in December 1969. Following Staff College LCol Landry was posted to Beirut, Lebanon as Military Attache for Lebanon, Syria, Iraq and Jordon. He and his family arrived in Beirut 14 days before the start of the 1973 October War.

In July 1976 LCol Landry was appointed Commanding Officer of the CFS Senneterre, and transferred in April 1978 to NDHQ as a staff officer for both Defence Minister Barney Danson and Allen McKinnon. After a brief tour in the Official Languages Division, in July 1981 he was appointed as the 15th Commanding Officer of 412 (T) Squadron, at CFB Ottawa, until December 1983.

In June 1983, LCol Landry was appointed and double-hatted as BOPSO, a position he held until his retirement in September 1989 from the Forces, after more than 36 years of loyal service.

MURRAY LEPARD, SQUADRON LEADER (Ret.), born Feversham Ontario in 1923. Joined RCAF July 1941, graduating at Moncton N.B. June 1942 as pilot. Served as a staff pilot until transferred overseas January 1944. Joined 412 Squadron at Heech Holland ending war at Wunstorf base Germany and the army of occupation. Returned to Canada December 1945. Released in January 1946.

Rejoined RCAF 1948. Served as pilot instructor at Flying Instructors School until 1955 then onto 1 (F) Wing Marville as Sabre pilot. Returned to Canada in 1959 as fighter controller then Sabre instructor on low level training at Chatham N.B. Base operations officer 1966-1970, retiring April of 1970 to take position as Business Administrator CFB Chatham Schools until 1984. Transferred as Executive Assistant to Director of Education in Lahr West Germany. Retired 1988 and returned to Canada.

Married the former Barbara Bradford, Belleville, Ont in 1943. They have five children and seven grandchildren.

He had a memorable moment during his air force career. On 4 May 1945, during armed recce north of Hamburg the engine quit. As terrain looked inhospitable, decided to bale out. Trimmed a/c for glide, opened coop top and side exit, undid

harness, tossed helmet off, hung onto windscreen and stepped out onto wing debating whether to slide off feet first or roll backwards when the engine exhaust at my face splattered and the engine caught. Eased back onto seat, throttle responded, so did up harness, closed side exit and tried to close coop top. As it stuck looked back to see helmet swinging wildly still plugged into radio. Pulled it in and on to head, closed the coop top looked up to see squadron circling above so joined and finished the flight.

CHARLES LOCKWOOD, (CHUCK) WING COMMANDER (RET.), born 1922 in Lacombe, Alberta, enlisted in the RCAF in 1941 and graduated from pilot training in April 1942.

Wartime service included operations overseas and in Canada flying B-17 and B-24 aircraft. In 1946 he entered the University of British Columbia completing his degree and post graduate studies in (industrial) psychology prior to re-enrollment in the RCAF in 1951. From 1951 until joining 412 Squadron in March 1955 he was employed in personnel research and development for aircrew and groundcrew. During his time on 412, he was selected to serve on the project team for introduction of the CC109 (Cosmopolitan) aircraft and was captain for the inaugural flight to Goose Bay in August 1960. Memorable 412 experiences include flying such distinguished passengers as Mr. J.A.D. McCurdy and Lord Mountbatten.

After leaving 412 in October 1960, he served in a number of senior personnel appointments in Toronto and Ottawa until his release in 1972. After his release he joined the Department of Transport where he utilized both his aviation and personnel background in appointments as senior manager and director until his resignation in July 1987.

Chuck presently resides in Ottawa where he is enjoying retirement with his wife, Mickey, and three daughters, combining his hobbies of motor homing and amateur radio—his call sign is appropriately VE3-CAF.

DONALD C. MACKENZIE, LIEUTENANT GENERAL, CANADIAN FORCES, RET., born 27 May 1931 in Mexico City. Received his secondary education at Trinity College, Port Hope, Ontario. He is a Bachelor of Commerce graduate of the University of Alberta.

Following training as a pilot, his early career included flying tours in northern aerial photography and mapping, flying instructing and airlift operations. He then attended the University of Alberta, and upon graduation was posted to Air Transport Command, first as executive assistant to the Commander, then as a staff officer in the personnel branch.

After completing the Royal Canadian Air Force Staff College course in 1965, he became Commanding Officer of the Canadian Forces VIP transport squadron in Ottawa, followed by promotion to Colonel and posting as Director of Air Force Equipment Requirements at National Defence Headquarters.

In May 1969, General Mackenzie was selected to attend the federal Government Bilingual and Bicultural Development Program at Quebec City. From July 1970 to June 1972 he was Deputy Base Commander, Canadian Forces Base Montreal. He next served three years as Canadian Forces Attache to the Canadian embassies in Rome and Madrid. He returned to Canada in September 1975 and became Director of Air Studies at the Canadian Forces Command and Staff College, Toronto.

On his promotion to Brigadier General in July 1976, General Mackenzie was named Commander, Air Transport Group, with headquarters at Trenton, Ontario, where he was responsible for all Canadian Forces' airlift and search and rescue operations. He was promoted to Major General in July 1979 and appointed Chief, Air Doctrine and Operations at National Defence Headquarters, Ottawa. In September 1981, he was assigned to NORAD headquarters as the Deputy Chief of Staff for Plans.

General Mackenzie was promoted to Lieutenant General in May 1983 and became Deputy Commander in Chief for the North American Aerospace Defence Command (NORAD), Colorado Springs, Colorado.

After he retired from the Canadian Armed Forces in August, 1986, he became a Senior Consultant with Public Affairs International, an Ottawa based government relations consulting firm until August, 1988.

GARRY B. MACLEOD, CAPTAIN, born Truro, N.S. 1941. After high school spent three years employed by Canadian Marconi administering supply of goods and services to military radar stations in Northern Canada.

He flew as a commercial pilot prior to joining RCAF in 1966. Graduated pilot training Portage la Prairie, Manitoba December, 1967. Posted to Maritime Command then to 429 (T) Squadron Winnipeg. Served as Training and Standards Officer, I.C.P. and Training Command V.I.P. Pilot; one year as Operations Officer and A/Mil. Cmdr. Air Defence Command.

While completing jet refresher course, prior to being posted to 412 Squadron in October 1973, he suffered a severe spinal compression during an aerobatic session in a tutor jet.

His career as a pilot at 412 was but a few short months, he became medically grounded and served the remainder of his military career administering 412 V.I.P. Operations and latterly base operations until his medical release in 1976.

He subsequently worked in security operations at the H. of C. Ottawa and is now permanently disabled as a result of the spinal compression. Captain MacLeod and former wife, Sheila, have three sons, Shawn, Kyle and Gavin.

ROY C. MANUEL, MWO, born in Vancouver in 1920. He began his RCAF career on enlistment in the non-permanent Airforce in March 1939 with the 111 (CAC) (coastal artillery cooperation) Squadron, Vancouver BC. Signed on wartime duties on declaration of war against Germany. First career posting, November 1939, was to 111 Squadron detachment at Patricia Bay, BC and became one of the original members in the RCAF to be stationed there. He was posted to No. 4 SFTS Saskatoon in September 1940, employed in the maintenance hanger. He was transferred in 1942 to 133 (F) Squadron (Hurricanes) at Lethbridge Alta. then on with the squadron to Boundary Bay and Tofino, BC. Back to 6 O.T.U. Patricia Bay, BC in February, 1944 and then RCAF Stn Comox and Greenwood N.S.

On disbandment of 6 O.T.U., he was transferred to RCAF Station Aylmer Ontario on an instructors course. On successful completion of course, he instructed in the Aero-engine trade in Aylmer and RCAF Stn Camp Borden until 1948 when he was transferred to 406 Auxiliary Squadron in Saskatoon Sask. where he worked as a Trade Advancement Instructor and also a tour in Squadron maintenance. Promoted to Sergeant and Flight Sergeant at this unit and then was transferred to RCAF Station, Penhold, Alberta. He served as NCO in line-servicing and in station maintenance on Harvard aircraft. He left Penhold as a Warrant Officer Two on transfer to 412 (T) Squadron at Uplands, Ottawa, Ont., where he served as Warrant Officer in line-servicing, as a member of a Maintenance Appraisal Team at Canadair in Montreal Quebec during the acquisition of the Cosmopolitan CC109 Aircraft and as the floor supervisor in 412 Squadron maintenance, also in Station Maintenance on the purchase of additional Hercules C130 aircraft, 436 (T) Squadron.

He was transferred overseas in 1967 to 1970, stationed in Sardinia, Italy and Lahr, Germany, on return to Canada he was transferred to C.F.B. Namao, Edmonton, Alta. with 435 (T) Squadron till he retired in July 1972 as a Master Warrant Officer. Moved to the city of Duncan, B.C. and worked a further 12 years for the municipality, finally retiring in 1985.

His lasting impression of his tour of duty with 412 (T) Squadron was the dedication of all members to ensure that squadron commitments were carried out efficiently and promptly.

ALAN MARTIN, S/L, joined the RCAF in February 1949 and was posted to #106 "K" Flight, Edmonton, in North West Air Command. Flew Canso's in the summer from detachment at Norman Wells and Dakotas from Edmonton in winter. The prime tasks were re-supply of isolated RCAF and DOT units, search and rescue and air-evacuation.

In October 1950 he was posted to Summerside, P.E.I. for the SNIN course and then instruction duties at the Air Navigation School. In

September 1952 he was transferred to 412 (T) Squadron.

Al was on 412 (T) Squadron for three years and then moved to Trenton first as OC the newly formed Air Transport command Air Assessment Team and then as chief instructor at the 4 (T) OTU ground school. In August 1960 he was assigned to the International Truce Commission at Saigon (Vietnam) for a one year tour of duty.

On return from the Far East, Al went to RCAF Staff College and from thence to AFHQ in Ottawa. He retired from the service in August 1968.

Before joining the RCAF, S/L Martin had completed six years of service in the Royal Air Force. These years saw initial training in Canada as an Observer, completion of OTU training at Penfield Ridge, N.B. on Ventura aircraft and then transfer to Ferry Command (45ATG) at Montreal. Between aircraft deliveries to the UK, the Middle East and India, he married Barbara Gardham, a student nurse who in off-duty hours was an Air Force House hostess. Returned to England in 1945 he flew Sterling and then York aircraft bringing service types back from India and Burma.

After retirement from the RCAF Al had a second "tour of duty". First, with the National Capital Commission in Ottawa and then with Canada Post. He retired, finally, in 1988 and he and Barbara now live in Ottawa.

Things remembered include: Having the Governor General, Viscount Alexander as our "guest" on a very non-VIP Canso for a tour of Northern Canada and a memorable visit to Dawson City to meet old-timers from the '98 goldrush. Trans AT flying - 19h 50m in a PBY in 1944; 5h 40m in the Comet in 1953; circumnavigating the world in three minutes (at the Pole in North Star 7518). Memorable, too, the first approach up the fiord to "Bluie West One" in Greenland in a B-25; the eerie tranquillity of islands in the mist in Baie d'Along as we patrolled the waters north of Haiphong, and the beauty of the Comet and pride in being one of the first in Canada to fly her.

FRED H.M. MAXWELL, SERGEANT CDI (RET.), born in Halifax, Nova Scotia, March 1936, he attended schools in Upper Sackville, Bedford and Halifax and enlisted in the Royal Canadian Air Force Regular, February 1954, as an Aircraftsman, Second Class.

Upon completion of basic training in St. Jean, Quebec, he attended trade school at Camp Borden, where he graduated as an Honor Student, becoming an Aero Engine Technician. Subsequently, he was posted to Winnipeg Communications and Rescue Squadron working on Dakotas, Otters, Harvards, Expeditors and T33s (Silver Stars), until his release in January 1957.

He re-enlisted in October 1958 with a rank of Leading Aircraftsman Group 3 and was posted to Uplands 412 Transport Squadron, servicing and maintaining Dakotas, North Stars, Expeditors, Comets, Mitchells, Cosmopolitans, C54s and C5 Aircraft. In 1968 he was posted to 4F.T.T.U., instructing on the CC117 Falcon. In 1973, he was posted to Greenwood, Nova Scotia, servicing and maintaining the Argus and Aurora. In 1983 he was posted to Shearwater, Nova Scotia, servicing and maintaining the SeaKing Helicopter with a short posting aboard H.M.S. *Iroquois*.

Maxwell retired in February 1985. He and his wife, Veronica, reside at Lewis Lake, Upper Sackville, Nova Scotia and have three children: Julie, Randall and Neil.

GEORGE E. MAYER, born in Montreal, Quebec in 1940. Following an avid interest in building and flying model aircraft and a rewarding three-and-one-half years in Air Cadets, he joined the RCAF Primary Reserve as an Airframe Technician in 1957. Immediately after returning from the 1959 Air Cadet Exchange visit to the United Kingdom, he joined the RCAF as a pilot and commenced training. Successfully completing courses at Centralia, Penhold, and Portage, he was awarded the coveted RCAF pilots wings and commission. His first flying tour was as staff pilot with the Air Navigation School in Winnipeg flying Beechcraft 18 and Dakotas. Volunteering for United Nations Service, he completed two tours of duty in one year - first at 115 ATU EL Arish, Egypt, and then at 134 ATU Sana, Yemen, for which he was awarded the UNEF and UNYOM medals.

Returning to Canada, he proudly served with 412 (T) Squadron from 1964 to 1968 flying Dakotas, Convair 540 and 580. After commuting trans-Atlantic in the Yukon for what seemed forever, in Aug, 1967 he married the former Joy Hartley of Ottawa who returned from teaching duties in Soest, West Germany to join the 412 Squadron family. A four-and-one-half year instructional tour on Chipmunks and Musketeers was followed by a posting to VP 405 Squadron Greenwood, Nova Scotia, on the mighty aging Argus. This six-year tour as an Argus crew commander, Squadron training officer and Instrument Check Pilot included many interesting detachments to exotic locations like Machrihanish, Scotland, Keflavik, Iceland, Gibraltar, Bermuda, Azores, Frobisher Bay (now Iqaluit) and added 3,685 hours to the log book.

Captain (R) Mayer is currently a Civil Aviation Inspector with the Department of Transport whose primary responsibility is for Instrument Flying Standards. He maintains currency on Cessna 182, BE90, Dakota and Cessna Citation II aircraft.

JOHN E. McALLISTER, FLIGHT LIEUTENANT, Medical Officer to 412 Squadron & 126 Wing February 1944 to September 1945. Born in Edmonton 1916. Education - M.D. University of Alberta 1939, Additional training - Edmonton and New York Hospital 1939 - 1941 and 1946-7 NYC.

Attached 412 from famed Biggin Hill through Normandy, Belgium and Holland. Hostilities ceased while at Wunstdorf near Hanover. Also had temporary duty with 52 Mobile field Hospital (Eindhoven) and M.O. at Megeve France Ski Resort. Outstanding memories - The Normandy Beach at Beny, Falais Gap days, joyful progress through Europe to Brussels.

Medical duties consisted of attention to a few shot up bombers commencing at Tangmere, such prosaic occurrences as entireties and wasps in Normandy. Above all, fraternizing with pilots, supposedly recognizing potentials for "the twitch." Despite the outstanding fighter performance of 126 Wing in general, stress did not prove too onerous to personnel, including maverick George Beurling. Regarding ground personnel, one can only express admiration for an ingenious and dedicated group.

Last memorable experience involved the crash landing of F/O G.M. Horter in boggy land on the west bank of the Elbe. The auxiliary tank had been dropped or exploded on impact, giving the impression to his mates and an adjacent army unit that survival was unlikely. With accurate pinpointing from the air and the help of the army unit, it was possible to locate the downed Spitfire. F/Ls Barker, Carew and McAllister were to find Hunter hanging forward in straps, with the buckled nose of his Spitfire immersed in a ditch. Despite multiple injuries, he survived.

Present status: Married Rita George in 1946. Practised Gynecology in Calgary 1948-1986. Eight children, fourteen grandchildren.

REG. MCGINNES, born 20 April 1923 in London, Ontario. He joined the RCAF in November 1942 and was assigned to 412 (T) Squadron in January 1945. He was stationed at No. 1 MD Toronto, T.T.S. St Thomas, No. 7 SFTS, Heesch, the Netherlands and Utersen, Germany. Rank achieved LAC. His memorable experiences  include running up a Spitfire, crossing the Rhine and hunting deers instead of Germans.

LOUIS McMILLAN, born on 1 October 1941, in Victoria B.C. His enrollment in the military took place in Victoria on 25 May 1959. He was indoc-

trinated at St. Jean Quebec as an Airforce AC2. On completion of basic training, he was sent to the Cooking School at CFB Clinton Ontario to complete F.S.A. requirements, (Food Services Attendant). The work continued to 1961 where at CFS Holberg B.C. he remustered to cook. A posting to CFS Falconbridge soon followed. After one year he volunteered to cross-train to Flight Steward and thus his exposure to 412 (T) Squadron life as an L.A.C. (Leading Aircraftsman).

This was a rewarding, eye opening, growing up process. He trained and performed cooking and serving duties on Dakota Aircraft, the C5, Yukon, Falcon Jets and the Boeing 727. All of this was climaxed by a three-year tour of Colorado Springs, CO under the direction of Capt Bill Long, serving Lieutenant General Ed Reyno. During these eight years world travel was indeed realized, from Hawaii to Tokoyo to Africa and most points in between. Shoulders were rubbed with Prime Ministers, Kings, and Queens from many nations during the Expo 1967 year. The most memorable experience was the refurbishing of the interior of "Smokey 02" by the Colorado Springs crew under the direction of a good friend and flight engineer Sgt Fred Quimet. The end result was being selected to transport the Queen and members of the Royal family throughout a seven day British Columbia Tour. He left the squadron as a Sergeant in July 1972 and resumed non-flying duties as the NCO i/c Food Services at CFS Kamloop B.C.

Much ground has passed by since those days but his love and respect for the squadron has remained. He is now a Captain presently serving as Base Food Services Officer at CFB Cornwallis Nova Scotia. There are seven more years to retirement. "Promtus ad Vindictam".

DICK MERRICK, FLIGHT LIEUTENANT,

born in Vancouver, B.C. in 1923. After graduating from Victoria High School in 1941 and attending Victoria College for one year, he joined the RCAF. Dick was selected for pilot training and received his wings at #7 S.F.T.S., Macleod, Alberta. This was followed by tours of instruction on the Cessna Crane at Yorkton and Saskatoon until April of 1945.

Dick was released in Vancouver where he attended the University of British Columbia, graduating in 1948 with a degree in Commerce.

After three years on "civie street", he joined the ranks of the "retreads" and returned to the RCAF. Initial assignment was as an instructor at Officers School, London, Ontario. From there he did a tour on Bristol Freighters with 137 (T) Flt. at Langar, Notts, England. Then, for almost five years, he flew with 412 (T) Squadron. After Uplands he did a two-year assignment at Goose Bay. From there he was transferred to Trenton for two years serving in A.T.O.C. and finally he served with 121 S.A.R. Squadron, Comox, flying the Albatross until his retirement from the Armed Forces in 1969.

The most memorable event of F/L Merrick's tour with 412 Squadron was the crash at Hall Beach of North Star 17520, one of the two V.I.P. Stars flown by 412 Squadron.

On 2 February 1962, this Dew Line inspection flight departed the Fox Main site for Ottawa with 10 crew and 15 passengers. Weather conditions were sky obscured, visibility about 1/4 mile in blowing snow, the temperature approximately -35 degrees F., and wind in excess of 30 mph with F/L Bud Whelan at the controls the aircraft took off and immediately lost both inboard engines. Fuel was jettisoned and the aircraft returned to the beacon. The intent was to hold until the weather cleared sufficiently to make a safe landing. However, a third engine developed trouble requiring an immediate approach and landing. Under minimum weather conditions a wheels-up landing was executed on the field. The expertise exhibited by F/L Whelan and flight engineer F/Sgt. MacDonald was outstanding.

The cause of the engine failures was related to oil dilution. Incidentally, N.S. 17520 was not salvaged and today lies buried in the Hall Beach area.

Dick has remained in Comox since leaving the Service. In addition to selling insurance he served for eight years on the Comox Municipal Council, six of those years as mayor.

Dick has been married to Olive for 39 years. They have three children and seven grandchildren.

GERARD MIGNAULT, (JERRY), MWO,

born in Isle Verte, P.Q. on 18 August 1920. He was the youngest of ten children, one of two boys who were overwhelmed with eight sisters.

Jerry received his education at the college in Levis, Quebec. He enlisted in the RCAF in 1939 as a general duties airman and subsequently served at Camp Borden, Halifax and Rockcliffe.

On 24 July 1946, Jerry married Madeleine Bellefeuille of Cap-de-la- Madeleine, P.Q. Jerry and Madeleine had three sons (Michel, Jacques and Daniel) and one daughter (Louise).

Jerry joined 412 Squadron in 1950 where he served as Flight Steward. It was on this squadron that the most distinguished aspects of Jerry's career unfolded. In his travels he served such dignitaries as Queen Elizabeth II and Prince Phillip, former Prime Ministers Louis St Laurent, John Diefenbaker and Lester B. Pearson, four Governor Generals, and 60 Heads of State. He logged more than 11,000 hours in the air.

After leaving 412 Squadron, Jerry became the Messing Officer at Sea Island, B.C. (1965) and at Uplands (1965-72).

Jerry retired from the RCAF in 1972 with the rank of MWOII. After 34 years of service, Jerry embarked on his second career. At a chance meeting with a former colleague (Group Captain Howie Morrisson) Jerry was asked to become steward of the Rideau Club. Jerry spent the next sixteen years with that renowned Club. Jerry retired from the Rideau Club in 1987 and passed away in Ottawa on 14 July 1989.

Jerry was a devoted husband and father who lived life to the fullest and enjoyed helping others. His personality and adaptability allowed him to handle difficult situations without offending people or principles. His poise, discretion and appearance reflected credit on the Armed Services. We will all dearly miss our "Flying Chef" who has left us to join that 412 Squadron in the sky.

GORD MILLER, W/C,

in December 1944 was posted to 12 Communications Squadron at Rockcliffe, in July 1947 was posted to ATC headquarters at Ottawa, in June 1954 posted as CP to 412 Squadron, Rockcliffe & Uplands, and on January 1959 posted to AFHQ.

Activities in the mid-forties consisted of a twice-weekly run from Rockcliffe to Montreal, Moncton and Halifax. The "Blueberry," as it was called, was usually a Lodestar. In April 1945, the Squadron was required to set up two flights a week from Rockcliffe to San Francisco to support the international conference which created the United Nations. Crews were changed at Chicago and Cheyenne, Wyoming. They used United Airlines facilities for the three months duration of the conference. His leg was Cheyenne to San Francisco. The aircraft used were Dakotas.

On the 23 June 1945, W/C Hale, the C.O., and Gord flew Gen. and Mrs. McNaughton to Rio de Janiero for the inauguration of President Dutra. The aircraft was Dakota 663, the rather plush pride of the fleet.

The following are some of the trips he captained on his return to 412 Squadron in 1954: 15 June 1955 Hon. Lester B. Pearson, Minister for External Affairs to London, England; 10 October 1955 Hon. Lester B. Pearson to Moscow, Singapore, Kuala Lumpur, Calcutta, Benares, New Delhi, Lahore, Peshawar, Karachi, Cairo, Paris, London; 3 April 1956 His Excellency Gov. Gen. Vincent Massey - Tour of the Arctic including a flight over the North Pole. Here His Excellency dropped a capsule which was expected to eventually drift on the ice flow to the coast of Greenland. 23 July 1956 Hon. Louis St. Laurent, Prime Minister, tour of the Canadian fighter bases at Baden Solingen, Zweibruchen and Marville; 9 September 1956 Hon. Mr. Campney, Minister of National Defence, to London and Paris; 11 November 1956 Hon. Paul Martin, Minister for External Affairs, tour to Wake Island, Guam, Manila, Saigon, Singapore, Bangkok, Djakarta, Darwin, Melbourne, Aukland, Sydney, Canberra,

Singapore, Kuala Lumpur, Rangoon, Colombo, New Delhi, Agra, Bombay, Chittagong, Peshawar, Karachi, Beirut, Malta, Gibraltar, Lages, Ottawa; 19 August 1957 Hon. Jr.R. Macdonell, tour to Wake Island, Guam, Manilla, Singapore, Kuala Lumpur, new Delhi, Karachi, Beirut; 16 October 1957 HRH Queen Elizabeth and HRH Prince Phillip to Patrick Henry Base, Va.

The above trips represent a small portion of the many tours undertaken by the very excellent and capable air and ground crews of the squadron whose unblemished record he believed is unsurpassed. W/C Miller passed away on November 26, 1992.

BERT MILLIKEN, SQUADRON LEADER, DFC, CD, born in Hamilton in 1916, died Ottawa, 1986. Bert was educated in Hamilton and Lobo. He passed an Air Frame Mechanics course then joined the RCAF in 1940. In 1942 he remustered to pilot (Course 72). Thence to 24 OTU at Long Marston, England and to 425 Alouette Squadron at Tholthorpe, flying Whitleys and Halifax. He completed a tour of 37 ops, including D-Day, earning the DFC.

His next posting was to Experimental and Proving Establishment at Rockcliffe, from 1945-1947 then training on the Sikorsky Helicopter and a transfer to 412 Composite Squadron in 1948. He flew the helicopter at air shows, and demonstrated its capabilities at fund raising events as well as search and rescue missions. As a pilot with 412, he flew all the transport aircraft.

In 1950, he was selected to become Aide-de-Camp to Governor General Lord Alexander, and thence to Vincent Massey, Canada's first Canadian Governor General.

In 1952, a transfer to London, Ont. to 2 Personnel Selection Unit (Officers) to select aircrew from the NATO trainees, was followed by a tour as OC 102 K Unit at Trenton, responsible for Search and Rescue. Then in 1960, OC Resolute Bay and finally a tour at AFHQ. Before his retirement in 1963, Bert had flown 23 different aircraft including Tiger Moth, Cessna Crane, Anson, Oxford, Whitley, Hudson, Harvard, Norseman, Canso, Lancaster, Liberator, Expeditor, goose, Halifax, Hadrian PG, Hadrian, Mitchell, Dakota, Privateer, Helicopter, Otter, North Star.

Following retirement, Bert taught school until 1981, in Nepean. He is survived by his wife, former F/O Dorothy Cole and his three children, Scot, Mark and Genevieve.

BARRY H. MOFFIT, COLONEL (RET.), DFC, AFC, CD, born in Toronto on 9 January 1920. Served as an officer in the RCAF/CF from October 1939 to December 1974.

Completed pilot training, including navigation and water conversion, in October 1940. Served in No. 5 (BR) Squadron at Dartmouth and Gander until mid-1943 on North Atlantic ASW patrols. Sank German U Boat on 4 May 1943. The war years were completed with a tour of duty at Air Force Headquarters, Ottawa and a year flying Trans-Atlantic ferry Flights (flying boats) with RAF Ferry command, Dorval.

After completing the RCAF Staff College Course in December 1945 two-and-a-half years were spent at Air Ministry London on a personnel exchange tour.

Upon promotion to Wing Commander, he was appointed Officer Commanding 412 (T) Squadron, Rockcliffe in August, 1949 and he held this post for one year. Following a year on staff at North West Air Command, Edmonton, he attended the U.S. Armed Forces Staff College, Norfolk, Virginia. Joined the staff of the Supreme Allied Command, Atlantic in April 1952 and in July 1954 was appointed Officer Commanding 404 (MP) Squadron, Greenwood.

In June 1957, he became RCAF Director of the Joint Maritime Warfare School, Halifax and after these proceeded to Ottawa for one year of intelligence and language training.

From August 1961 to August 1964 held the position of Air and Naval Attache, Canadian Embassy, Warsaw, Poland. Upon return to Canada, he became Director of Intelligence Production in the newly integrated Intelligence Division of the Canadian Forces in Ottawa.

From July 1967 until mid-1977 he served as Director Exercise and Evaluation at three different NORAD Region Headquarters at San Francisco, Kansas City and Tacoma. And the final tour of duty was as Chief of Staff, Operations, Maritime Command Pacific, Esquimalt, BC.

After retiring from the service, he spent 10 years at Branch Director Level with the Ministry of Housing, Government of Ontario.

Married to the former Betty Parrott of Stacy Creek, Ontario; they have two children and four grandchildren.

Most significant event while commanding 412 Squadron was the round the world trip for the Prime Minister with a VIP North Star captained by F/L Smith. Barry left Ottawa and 412 Sqn. in December 1949.

J. IVAN MORESIDE, (F/L), was born in Strasbourg, Saskatchewan in 1919. He helped on the family farm and drove a transport truck until he enlisted in the RCAF in 1941. Graduated as a pilot the following year.

During the war years he completed two tours of bombing operations on Mitchell aircraft. The last operation was on the night of June 6th (D day). The following day he was transferred to Canadian Army Tactical Headquarters to be the personal pilot of General Crerar. He remained with the general and his staff until the end of the European war. Returned to Canada in August 1945 and was demobilized two months later.

He married Marjorie Chapin of Strasbourg in 1950 and re-enlisted in the RCAF in 1951. Spent two years as a line pilot at ANS Winnipeg before joining 412 Transport squadron in 1954. He and Marjorie have many fond and happy memories of the four years in Ottawa.

In 1958 he was transferred to CJS London as O.C., Station Flight Northolt, a great 4-1/2 years there before completing a most enjoyable airforce career at ANS Winnipeg - being retired from the service in 1964.

He was employed in the Credit field with Dunlop and General Tire companies (Winnipeg) for five years before moving to Victoria B.C. in 1969.

After working for Revelstoke Building Supplies as credit manager of their West Coast Division for 13 years. He retired from the work force in 1982 and is now enjoying a retirement of golfing, fishing, gardening ,etc...

He and Marjorie have two children and six grandchildren.

LAURENCE MOTIUK, WING COMMANDER, born in Vegreville, Alberta in 1925. He attended Mundare High School and joined the Royal Canadian Air Force in 1943. He served as a Bomb Aimer with RAF Bomber Command in the United Kingdom during World War II and as a Navigator with RCAF Transport Command in support of United Nations Operations in Korea, the Middle East, the Cong and Cyprus.

He served with 426 (T) Squadron, Dorval, Quebec 1951-1952; instructed at No. 1 Air Navigation School and Central Navigation School Summerside, P.E.I. from 1952 to 1954; was assigned as Staff Officer, Officers' Postings at Training Command Headquarters in Trenton, Ontario, from 1954 to 1959 where he rejoined 426 (T) Squadron serving as Navigation Leader. In 1961 W/C Motiuk attended the RCAF Staff College, spending the next three years on staff of the Air Force College.

After a brief posting to Canadian Forces Headquarters in 1965 (Personnel Branch), he joined 412 (T) Squadron, Uplands serving as Radio/Navigator Leader and Deputy Commanding Officer. From 1967 to 1969 he was assigned to the Officer Development Board at Canadian Forces Headquarters as Project Leader. In 1969 W/C Motiuk joined Transport Canada in Ottawa, Ontario and since 1987 has been Vice-President, Academic Affairs at the International Aviation Management Training Institute in Montreal, Quebec.

He is a graduate of the Universities of Alberta (1950) and Toronto (1965). W/C Motiuk was awarded the Honorary Wings of the French Air Force for NATO training activities and those of the Chilean air Force for disaster relief operations. W/C Motiuk is married to the former Margaret MacArthur of Summerside, P.E.I. They have a son, Laurence, and daughter, Mary Lee and two grandchildren.

KEITH C. MURPHY, W/C, D.F.C., C.D., (RET), born in Ottawa, graduated from Lisgar Collegiate Institute in June 1940. At 20 years of age he joined the RCAF and graduated as on Observer from No. 1 Air Navigation School, Rivers with the rank of Pilot Officer.

In October 1941 he arrived in Britain and after 3-1/2 months O.T.U. training for Bomber operation, he joined 115 Squadron, RAF 3 Group and commenced Bomber operations over Germany and France. During this first tour of operations, he was promoted to F/L, assumed the duties of Navigation Leader and was awarded the D.F.C. For the last ten operations over Germany, he was appointed Captain of the Bomber aircraft.

In December 1942, he was posted to 424 Squadron, RCAF in 6 Group as Navigation Leader. 424 was a new squadron fresh from Canada and Bomber O.T.U. training In a short time they were in the thick of the battle over Germany.

In the Spring of 1943, the squadron flew to North Africa and formed a wing of three squadrons and commenced bomber operations over Sicily and Italy. As Navigation Leader and Assistant Flight Commander, he started his second tour of Bomber operations on Wellington aircraft and before the wing was returned to England in the Fall of 1943, he completed his second tour.

After a short stay at No. 82, O.T.U., as an instructor, he was repatriated to Canada.

In February 1944, he took time off to marry Gladys Pearce, also of Ottawa, and soon the newlyweds were at No. 9, A.O.S. St. Jean, P.Q. on instruction duties. This was a short-lived stay and by August they were back in Ottawa at 168 Squadron on transport duties, flying the mail to Canadians troops in England, Africa, Southern France, and Egypt.

In June 1950, the transport experience led to exchange duties with 511 Squadron, (R.A.F.) at Lyneham, England. This period also returned him to S/L rank and duties as Flight Commander and Deputy Commanding Officer in his squadron.

On return to Canada, he commenced five years of duties as a Staff Officer in Aircraft Requirement in A.F.H.Q. Ottawa. In July 1957, and after refresher training at 2 A.O.S. and 4 O.T.U., Keith joined 408 Reconnaissance Squadron at Rockcliffe, Ottawa. In addition to Photo and Recce flying he was responsible for Navigation and then operated as Senior Training Officer.

Staff College put an end to serious flying duties in September 1960 but led to some very interesting postings, first to Air Transport Command H.Q. as Staff Officer, Joint Ops.

The next move was to Station Armstrong as Commanding Officer with a promotion to Wing Commander, and finally in July 1964, to No. 4 Wing, Baden-Solingen, Germany as C.A.D.O. Although he operated in the newly-formed unified Armed Forces as Lt. Col., he retired in February 1969 as a Wing Commander. The Murphy's have two children, David in Vancouver, and Diane, who lives in Waterloo, Ontario.

Two incidents stand out in this career worthy of note. While with 511 Squadron, Keith was involved in a fatal crash when five members of a Hastings crew were killed. Other lives probably were saved by the passengers being in backward-facing seats. The report of this crash was partially responsible for the RCAF installing backward-facing seats in its first C.L. 44 model.

The second event was his participation in the first Round-the-World-trip by the RCAF when transporting Lester B. Pearson to the Columbo Conference in 1950.

FREDERICK T. MURRAY, born in 1922 and lived in Saint John New Brunswick. He enlisted in the RCAF in August 1941 and trained at Valcartier, Victoriaville, Ancienne Lorette, and Uplands. He received his wings and rank of Sergeant Pilot in July 1942, and sailed from Halifax August 1942 aboard the Strathmore in convoy for Glasgow, Scotland.

Operational training from September 1942 to December 1942 when he joined 412 Squadron at Kenley, England. Duties included bomber escort, fighter sweeps, low level sorties and sea patrol. He received his Pilot Officer's commission in September 1943 and completed his first tour in March 1944 when he became an instructor at 83 Group Support Unit.

He rejoined 412 Squadron in October 1944 and flew from airdromes at B 84, Volkel, and Heesch in Holland. In December 1944 he was posted to 401 Squadron as a Flight Commander with a rank of Flight Lieutenant, and awarded the Distinguished Flying Cross in January.

In February 1945 his aircraft was hit by flak, and he parachuted from his burning plane and was captured. Liberated by General Patton's army in April 1945, arrived in Canada in June and was discharged August 1945.

He graduated in 1949 from U.N.B. with a B.Sc. degree in Forestry. He is married with three children and six grandchildren, and lives in Erie, Pennsylvania.

W. BARRY NEEDHAM, born 8 August 1920 at Simpson, Sask. Early education at Saskatoon, Sask, before moving to Wynyard, Sask. for high school. Following high school Needham joined the RCAF at Regina on September 1940. After guard duty at Prince Rupert, BC and ITS at Regina, Needham commenced pilot training at Regina Flying Club in January 1941. Service flying was at Yorkton, flying Harvards. Posted overseas in July 1941.

Needham was also at #61 OTU Heston, England in September 1941; 412 Squadron, Wellingore, Lincolnshire, from September 1941-May 1942; 57 OTU Eshott Northumberland from April 1943 to November 1943; 401 Squadron Biggin Hill in February 1944; 412 Squadron Biggin Field from 16 March 1944 to 7 July 1944; 124 and 170 Ferry Squadron December 1945 to November 1945; and 412 Squadron, Utersen, Germany from February 1946 to March 1946.

Needham joined 412 Squadron as a sergeant pilot on 7 October 1941 at Wellingore, Lincolnshire. He received his commission in December 1941. Made "B" Flight Commander in 1942.

Some of the squadron's notable actions in which he took part included attacks on five German E boats; escorting torpedo bombers on their attack on the Sharnhorst and Gneisenav; a large number of bomber escorts; Dieppe raid; several Rhubarbs; dive bombing of V1 sites; patrolling beachhead on D-Day.

Moved with the squadron to France (Beny-Sur-Mer); shot down by flak 7 July 1944. Taken prisoner to make-shift hospital in Rennes, but later abandoned by Germans when allies reached the city. Returned to England and later to Canada and joined 124 Ferry Squadron.

ROBERT NEWMAN, MAJOR, born in 1928 in Hyas, SK. Joined the RCAF in 1947, graduating as a pilot with course 4 at Centralia, Ontario. First posting was to the Joint Air Training Centre at Rivers where he flew the Dakota (and completed the Army paratroop course, six jumps). He then instructed on Harvards at Gimli and on Expeditors and Mitchells at Saskatoon. A tour at AFHQ came next, followed by a posting to Winnipeg where he flew the Mitchell and Dakota. In 1960 he was posted to 426 Squadron, Trenton, flying the North Star, and in 1962 was assigned to 412 Squadron, Ottawa. While at 412 Squadron he flew the Dakota, Cosmopolitan and Yukon, and acted as Flight Safety Officer and Instrument Check Pilot.

Promoted to Major in 1966, he attended the Canadian Army Staff College at Kingston, and in 1967 was posted to CFHQ. His final posting was to Winnipeg where he served as Chief Pilot, ANS Flying Wing and D/CO 429 Composite Squadron.

Major Newman married Sigrid Suhr in 1952. They have two sons and four grandchildren. Following retirement in 1974, the Newmans moved to Hyas, SK where they have been involved in various business enterprises. Maj. Newman still enjoys flying and owns a Grumman Cheetah.

DENNIS B. O'CONNOR (DOC), SQUADRON LEADER, born in North Bay in 1933. Attended schools in North Bay and Capreol, Ontario. Finishing high school at 17 he spent 11 months working underground at Falconbridge until he was able to join the RCAF in 1951. He trained as a pilot in Centralia graduating with course 26 in 1952; short courses in advanced flying and gunnery confirmed that Buzz Beurling's records were safe and he was posted to RCAF Summerside to fly Dakota aircraft in July 1952.

In August 1953, the first of six consecutive transport postings came with a move to 436 (T) Squadron in Lachine to fly C-119 aircraft. The tour was survivable despite the aircraft and was followed by full tours with 408, 4 (T)OTU, 437, 511 (RAF), and 412. Joining 412 Squadron during centennial year saw many distinguished guests and heads of state flown by the squadron and as pilot leader it was a challenging and satisfying task. In 1969, he participated in the England - Australia Air Race as captain of a 412 Falcon 20C. This race was part of the Australian Bi-centennial celebrations and resulted in several world records being set by the 412 aircraft which still stand.

During his tour at 408 Squadron, Doc met and married his wife Agnes McNamara, who was a serving RCAF Nursing Sister, and to this day is one of the few retired RCAF members with a permanent AO'C. Knowing a tour with 412 (T) Squadron could not be topped, Doc retired in 1974 to pursue a civilian flying career.

CLAYTON STUART OLSEN (RET)

COLONEL, born in Wilkie Sask, enlisted as a pilot in the RCAF in April, 1942, and had continuous service until retirement with the rank of Colonel 30 December 1975. Joined 412 Squadron as an acting Flight Lieutenant January 1946, reverted to Flying Officer in peacetime force about September 1946.

Stuart served on 412 (T) Squadron January 1946 to September 1949 and again January 1953 to June 1954. Promoted to Squadron Leader on rejoining squadron in January 1953. Came back the second time to fly the Comet 1A Jet Transport. They were grounded in late 1953 after a series of spectacular crashes with BOAC Airlines. Subsequent testing revealed pressurization was causing weak spots to blow out. They were modified and returned to service about two years later with 412 Squadron.

In addition to World War II, when he served on 115 and 8 Bomber Reconnaissance Squadrons in anti-submarine patrol on the West Coast of Canada, Stuart saw service with United Nations operations in the Gaza Strip, Egypt, Yemen, Vietnam, Congo and the Arab/Israeli War, October, 1973.

The early part of Stuart's career was as a pilot with Air Transport Command 412 VIP Squadron and 426 Transport Squadron on North Stars. He was one of the original pilots trained on the first Comet Jet Transports operated by a military service in 1952.

Following graduation from the Canadian Army Staff College in 1956, Colonel Olsen was appointed as Executive Assistant to the RCAF Comptroller. Four years later he became Officer Commanding of Air Transport Command Aircrew Assessment Unit. In the following year he was transferred to the Gaza Strip as Air Advisor to the United Nations Emergency Force Commander. On return to Canada in 1963 he was appointed Officer Commanding four Transport Operation Training Units at Trenton. From Trenton Stuart served a year with the Canadian Air Division Headquarters in Metz, France and then became Canadian Air Force Member at Nato Military Agency for Standardization, London, England.

Colonel Olsen was transferred back to Canada in 1969, promoted to Colonel and appointed Base Commander of Canadian Forces Base, Rockcliffe, Ottawa, Ontario. In 1972, he went to Egypt for the second time and served three years as Canadian Forces Attache at the Canadian Embassy in Cairo. On retirement, Stu and his wife, June, moved to Kelowna, BC and became partners in Century 21 Black Mountain Real Estate Ltd. where they are active sales people.

RAY PAQUETTE, reported to RCAF Stn Uplands fresh off a nine-week loadmaster course in April 1962. He held the classification of Leading Aircraftsman and had just re-mustered from a boring job in the supply Trade to this newly formed trade of Transportation Technician.

If it was "excitement" he was looking for; he certainly found it at 412 Squadron. Loadmasters were actually on Air Movements personnel strength and if they weren't checking in passengers or loading aircraft they were flying on the aircraft, often performing all three functions and then climbing aboard as the loadmaster. He often wondered if it was a way of keeping them honest in their weight and balance calculation.

The squadron had four types of aircraft at that time. The Comet passenger jet, the C5 North Star, four old C47 Dakotas and a fleet of nine brand new Cosmopolitans CC109s. Most of them preferred to fly on the old reliable Dakotas, at least with them you knew when you would get back to home base. Not so with the shiny new Cosmos. It's Napier-Eland engines were said to be underpowered and he could almost be guaranteed one emergency of some kind on any given trip. Different aircraft flight crews were easily identified by the amount of luggage they carried. Even on a short hop to Trenton by Cosmo, they would carry at least an overnight bag. On the old Dak, he took his shaving kit; "maybe."

Many Cosmo flights were delayed due to mechanical failures and if they were unfortunate enough to be away from base during this period, they sometimes forfeited their days off due to the delays or worse still; arrived back, just in time to start their next shift in A.M.U.

After four years of that, he was glad to accept a posting to #1 Fighter Wing at Marville France, and later to Lahr Germany. On his return to Canada three years later, he was enjoying a posting at 3 A.M.U. Uplands again when a message came in transferring him back to 412 squadron. There were black rubber heal marks across the hangar floor as he reluctantly reported to Major Al Chapman, the squadron Flight Crew Leader at the time. The squadron had matured during his absence and had evolved as a 1st class V.I.P. service that was second to none. The cabin-crew personnel had gained respectability and were recognized as an integral part of the aircraft crew. As Captain Gord Howard often said, "It doesn't matter how smooth I grease that bird in, if the service in the back is poor, the V.I.P's are going to be unhappy."

The flight meals were cooked from scratch in electric fry pans and boilers by the flight steward and some of our trips were hectic with up to 27 V.I.P. passengers to serve a three-course meal to, plus bar service. They all worked as a team and it was not uncommon for one of the pilots to climb out of the cockpit and give them a hand in the galley. He still recalls Captain Pete Jenning's huge frame struggling out of his seat and turning the fillet mignons over for us. His culinary talents were invaluable and on many occasions he saved the day for them in the back.

They all worked together and there was never any hesitancy on the part of the officers to form a baggage chain along side the men. Captain Kip Powick was usually first there with his sleeves rolled up. Some of this V.I.P. baggage was bigger then he was, but that didn't deter him and they all loved him for it.

They had an excellent C.O. in the person of Lieutenant Colonel Glen Parslow and morale was high. He always included the families whenever possible and they were able to take their wives along with them on some of their better training trips south and to Europe. Whenever family members were on board, the V.I.P. treatment was put aside and they were given treatment normally reserved for Royalty only and it was things like that, that made 412 squadron what it was at that time.

Thanks to the 412 (T) Squadron for some of the best years in his service career.

CHARLES H. PARENT (CHUCK), COLONEL, joined the RCAF in 1954 and after graduation went to RCAF Station Centralia as a flying instructor. In 1959 he was posted to 426 (T) Squadron at RCAF Station, Lachine, Quebec, on North Stars. Exchange duties at RAF Station Lyneham, England flying the Britannias followed in 1962 and lasted until the end of 1964.

Upon his return to Canada, he was posted to Air Transport Command HQ as a staff officer in the Operations Branch, and in 1967 he was selected to become the Executive Assistant to the

Commander of Air Transport Command. In 1970, he attended Course 5 at the CF Staff College and after graduation was posted to CF Staff School on the directing staff. A tour at CFS Senneterre as Commanding Officer followed in 1973.

1976 saw his selection as Commanding Officer of 412 (T) Squadron where he flew both the Cosmopolitan and Falcon aircraft. The highlight of his tour was the awarding of the CDS Commendation to the Squadron in 1977 and presented personally by General J. Dextraze.

While CO of 412 Squadron, he presided over the dedication of the 412 Squadron crest at St. Clement Danes Central Church of the Royal Air Force. Their crest now rests on the floor of the church along with most other Commonwealth and allied Air Force Squadrons who flew on operations during WW II.

Colonel Parent was posted to Air Transport Group HQ as Deputy Commander in 1978, which was followed in 1981 by a four and one half year tour as Base Commander of CFB Summerside. In the summer of 1985, he went to Spain as the Canadian Forces Attache and in 1989 retired after 35 years of service with Canada's Defence Forces.

Colonel Parent and his wife Beverley live in Manotick, Ontario, with the No. 14 hole of the Carleton Golf and Yacht Club (of which they are members) just out their back door. He also found the time to complete his Bachelor of Art's degree at the University of Manitoba and is presently embarking on a Masters degree programme.

GLEN S. PARSLOW, WING COMMANDER,

was born in Ottawa in 1929. He attended Nepean High School, and joined the Royal Canadian Air Force in 1949. He graduated as a pilot from Centralia in 1950 as a member of Course 15 whose members, because of the needs of Korea and NATO, became the first post-war instructors. Wing Commander Parslow married the former Dorothy Rourke in 1951. From then until 1954, he served as a flying instructor at Centralia and at the Flying Instructors' School and the Central Flying School in Trenton.

He later served with 412 (Transport) Squadron from 1954-1958 as a line pilot, training officer and check pilot. He became the personal pilot to Air Marshal W.R. MacBrien, Commander of Air Defence Command; then in 1963 attended the Royal Canadian Air Force Staff College. From 1964-1967 he served as the Executive Assistant to the Assistant Chief of Staff in SHAPE, Paris, France. He returned to Ottawa as Chief Pilot with 412 (Transport) Squadron for two years.

A tour in National Defence Headquarters must have gone right for a change since following that tour he was, for the third time, dispatched to 412 (Transport) Squadron becoming its Commanding Officer in July 1971. While there he organized the Squadron's first reunion bringing together for the first time members of the units from which the Squadron evolved. A tour in National Defence HQ from 1974-1979 terminated his military career which was followed by nine years with Transport Canada from which he retired as Executive Officer Air Operations Contingencies in 1988. Wing Commander Parslow and his wife are now thoroughly enjoying the family lives of their four children and ten grandchildren.

CARMELO PATAFIE,

born in Ottawa Ontario in January 1923. After a short period of employment in the Civil Service, he began his military career in September 1942 by enrolling in the RCAF as an Airframe Technician. He successfully completed his training at Galt and St. Thomas, Ontario. In early 1943 he was transferred for a short period to #8 S.F.T.S. Moncton N.B. This followed by a period of 1-1/2 years at #9 R.D. St. Jeans P.Q. A transfer to 12 Comm Flight Ottawa in late 1944. Spending 10 good years at 412 Squadron. From here transferred to #1 (F) Wing in Marvel, France. Following this a tour of eight years to Greenwood N.S. employed on newly acquired Argus Aircraft and a stint in the A.E.C.R.O. Section. His service career was completed with 2-1/2 years at Material Command. Following this, an 18-year second career with the Air Service Branch of the Department of Transport, employed in the Aircraft Technical Records Section.

Having been a member of 412 (T) Squadron for a period of 10 years, one must reflect: arriving in late 1944 and leaving in 1955. Carmelo had served under many of the Squadrons distinguished Commanding Officers; (ie W/C G.G. Diamond, S/L. A. Tilley, W/C E.B. Hale, W/C W.H. Swetmen, W/C B.H. Moffitt, W/C R.I. Trickett, W/C H.A. Morrison, and finally W/C W.G. Miller. Many moments are cherished during this tour of duty.

During this tour at #12 Squadron, 412 Composite & 412 (T) Squadron, he had been employed as an Airframe Technician on several various aircraft types: Hawker Hurricane, Harvard, Anson, Beech Expeditor, Liberator, Lockheed Loadstar, Douglas DC-3, Grumman Goose 11, North Star, Canadair C-5 etc. The thoughts he recollects mostly at the present time are: When one was required to straddle over the tailplane of Hawker Hurricane aircraft during run-ups to prevent aircraft nose down tendency; dismantling of DC-3 wheels with the use of wooden wedges and sledge hammer in removing tires and tubes in order to carry out wheel inspections. (No such modern equipment in those days to carry out this task;) stripping and removing exterior camouflage paint from DC-3 Aircraft; re-configuring these aircraft from troop and cargo carriers to passenger roles used for the transport of dignitaries, and Blueberry run; re-configuration of a Liberator which was used by the late Hon. W.L. McKenzie King to attend the "League of Nations" conference in San Francisco, CA.

The knowledge and experience gained during this tour of duty with 412 (T) Squadron had conditioned and allowed him in many ways to strive for the ultimate in all future endeavors during both service and civilian career employment.

These accomplishments not only made him quite proud to be associated with 412 (T) Squadron but proved to be a driving factor in such achievements.

As a young lad, he always ventured to both Uplands and Rockcliffe Airports to watch vintage aircraft take-off and land. It was always his dream and intention to enlist in the RCAF. All he can say is it happened and if he were to have it to do all over again, he would want it to happen exactly in about the same manner, (with the exception of hostilities breaking out in order to make it a precondition).

PAUL PAWLIUK, WARRANT OFFICER,

joined the RCAF July 1946. After completing Manning Depot at Portage La Prairie Man., he was transferred to 6 RD RCAF Stn Trenton, to await the commencement of Post War technical training courses. Graduated from a one year AEM course, transferred to CEPE RCAF Stn Rockcliffe November 1947. Seconded to 412 (T) Squadron, and worked in the A/C Refueling Section.

With the outbreak of the Korean War he was transferred to 426 (T) Squadron Tacoma, Washington, July 1950. It was with 426 Squadron that he began his flying career as Flight Engineer on North Star A/C.

After approximately two years with 426, he was transferred to 412 (T) Squadron Rockcliffe, June 1952 and thus began an association with this squadron which was to last for 17 years. His flying duties included a variety of VIP A/C, which also included DAK 1000 and AIRFORCE 10,000 the C-5. He was one of the last engineers on this A/C when it was retired from service.

In 1961 he was transferred to 107 RU RCAF Stn Torbay Nld, as Flight Engineer Leader. After approximately one year the Base was closed, and he was transferred to 4 OTU RCAF Stn Trenton and continued flying North Stars mostly on Global Operations. With the phase-out of the North Stars, he converted to C130 Hercules A/C, and was transferred to 436 (T) RCAF Stn Uplands. After accumulating 15,000 flying hours, he was assigned to the Herc Flight Simulator as Chief FE Instructor. When the Simulator was moved to Trenton, he again was transferred to 412 Squadron in June 1971, and served as Squadron Adjutant until his release in June 1973. However his association with DND was to continue for another 12 years, working in NDHQ/DCI, and finally retiring in June 1987. Paul and his wife, Joan, live in Ottawa. They have four children and 6 grandchildren.

WILLIAM JOHN PENFOLD (BILL), COLONEL, joined the RCAF in 1951, trained as a Radio Officer and was subsequently posted to 412 (T) Squadron in late 1951. While on 412, he flew on the C5, North Stars, and both wheeled and ski-wheeled Dakotas. His most memorable trip was as a member of the C5 crew on the 1953 South American tour of CD Howe with Flight Lieutenant Jack Reid as Captain. He was then posted to Victoria on recruiting duties and cross-trained to Navigator in 1958. Two flying tours followed, one on 419 (AW) Squadron in Baden-Soellingen and one on 405 (MP) Squadron in Greenwood. He was posted to his fourth flying tour on exchange to 10 (MP) Squadron in Townsville, Australia. After attending Staff College in 1969, he took a command position in Halifax and then was posted to personnel in NDHQ. After serving as BAdO at Greenwood, he was then promoted to Colonel and became the National Military Representative at SHAPE HQ in Belgium. His last posting was as Base Commander at CFB Toronto and, on his release in 1983, he took employment as General Manager of the Hamilton Convention Centre. He now lives in Ottawa and runs a meeting and exhibition planning company. He is married to the former Pat Regan of Hamilton and has two daughters, three grand-daughters and a grandson.

JOSEPH CHARLES PITRE (CHUCK), MASTER WARRANT OFFICER, born in Bathurst, New Brunswick in 1939. After completing his secondary education, he joined the RCAF in 1957 and did his basic training in St. Jean, Quebec. Upon completion of an Airframe Technician course in Borden, Ontario, his first transfer was to 412 (Transport) Squadron where he served from 1958 to 1969. During his tour, he worked on a variety of aircraft including the North Star, Comet, C47, B29, C45, CC109 and CC106.

In early 1959, he was the first airman to receive the "Airman of the Month" award for which he was granted a world tour. In 1969 he was transferred to 447 SAM Squadron (Bomark Missiles) in LaMacaza, Quebec, and in 1972 to 416 Fighter Squadron (Voodoos) at CFB Chatham, New Brunswick. A transfer in 1975 brought him back to Quebec, CFB Bagotville, where he served with 425 All-Weather Squadron as Deputy Aircraft Servicing Officer, Deputy Transit Servicing Officer (410) Squadron and finally as Base Technical Adjutant.

In 1985 he was transferred to 409 Squadron (F-18s) at Baden-Soellingen, West Germany, where he retired in 1987. Chuck married the former Rita Mazerolle also from Bathurst. They have three children and four grandchildren.

JOHN LAWRENCE PLANT, CBE, AFC, CD., LL.D, BASc, AIR VICE MARSHAL RCAF (RET.), was born at Swansea, Wales on 20 August 1910. He obtained an Honors Degree of BASc in Mechanical Engineering at the University of British Columbia in 1931. He joined the RCAF in 1929 and commenced flying training as a Provisional Pilot Officer. He obtained his pilot's wings and a permanent commission in 1931. His first posting was to Jericho Beach, B.C. where he participated in the first major air supply operation in Canada by dropping 6,000 pounds of food on four sorties from a Vancouver Flying Boat to the storm-stranded residents of the Fraser Valley.

A "whirlwind" flying instructor's course at Camp Borden in June 1936, preceded posting to No. 20 RCAF Auxiliary Bomber Squadron at Regina. He organized a squadron pilot training program with both ground and air training.

Following this, he was posted to Air Force Headquarters as a staff officer in the personnel branch. In September 1940, Squadron Leader Plant was posted from Air Force Headquarters to lead No. 12 (Communications) Squadron, newly formed at Rockcliffe, with orders to provide safe transportation for senior officials following the crash of a Hudson aircraft in which the Minister of National Defence was killed.

Early in 1941, he flew a Trans-Atlantic Ferry trip in a Catalina from Bermuda to Greenock, Scotland in a record time of 20:05 hours.

On 7 May 1941, he was posted with the rank of Wing Commander to RCAF Station Patricia Bay, B.C. as Commanding Officer where he flew the various types of aircraft on the station. As C.O. he placed the station on full alert after the Japanese attacked on December 7, 1941. He also arranged to have senior US pilots checked out on wartime Hudsons because of serious crashes in the Seattle-Tacoma area.

On 3 March 1942, he was posted to the United Kingdom to command 413 Squadron which was to proceed to Ceylon. He flew his own aircraft, a Catalina, from the U.K. to Ceylon. He flew many patrols from Ceylon against active Japanese operations, one of which was a cover operation for the British landings on Madagascar.

On 1 January 1943, he was posted to the United Kingdom as Commanding Officer of RCAF Station, Dishforth, Yorkshire which housed 425 and 426 Squadrons and satellite housed 432 Squadron. When Dishforth closed in midsummer, he was posted to RCAF Station Leeming which housed 408, 427 and 429 Bomber Squadrons.

He returned to Canada in December 1943 and was posted to Army and Navy College in the United States, graduating in April 1944. In May 1944, he was posted to Air Force Headquarters in Ottawa as Deputy Air Member, Air Staff (Plans). He continued, along with his normal duties, to do a considerable amount of flying and qualified for No. 1 Green Instrument Rating which he kept current until his retirement in 1956.

On 31 May 1945, as Air Commodore, he was appointed Air Officer Commanding, No. 9 (Transport) Group with headquarters at Rockcliffe. He immediately qualified himself as a captain on all types of the Group's aircraft, including the B-24 Liberator and the B-17 Fortress. He did a lot of flying to all units in the Group, both in Canada and overseas. In November 1945, he flew as captain of a B-17 from Canada to Warsaw, Poland, carrying the third 2,000 pounds load of penicillin donated by the Canadian Red Cross to the people of that shattered country, the second load having been lost with the aircraft and crew in Germany. The flight was very risky at that time and resulted in his being awarded the Air Force Cross. In January 1945, he set a flight speed record between Vancouver and Ottawa flying a B-17 aircraft.

On 16 February 1946, he was appointed Air Officer Commanding Western Air Command. During his time there he qualified on all types of aircraft in the command.

On 1 December 1947, he was posted to Air Force Headquarters as Air Member for Personnel. In 1950 while the European Air Division was being established, facing considerable opposition, he succeeded in having the government authorize dependents to accompany RCAF members of squadrons and supporting units. This had a profound effect on the morale of the Air division and was one of the factors that helped make it the most efficient of the NATO air elements.

After 22 August 1951, he saw these effects first hand while serving in the headquarters of the Allied Air Forces, Central Europe, when his overall contribution to the NATO alliance was recognized by his appointment in 1953 as Chief of Staff at that headquarters and his promotion to the rank of Air Marshal. For the first time the RCAF had two serving officers with that rank.

In 1954, on return to Canada, he reverted to his permanent rank of Air Vice Marshal on appointment to the post of Air Member for Technical Services. In 1956 he served as Air Officer Commanding, Air Material Command and then resigned his commission.

He was appointed Executive Vice President of Collins Radio Company, for whom he worked until 1958, when he joined Avro Aircraft Ltd as President and General Manager. At Avro he led a team that developed the Avro Arrow. Six aircraft made their maiden flights. John Plant resigned from Avro six months after the cancellation of the Arrow program. He rejoined Collins in 1960.

His honors, decoration and awards are: Companion of the British Empire, Air Force Cross, 1919-1945 Star, Aircrew Europe and Atlantic Star, North Africa Star, Burma Star, Defence Medal, C.V.S.M. and Clasp, War Medal 1939 - 1945 and Palm, and Canada Decoration and Clasp. *Editor regrets to advise that the A/V/M is now deceased.*

D.K. POWICK (KIP), CAPTAIN, born 1942, Kelowna B.C. He joined the RCN in 1961 and a year later transferred to the RCAF. Awarded pilot wings on T33s in 1964 at Portage la Prairie and was then trained on the C45, RCAF Station Rivers, and spent three months flying at the Nav School in Winnipeg. He then flew for three

months at RCAF Station Camp Borden, where he met and married the former Diane Hansen.

In 1965, he was trained on the DC3 and posted to 131 KU North Bay. Three years later the unit was closed and he was posted to CFB Gimli as a T33 instructor. In 1969, he was assigned to instruct T33 pilot instructors at the jet FIS, Portage la Prairie and moved with the FIS back to Gimli when jet flying ceased at Portage. In 1971, he was posted to 412 (T) Squadron, Cosmos, Ottawa for three years followed by a posting to Colorado Springs flying Smoky 02.

Year of 1977 saw Powick as the OIC of the Halifax Rescue Centre and in 1981 he was posted to 436 Squadron, C-130s, Trenton and thereafter became a C-130 pilot instructor at 426 Squadron.

The spring of 1988, saw Captain Powick request his release after 27 years in the Forces. He is currently employed as a pilot with Canadian Airlines International. Kip, Diane, and their three children reside in Trenton.

J.W. RATCLIFFE, CD, LIEUTENANT-COLONEL, was born in Cambridge, England in 1933. He attended Cambridge High School and on graduation in 1949, enrolled in Cambridge University where he attained a diploma in Organic and Inorganic Chemistry in 1951. In May 1951, John enlisted in the Royal Air Force as a Cadet Pilot. He was presented his pilot wings at Claresholm, Alberta in May 1953 as a member of the NATO training plan. John then trained as a jet fighter pilot on Vampire and Meteor aircraft. At the time of his transfer to the RCAF in September 1955, he commanded B Flight, 64 (F) Squadron RAF.

After a variety of single and multi-engined flying tours from 1955 to 1963 including instructional duties, acceptance and ferry flights and instrument check pilot (ICP) school, John served as Command ICP (CICP) at Air Material Command Headquarters in Ottawa from November 1963 to April 1968. He was promoted to Major in 1968 and posted to 412 (T) Squadron. As a measure of his versatility, he served as squadron Chief Pilot for both CC 109 Cosmopolitan and CC 117 Falcon aircraft. Before being posted to Staff College in 1971, John was proud to have flown the Queen Mother, Queen Elizabeth and Prince Phillip, the Governor General, Prime Ministers Trudeau and Diefenbaker and many other senior civil and military VIPs.

On completion of Staff College, John became CICP Cosmo and Falcon at ATCHQ Trenton. This service was interrupted by six months of duty with the ICCS Vietnam, January to August 1973. From September 1975 to January 1978, John served as DCO 437 (T) Squadron flying the CC 137 Boeing aircraft. He was promoted to Lieutenant-Colonel and returned to ATGHQ as SSO Standards and Evaluation after which he returned to 437 (T) Squadron as Commanding Officer. In December 1981, John joined the NATO AWACS serving in Tinker Air Force Base (December 1981 to June 1982) and Geilenkierchen, FRG (July 1982 to August 1986). During this time, he accepted the challenge of building a multinational squadron from its inception to combat-ready status. In August 1986, after a most successful squadron tour, John became EA to the Commander, NATO AWACS in Belgium where he served until his retirement in 1989. He amassed more than 17,000 flying hours in 36 types of aircraft during his military career.

John married the former Kaye Clark of Kipling, Saskatchewan in 1961. They had no children. After a short illness, he passed away in January 1990 while on rehabilitation leave.

PETER W. REBEK, born in Wolfsberg, Austria, moved to Canada a year later in 1950 where he grew up in Sault Ste. Marie, Ontario. He joined the Canadian Forces in 1968 under the ROTP program at the University of Western Ontario - King's College. After graduation in 1971, he commenced and successfully completed flying training at Portage la Praire, then Moose Jaw and Cold Lake.

His first assignment was the appointment as Assistant Base Personnel Services Officer in Moose Jaw. Shortly thereafter came his posting to 429 Squadron in Winnipeg, where he served until 1975, gaining a great deal of experience. He then spent a three-year challenging and rewarding tour with 412 Squadron at Uplands. A pleasurable but short posting followed at NDHQ with a superb boss, Lt. Col. Glen Parslow and a great cohort, Harry Smith, better known as "Old Weird Harold." In 1979 he left the forces to fly for Norontair - Air Dale Ltd. in his hometown of Sault Ste. Marie. Ten years later the opportunity and circumstances allowed Peter to join Boeing Canada - de Havilland Division as a production, test and training pilot, his current position.

The move to Toronto was very beneficial, providing interesting world travel working with various airlines as well as allowing progress to management. Nevertheless, the military background and experiences have kept him in good stead, and this shall never be forgotten nor the friendships created.

KENNETH ROBB, F/LT, born in London, England in 1921 and has resided in Montreal, Quebec since 1923. He joined the Royal Canadian Air Force in 1940, did his basic training in Canada and completed his operational training on Spitfires at No. 57 O.T.U. Hawarden, England.

He joined 412 (Fighter) Squadron at Wellingore in October 1941 and completed his first tour of operations in October 1943. During this period he was stationed at many of the well known Fighter Command bases such as Biggen Hill, West Malling, Redhill, Tangmere, Kenley, etc., and was engaged in a variety of operational activities including fighter sweeps; bomber escort; reconnaissance patrols; anti-shipping and train-busting including three sorties with the Squadron at Dieppe.

As a rest from operations he attended the Central Gunnery School at Sutton Bridge, England and taught air gunnery at No. 55 O.T.U. on Hurricanes.

In July 1944, he joined 411 Squadron at 126 Airfield at Caen, France for his second tour of operations when, amongst other duties, he participated in dive bombing ground targets with the Spitfire Mark 1X-E.

F/Lt Robb, presently a practicing architect in Montreal, married Elizabeth in 1942 in Wales. They have three children and three grandchildren all residing in Canada.

WILLIAM O. ROBERTS (BILL), born in Winnipeg, November 1915. Enrolled in RCAF April 1940. Basic training at Toronto Manning Depot. Took 11th entry airframe course at St. Thomas, Ontario. First posting to Trenton, Ontario September 1940. Re-posted to Picton, Ontario to Conversion Training Unit for Americans volunteering in RCAF in November 1940. Served in France as of 11 December 1944 at Benny-Sur-Mer and across France through Belgium into Holland.

Repatriated in 1945. Worked in printing plant after discharge but unable to settle down in civilian life yet. Re-enlisted in RCAF, November 1946.

Married Evelyn Howorth October 1946. Parents of two children, David and Ruth.

Postings to Rivers and Winnipeg bases. Served one year, 1950-1951, active service with detachment to 426 (T) Squadron at McCord AFB, Washington during Korean conflict. Completed five years enlistment in September 1951.

Left Air Force and joined a defence contract in Winnipeg operated by Air Canada, then known as TCA. Became part of Air Canada's Winnipeg staff in April 1955 when the Viscount turbo prop service began. Retired from Air Canada December 1, 1980. Relocated to Burnaby British Columbia in January 1981.

S.L. ROMARD, MWO, enrolled in the RCAF January 17, 1957. Employed in 412 Squadron December 1958 to May 1964. Tech crewman 412 Squadron October 1960 to May 1963, 21 years old.

Shortest flight in a Dakota: Charlottetown - Summerside, 29 December 1960, Dak 1000, Captain F/L Goddard, Total time .20 min. Longest Flight in a Dakota: Ottawa - Winnipeg, 10, November 1961, Dak 661, Captain F/L Auld, Total time 07.50 hrs. Most flying hours in one month: March 1963 total 88:15 hours.

Important Flights: St. Hubert - Sydney N.S., 8 July 1961, Captain F/L Fassold, transported Dr. J.D. McCurdy's body to Sydney N.S. for his funeral; Ottawa - Kingston, Ontario, 21 June 1962, Captain F/L Goddard, Queen's mother, Elizabeth, Royal tour.

Presently employed as a Lead Life Cycle

Material Manager (LLCMM) at NDHQ Ottawa since June 1986.

Career Manager for AE Tech Ptes-CPLs December 1981 to June 1986 NDHG Ottawa. Senior Aircraft Technician July 1977 to December 1981 CFB Ottawa (S) Bameo. Aero Engine Technician May 1969 to July 1977 Greenwood, N.S. Aero Engine Technician May 1967 to May 1969, CFB Lahr Germany. Aero Engine Technician May 1964 to May 1967, 1 Wing Marville France. Aero Engine Technician and Tech crewman December 1958 to May 1964, 412 VIP Squadron Uplands Ontario. Aero Engine Technician November 1957 to December 1958, NAMAO Edmonton Alberta.

Basic Aero Engine Course, April 1957 to November 1957. Recruiting course, January 1957 to April 1957.

Worked on the following aircraft: Harvards, Otters, C-45 Beechcrafts, CT133 T-Birds, Dakotas, North Stars, Mitchells, USA C-47 and C-54, Comets, C-5 VIP A/C, Bristols, Argus, Cosmos and Falcons.

ROBERT J. ROSE, CAPTAIN C.D., born 1929 in Windsor, Ontario, enlisted in the RCAF in 1951 and trained as a Radio Officer at RCAF Station Clinton Ontario. Following training at 4 (T) OTU, he joined 426 Transport Squadron at Lachine Quebec. The squadron at that time was involved in the Korean Airlift. He received the Canadian Forces Decoration and the Korea Medal.

In 1955, he transferred to 412 Squadron Ottawa where he flew in Dakota, North Star, C-5 and Comet aircraft. From 1958 to 1962, he served as Executive Assistant to the Chief of Telecommunications at Air Force HQ Ottawa. In 1962, he returned to flying duties with Canadian Station Flight, CJS (London) based at RAF Station Northolt England. In 1965, he served on the Administrative staff of the newly integrated Canadian Defence Liaison Staff London. He returned to Canada in July 1966 to 435 Transport Squadron Edmonton, flying C130 Hercules aircraft. Posted to Air Transport Command HQ in 1969 as Command Protocol Officer and also served two years as Executive Assistant to the Commander ATC.

Capt. Rose retired from the Regular Force in 1975 and joined the Public Service as Civilian Personnel Officer at CFB Kingston. In 1976, he returned to Trenton to the Regional Civilian Personnel Office until retirement in 1988. He and his wife Ann currently live in Belleville Ontario.

JAMES S. SHIPTON, FLIGHT LIEUTENANT, was born in Kingston in 1929, graduated from Verdun High School in 1948, whereupon, he enlisted in the RCAF in October of that year. Graduated as a Radio Officer in 1949, he was posted to 426 (T) Squadron and flew on the Korean Airlift from 1950-51. In 1952 F/L Shipton married the former Joan Louise Osborne.

Upon receiving his Navigator wings, he returned to 426 (T) Squadron in 1952 and participated in further flights until 1954.

Upon completion of a tour in the Operations Branch Air Transport Command Headquarters from 1954-58, he was posted to 412 (T) Squadron. From 1958-62 he flew in Squadron Comets, North Stars, and the C-5 as crew navigator.

After completing the Electronic Warfare Officer Course at Mather AFB, Sacramento California, F/L Shipton was posted to the Air Navigation School at Winnipeg. After a short tour as an instructor, he was posted to the Central Navigation School Navigation Standards Section.

In 1968 F/L Shipton was posted to 111 KU/ 440 (Transport and Rescue) Squadron at Winnipeg, where he participated in many searches above 60 Degrees North. A second posting to 412 Squadron occurred in 1970 during which time F/L Shipton was crew navigator on Arctic, TransAtlantic, and Caribbean and South American flights in the Cosmopolitan a/c.

From 1975-85, he served in staff positions at NDHQ from where he retired.

F/L Shipton and his wife have two daughters, three granddaughters, and one grandson.

KARL H. SJOLIN, F/SGT, born at Falun, Alberta in 1925. He attended public school there followed by one year of high school in Wetaskiwin and two years at Olds Agricultural College.

He worked on his father's farm for one year before moving to Wetaskiwin to obtain his automotive mechanics license.

In 1946 he joined the RCAF as an Aero Engine Technician. His basic training was taken at Portage La Prairie. From basic it was on to Camp Borden to take his technical training, graduating in the fall of 1947, when he was posted to 435 Squadron in Edmonton.

Early 1948, he moved on to 412 Squadron at Rockcliffe. In 1953, he was married to the former Bev Hargroves of Ottawa. From 1950 to 1954, he was employed as flight Engineer on the C-5 aircraft which was used only for VIP transport. The highlights of this duty was the 1953 trade mission tour of South America with the late C.D. Howe and the 1954 world tour with the late Prime Minister Louis St Lourent.

In the fall of 1957, he moved on to Fort Churchill in Manitoba. Spring of 1959 saw him posted to the transport OTU at Trenton where he remained until early 1963. At this time he was sent to 426 Squadron at St Hubert.

After only nine months there, the squadron was disbanded so it was back to 412 Squadron at Uplands. The fall of 1965 saw him move again to the TSU at Downsview where he was employed as a Quality Assurance Inspector in the petroleum products field.

In 1970, he retired from the RCAF and found his way back to Weteskiwin, where he and his wife now reside. F/Sgt Sjolin and his wife have four children and six grandchildren spread from Vancouver to Halifax.

EDWARD W. SMITH, LT. COL., D.S.O., C.D., born in Metis Beach, Quebec on 11 November 1920. On 20 July 1940, he joined the RCAF in Sherbrooke, Quebec, where he had just received his diploma as an accountant from O'Sullivan Business College.

After pilot training he went overseas as a Sergeant Pilot in February 1941. He completed two tours of operations in Bomber Command. During his first tour with 102 RAF Squadron he ditched once, and was shotdown over his own base shortly after. He received his commission in 1942 while instructing at OTU in Kinless, Scotland.

On completion of his second tour with 424 (RCAF) Squadron, he was awarded the Distinguished Service Order. Having completed the Empire Central Flying School Course in September 1944, he returned to RCAF station Trenton where a course was completed at the Instrument Flying School. This was followed by a tour at the Test and Development Establishment in Rockcliffe, Ontario. During Operation "Muskox", he flew gliders in the Arctic with USAAF members of the 5th Air Force.

Shortly thereafter, he was transferred to the USAAF Air Transport Command in Washington, as an Exchange Officer. During the two years he flew out of Westover and Fairfield AFBs, this program also included fifty trips on the Berlin Air Lift and Atomic tests in the Pacific. During this period the USAAF became the USAF and ATC became MATS. President Truman defeated Mr. Dewey during his stay in Washington.

On returning to Canada in 1949, he joined

412 (T) Squadron at Rockcliffe, Ontario. There he had the honour of flying many VIPs and was captain of the first RCAF Round the World flight, with the Hon. Lester B. Pearson then Minister of External Affairs and later Prime Minister.

He was taken off flying and served as a Staff Officer Air Transport Operations at Air Force Headquarters under the great Frank Pearce. On promotion to Squadron Leader, he spent the next three years in Vancouver, BC, as Officer Commanding, 442 Auxiliary Support Units. This was followed in 1954 with a transfer to the All Weather OTU at North Bay, Ontario and promotion to Wing Commander to Command 428 All Weather Fighter Squadron.

In 1958, he was transferred to RCAF Stn. Cold Lake as Commander of the All Weather Operational Training Unit. A year at Staff College in 1961 was followed by three years as Commanding Officer of RCAF Stn. in Quebec, a radar station under Bangor Sector.

In July 1964, he was transferred to Allied Air Forces Central Europe in Fontainbleau France as Staff Officer Ground Environment. On returning to Canada in 1964, he was appointed Deputy Director Bilingualism at Air Force Headquarters until retirement in 1970.

Thirty years service - 10,000 hours flying - 75 types of aircraft.

Married Jane McDonough of Glasgow, Scotland and is the father of Rosemary, a McGill graduate, and two sons, Ronald and Kevin, both graduates of the Royal Military College.

Second career was with the Department of Energy Mines and Resources as Director of Security. Third career is with Statistics Canada as a Senior Labor Force Survey Interviewer. While employed by Energy Mines and Resources, he obtained his B.A. in Political Science at Carleton University during evening and summer courses.

RODERICK I.A. SMITH, (ROD), born in Regina, Sask., 11 March 1922. He joined the RCAF 30 September 1940. He flew Spitfires (Marks I, II, V, and IX) and made about 380 operational flights during World War II, totalling 470 operational hours.

He was a pilot officer and a flight lieutenant while serving in 412 Squadron; he became a squadron leader (and CO of 401 (F) Squadron) at the end of September, 1944; in the postwar Auxiliary. He became a wing commander (and CO of 411 (F) (Aux) Squadron) retiring in 1953. He was awarded the DFC & Bar, and was discharged from the RCAF, 31 May 1945. He is single and a retired lawyer.

He joined 412 Squadron as a pilot at Digby, Lincolnshire on 30 June 1941, the day it formed. On July 8th the CO put Smith's name in the flight book for the squadron's first flight but when he got out to the aircraft, a Spitfire I, it was about five minutes from being ready, so the honour of being first to get airborne went to Lloyd (Pipsqueak) Powell, who later became a noted train buster and was killed in action.

On 8 November 1941 he was with the squadron on its most disastrous operation, a patrol near Dunkirk, in which they lost Kit Bushell (our acting CO), Owen Pickell and Ken Denkman, a quarter of the airborne squadron. With them on that patrol was 19-year-old John Magee, author of the famous poem "High Flight." They were attacked by some radial engine fighters they had never seen or heard of before, and which they found out much later were the formidable Focke-Wulf 190s. It was John's first operational flight but he fired at an Me 109 nevertheless, albeit without result.

On 11 December 1941, south of Digby, Smith found the burning wreckage of a Spitfire which turned out to be John Magee's. He had collided with an Oxford training aircraft and did not survive. They did not know until after he died that he had written poetry.

In late September, 1944, he had the honor to lead 412 for three days over the Arnhem and Nijmegen bridges during which it shot down 26 enemy aircraft, more than a third of the number shot down by the whole of 83 Group of the Second Tactical Air Force.

J. ALLAN SNOWIE, LIEUTENANT, CD, RCN, born in Scotland, Allan joined Canada's Senior Service in 1965 and spent five happy years before unification and the demise of the aircraft carrier Bonaventure dispersed naval aviators throughout the Armed Forces.

Thus he came to report aboard as Senior Naval Officer within Escadrille 412 and was promptly told to shave off his RCN issue beard. As it was the time of the October Crisis, and not wishing to be shot as a suspected terrorist by gun wielding airmen sentries, he complied.

So Allan learned that 412 was a great squadron to get away from. Cosmo crew deployments out of Ottawa's NDHQ sight and mentality were excellent - great fellows, great flying, great fun - European Ops, Northern flights and VIP Tours. For trivia interest, his logbook records that the unit's first integrated flight was 1 December 1970 when Buzz Currie (Air) completed a training session on Trev White (Land) and Co-pilot Snowie (Sea). Best memory was the Squadron Honour Guard that presided at his wedding - try teaching sword drill to RCAF types an hour before going to the altar! Bride Lorna-Lee is now a lawyer practicing in Guelph, where they live and Allan flies for Air Canada and writes, his latest book being "The Bonnie."

RAY SOWERBY, S/L, 1939-45 WAR MEDAL, C.V.S.M., C.D., born Merritt, B.C., 9 September 1925; son of Alfred and Hannah (Telfer) Sowerby; married Marion Ann (Macdonald) 29 June 1957; children: Sheila, Jane, John. Sowerby was educated at Merritt high School, Jr. Matric, 1943; University of B.C., B.A. 1949; University of Ottawa, post-grad 1960; Carleton University, post-grad 1965; University of Colorado, post-grad 1968; Queens University, post-grad 1971.

RCAF 1943 to 1945 and 1952 to 1972. Maritime command, Training Command, A.F.H.Q., Air Transport Command, NORAD, R.M.C. Retired to Kelowna, B.C. in 1972. Owner/Manager of Century 21 Black Mountain Realty 1973 to 1988. Retired in 1988.

GORDON U. SPRINGER, FLIGHT LIEUTENANT, born in Weyburn, Sasketchewan in 1920, completed secondary education in Weyburn, then at the beginning of WW II enlisted in the RCAF as an airframe mechanic.

In 1943 he married Elta Wickey. They have five children - Raymond, Gary, Cheryl, Joanne and Sandra.

During 28 years of service, he performed a variety of aircraft maintenance assignments. From 1949 to 1953 he was transferred to the RCAF Recruiting Unit in Winnipeg, Manitoba

In 1957, while with 426 (North Star) Squadron in Lachine Quebec, was commissioned from the rank of flight Sergeant in Technical (Aeronautical Engineering), served three years as engineering officer with 408 (Lancaster) Squadron at Station Rockcliffe, Ottawa then one year as engineering officer with 115 Air Transport Unit, United Nations Force in Egypt.

On return to Canada in 1961, transferred to 412 (T) Squadron to occupy positions of Aircraft Engineering control and Records Officer, Aircraft Repair Officer then Senior Aircraft Engineering Officer.

In 1968, F/L Springer retired from 412 Squadron to accept employment in "personnel" with Public Works, Canada and later Canada Post.

He retired from the Federal government in 1982 and now resides in Brockville, Ontario and Ellenton, Florida.

ROY STURGESS, MAJOR GENERAL, born in 1929, in Toronto. He joined 412 Squadron in 1951 following wings graduation. In 5 1/2 years he accumulated 4,500 hours, and was captain-qualified on Expeditor, Dakota, North Star, and C5 aircraft. Appointed squadron check pilot in 1953 and chief check pilot in 1955.

During his time with 412, he flew to all continents and carried such distinguished passengers as the prime minister of Canada, Prince Phillip and many foreign heads of state.

After leaving 412 Squadron, he served as both a Squadron and a Base Commander and was the last secretary of the Air Council prior to integration. Appointments which followed included Director of Maritime Aviation, DG Organization and Manpower, Commander Maritime Air Group, COS Operations and Deputy Commander of Air Command.

His last assignment was Commander, CDLS and Defense Attache to the USA. Retiring in 1984, he was appointed senior VP of Operations and executive VP of Canadian Pacific Airlines.

When the airline was sold in 1987, he entered management consulting as a principal in a Vancouver firm. He was appointed associate fellow of CASI in 1978, and Commander of the Order of Military Merit in 1980.

He is a graduate of RCAF Staff College, National Defense College, and the USN postgraduate school.

R.B. SUTHERLAND (BRUCE), LIEUTENANT-COLONEL, born in Calgary, Alberta on 31 August 1944. He was raised near DeWinton in the Alberta foothills and attended school in Okotoks.

Lieutenant-Colonel Sutherland joined the Royal Canadian Navy in May 1964 as an Ordinary Seaman and served as a Sonarman on board HMCS *Qu'appelle*. He was commissioned as a Sub-Lieutenant under the Naval Venture Officers' Training Plan on October 20, 1967.

His first tour of duty was with VS 880 Squadron in Shearwater, Nova Scotia, where he flew the CS2F "Tracker" both ashore and onboard the aircraft carrier, HMCS *Bonaventure*. His next posting was to 412 Transport Squadron in Ottawa. Over the next seven years, he accumulated 3500 hours on the Cosmopolitan aircraft; four years were spent flying VIPs in Ottawa and three as a pilot instructor with 426 Training and Transport Squadron in Trenton, Ontario.

In 1978 he attended the Canadian Forces Command and Staff College in Toronto and stayed for a subsequent two years as a member of the College Air Planning Staff. Lieutenant-Colonel Sutherland left Toronto for a year long French course and joined 415 Maritime Patrol Squadron at Greenwood in 1981. He was promoted to the rank of Lieutenant-Colonel from the position of Deputy Commanding Officer 415 Squadron on July 25, 1986, and assumed Command of 407 Maritime Patrol Squadron in Comox, BC, the following day.

Lieutenant-Colonel Sutherland joined the Canadian Forces Maritime Warfare Centre as Deputy Commanding Officer on July 30, 1988.

Lieutenant-Colonel Sutherland and his wife, Jill, live in Dartmouth, NS, with their two children, Alexis and Geordy. His daughter, Paige, resides in Penticton, BC.

GARTH THOMSON, L/COL, born in Toronto in 1930. He grew up in Alexandria, Cornwall and Napanee, Ontario before entering the Royal Military College in 1949. While at RMC, he trained as a navigator at Summerside. He completed his education at the University of Toronto.

His tour with 412 (T) Squadron was from 1955-58 as a navigator on the North Star, the Dakota - including a memorable Trans-At ferry flight in a Dak - and latter, on a Comet crew. He spent 13 years with Air Transport Command: in addition to 412 Squadron, he served with 426 (T) Squadron; 435 (T) Squadron; on United Nations service in the Middle East with 115 ATU; and as a navigation instructor with 4 (T) OTU.

In 1963 he was appointed Commanding Officer of RCAF Station Flin Flon. In 1965 he attended the RCAF Staff College and later returned to Armour Heights on the Directing Staff. He also served as a plans staff officer at National Defence Headquarters, Air Transport Command and SHAPE, where he retired in 1980.

L. Col. Thomson is married to the former Patricia Telfer of Rossland BC where they now reside. They have a daughter Peigi, and two sons, Rob and Murray.

J.M. TRUDEAU (JOHN), MAJOR, born in 1931 in Alfred, Ontario, joined the RCAF in 1954 after working three years for Canadian Aviation Electronics. After graduating at No. 1 Flying Training School, Centralia, Ontario in 1955, he completed Advanced Flying at Gimli and CF-100 OTU in the Spring of 1956.

Following a short tour with 428 (Ghost) Squadron in Ottawa during which he married Rollande, he was posted to Centralia as a flying instructor and then as a Course Director until 1963. He then was appointed PA/AOC at 1 AIR DIVISION, Metz, France until the Fall of 1966 when he was transferred to 412 Squadron. This was his best flying tour, being the most interesting and gratifying for the next five years. Between 1971 and 1974 he held the position of Squadron Commander, 7 Wolfe Squadron (bilingual) at RMC, Kingston, where he was promoted to the rank of Major. He spent his last three years before CRA at NDHQ, Ottawa, in the Directorate of Recruiting and Selection.

In 1977, he joined the other Air Force, TRANSPORT CANADA, where most ex-RCAF pilots continue their flying career. As an Air Carrier Inspector he took the DC-9 course in 1978, the DC-8 in 1981, and the B767 in 1983, all with AIR CANADA. In addition he has flown the Queen Air, Twin Otter, and C182 with Transport Canada. Rollande and John have two children, (one presently in the CAF), and one grandchild. He is planning retirement at age 60.

R. TURCOTTE, SGT., born in Drummond-Ville Quebec on 19 September 1951. Joined Canadian Armed Forces on 28 June 1972 in Trois Rivieres Quebec. In that first year went to Boot Camp and English course at St-Jean, Quebec and Camp Borden, Ontario; followed by the traffic school in Borden and his first transfer to CFB Trenton in September 1973 at 2 Air Movement Unit. After learning on how to plan, process and load passengers, freight, and vehicles aboard an aircraft, he was transferred to 437 (Transport) Squadron in Trenton as a Loadmaster on CC137 Boeing 707 from 28 June 1977 to 21 February 1983.

After a conversion course to CC109 Cosmopolitan in 1983, he was transferred to 412 (Transport) Squadron in Ottawa as a Loadmaster. In four years of flying at 412 Squadron, he was NCO i/c training cell, except for six months spent at CFS Alert N.W.T. He really enjoyed flying at 412 (T) Squadron where he accumulated 1800 hours on CC 109 for a grand total of 4800 hours of flying on both aircraft. He said goodbye to 412 (T) Squadron on July 6, 1987 for two service Battalion Canadian Forces Base Petawawa Ontario where he was still serving as of April 1990.

As a family man, Sgt. Turcotte and Mrs. Turcotte have two children, Sandy,14 and Eric, 11.

W.A. VERMUE (BILL) CAPT., born in the Netherlands, in 1948 and with his entire family, immigrated to Canada in 1953. The family settled in southern Ontario and call London their home.

Captain Vermue was selected by the RCAF for pilot training in 1967; however, enrollment did not take place until after integration the following year.

After pilot training in Camp Borden, Gimli and Portage la Prairie he graduated with the last pilot course to obtain their wings on the Expeditor (Beech 18). From 1970 to 1973 he stayed in Portage as an instructor on the Chipmunk and Musketeer.

This was followed by two tours in Trenton,

with 424 Squadron and as Staff Officer Airlift Planning in ATG/ATOC, respectively. In 1979, he was transferred to Lahr, West Germany, as one of the original four pilots on the Dash 7. In 1983, he was assigned to the continuous French course in Trenton and St. Jean, followed by one year as Staff Officer Language Training with Training Systems HQ in Trenton. He was transferred in 1985 to Canadian Forces Recruiting Detachment in Hull, P.Q., serving as its CO for his final two years.

In 1988, he was transferred to 412 Squadron again, this time to the mother squadron in Ottawa to fly the Cosmopolitan. Shortly thereafter, he terminated his military career to take up a position with Flight Safety Canada, Ltd., as their Program Manager for the Dash 7 and Twin Otter aircraft.

Captain Vermue is married to the former Betty Jean Grobb of Portage la Prairie, Manitoba. They have two children, Marl and Reg, and currently reside in Guelph, Ontario.

JOHN H. WALDIE, SQUADRON LEADER, born in Sherbrooke, Quebec in 1928. He graduated from Sir George Williams University in 1950. While at the university he learned to fly at Curtiss-Reid Flying Service at Cartierville airport. He left a flying instructing job at Curtiss-Reid in the fall of 1950 to join the Royal Canadian Air Force. He earned his wings at Centralia and after Pilot Gunnery School at MacDonald, Manitoba, he was transferred to 412 (T) Squadron at Rockcliffe. In the summer of 1954 he moved down the hanger line to the Central Experimental and Proving Establishment and was sent to the Empire Test Pilots School at Farnborough, England in 1955.

He returned to CEPE in January 1956 and married Diana E. Winter of Enfield, Middlesex, England. His first project was the Air Force handling and performance testing of the F86 "Sabre" MKVI. Later he did the initial RCAF testing of the Canadain Argus.

After six years of test flying, he was transferred from CEPE (now at Uplands) to ATCHQ, Trenton as Command Flight Safety Officer. He attended the RCAF Staff College in 1964/65 and was transferred back to 412 (T) Squadron now at Uplands, for a second tour, this time as Pilot Leader. He resigned from the RCAF in August 1966 to pursue a career in commercial aviation.

His first airline job was with World Airways of Oakland, California, based in Tokyo, Japan flying B 727s supporting US military operations in Vietnam. Since 1974 he has moved extensively. He has flown for Air Mali, Japan Airlines, Uganda Airlines, and Iran Air.

He returned to Canada in the fall of 1978 to join Ontario World Air. In 1981 he started flying for Worldways Canada and at time of writing is a senior Lockheed L1011 Captain.

PAUL RHODES WILLIAM WEBB, SQUADRON LEADER, (RCAF RETIRED), was born in Trinidad, British West Indies, in 1926. He was educated in England at King Edward's School, Whitley, and London University. Prior to coming to Canada in 1948 he served as an engineer officer in the British Army on bomb disposal and mine clearance duties.

Joining the Royal Canadian Air Force in 1948 he trained as a radio-navigator, serving on 412 (T) Squadron, Rockcliffe, from 1949 to 1950 and from 1951 to 1954. He attended the Aerospace Systems Course at Central Navigation School, Winnipeg, from 1954 to 1955, followed by a year on CNS staff. From 1956 to 1963 he served at RCAF HQ, Ottawa, as a project engineer on design and development of air navigation systems. He returned to Winnipeg in 1963 as Station Telecommunications Officer and in 1965 he was posted to 53 Radar Squadron, Holberg, as Chief Ground Environment Officer. Transferred to Fourth Allied Tactical Air Force HQ, Ramstein, Germany in 1967, he served as Communications Planning Officer until retirement from the Canadian Forces in 1972.

From 1972 to 1987 he was a project engineer and management consultant with the Department of Industry, Trade & Commerce, and the Canadian Customs Service. Married with three children, he resides in Ottawa.

F.W. WHEELER, (BILL) WARRANT OFFICER, was born in Collingwood, Ontario in 1936 and was educated in Hamilton, Ontario. He joined the RCAF in 1953 and trained as an AE Tech at Camp Borden. Upon completion of his training, he was stationed at Centralia where, in 1955, he married the former Patricia Bowden. In 1957 he was transferred to Borden as an AE Tech and crewman. In 1959 he remustered to AMU and upon completion of training at Trenton was transferred to 3 AMU as Loadmaster with 412 Squadron from 1959 until 1962.

He was transferred in 1962 to 3 Wing Zweibrucken, Germany, as the AMU Rep., and in 1965 was transferred to AMU Sardinia, Italy, in charge of the AMU detachment.

In 1967 he transferred to 2 AMU Trenton where he was on the 2 AMU MAMs team and then NCO I/C warehousing.

He was transferred in 1971 to 426 (T) Training Squadron where he became WO I/C of the Advance Air Movements and Loadmaster Training school until retirement in 1974.

Bill is presently the Air Operations Manager for Echo Bay Mines Ltd. in Edmonton, Alberta, and resides in Devon, Alberta.

Pat and Bill have four children and six grandchildren.

R.H. WHELAN (BUD), MAJOR, born in Ottawa in 1928. He attended Ottawa Technical High School and was one of the first three air cadets trained as a glider pilot in 1945, attaining his private pilot's license in 1946. He graduated as an RCAF pilot in May 1951 on the occasion of the first NATO pilots graduation. Major Whelan married the former Ruth Mary Rock in October 1951.

He served as a Staff Pilot at Summerside, P.E.I., and from 1952-1956 was a Flying Instructor, Standards Officer and Instrument Check Pilot at Centralia. From 1956-1959 he was the Transport Check Pilot at a 2 (F) Wing, Gros Tenquin, France. In October 1959 he began his first tour at 412 (Transport) Squadron where he flew Dakotas, North Stars and D.H. Comets. A short tour as a Line Pilot at 107 Rescue Unit, Torbay, Nfld., was followed as the Commanding Officer, RCAF Recruiting Unit, St. Johns.

Following that tour, he was posted back to 412 (Transport) Squadron in time to help introduce the fan-jet Falcon to VIP service, where he served as a Line Pilot, Training Officer and Check Pilot, and was promoted to Squadron Leader. This was followed with a posting to Air Transport Command Headquarters in Trenton as Staff Officer Pilot Training Standards.

In 1972, Major Whelan returned to St. Johns, Newfoundland as the Commanding officer, Canadian Forces Recruiting and Selcection Centre. He retired from the Canadian Armed Forces in October 1975. In March 1979, Major Whelan became a Flight Operations Instructor on Boeing 727 with Air Canada, and continues serving in this capacity.

Major Whelan and his wife have three daughters and four grandchildren.

TREVOR L. WHITE, LT. COL., born 1933 in Estevan, Saskatchewan, He joined the RCAF in September 1952 after completing high school in Nelson, B.C. He graduated from pilot training in Penhold, Alberta in November 1953. After completing advanced training and gunnery school on the T33 Silver Star, he was posted to 1 (F) OTU Chatham, N.B., where he trained on the F86 Sabre. He married the former Marjorie Hamilton in 1954 and was posted to 444 (F) Squadron in Baden, Germany, where he served until expiration of his short service commission in November 1958.

White re-enrolled in the Royal Canadian Army Service Corps in 1962. After Corps training he was employed as an instructor in Army Aviation at Rivers, Manitoba from 1963-67, at which time he was posted to 412 (T) Squadron to fly the Cessna 182 (L19L) aircraft. In February 1968 he became the first "Brown Job" to be trained on the CC109 Cosmopolitan, which he flew from Ottawa until January 1971. He served in Yellowknife from 1971-73 then joined the Cosmo Detachment in Colorado Springs, where he flew Smoky 02 for four years. He served as detachment commander from 1974-77, having been promoted to major in 1974

Following a tour as Commandant of the Junior Leaders School at Penhold and Base Operations Officer at North Bay, White returned to 412 Squadron and Commander of the Lahr (Dash 7) Detachment, where he served until September 1984.

White retired from the Regular Force in May 1986. However, he left to become the Deputy Air Operations Officer at the Regional Cadet Office in Trenton, Ontario. He was promoted to his present rank in July 1987 and assumed the duties of air operations officer, responsible for Air Cadet Camp, as well as gliding programs for Ontario.

As a family man, Lieutenant Colonel and Mrs. White have two children and four grandchildren.

CHARLES C. WILLIS, S/L, on 9 July 1937 joined the RCAF after graduating from Nepean High School in Ottawa. He went to No. 2 T.T.S. at Camp Borden with 204 other airmen from all parts of Canada. They drilled for two months before commencing their Technical Training School Courses as Airframe and Aero-engine mechanics. The esprit de corps they established was terrific and the class of 1937 has had periodic reunions ever since. In September, 1987, they celebrated the Fiftieth Anniversary at Winnipeg - 75 classmates plus wives or girlfriends attended.

Upon graduation in June 1938, he was posted to No. 6 TB Squadron at RCAF Station, Trenton, While there he was selected along other airmen to train as Household Guards at Rideau Hall in Ottawa for the May, 1939, visit of King George and Queen Elizabeth.

From there he was posted to RCAF Station

Camp Borden in January, 1940, as a Corporal and then to No. 2, B & G School, Mossbank, Sask. in October, 1940, and promoted to Sergeant. Fairey Battles were used for Bombing and Gunnery and he was in Maintenance.

In April 1941, he was posted to No. 5 B & G, Dafoe, Sask. and promoted to Flight Sergeant. Then in May he was posted to No. 7 B & G School, Paulson, Manitoba, to help open the station. In September/October 1941, he took a Senior N.C.O.'s course at Trenton and was recommended for a commission in engineering or administration. He turned it down as he wanted to go overseas as aircrew. Remustered to aircrew in 1942 and graduated as a Bomb Aimer with his commission in April 1943. Posted to No. 6 B & G School in Mountain View, Ontario as Bombing Instructor. Posted overseas in February 1944.

Crewed up with four other RCAF aircrew and two RAF and after OTU and Conversion Unit, went to 153 Squadron RAF at Scrampton in 1 Group. In March, 1945, he was posted to RAF Station Wellesbourne, Mountford as a Bombing Instructor. By this time, he was a Flight Lieutenant. Came back to Canada in August, 1945.

He remained in the RCAF after the war on a short service commission and worked as a Staff Officer in the Construction Engineering Branch at Trenton disposing of surplus heavy equipment at stations that were closed down.

In 1947, 30 Bomb Aimers and Air Gunners were sent to the Institute of Aviation Medicine in Toronto to check out on the Link Trainer G. machine, etc. and then 15 were sent to radio school at Clinton. The other 15 including Willis were posted to the RCAF Station, Centralia for the first post-war pilots course flying Harvards. A most interesting course with great instructors. They all graduated in June, 1948, and A/M W. Curtis, the Chief of Air Staff gave them their Wings. He was posted to 408 Squadron, Rockcliffe, and then to 412 (T) Squadron on February 15, 1949.

This was an interesting and rewarding tour of duty with 412. To fly prime ministers, cabinet ministers, ambassadors, generals was quite an honour.

He received his permanent commission while on 412 and was posted to Air Operations Transport in AFHQ on 12 September 1951. He was promoted to Squadron Leader while at AFHQ and was transferred to Allied Land Forces Central Europe, Fontainbleu, France, in July, 1953. He was the Air Transport Advisor at ALFCE and the only Air Force Officer working with 139 Army officers of different nationalities. He was promoted to Acting Wing Commander - a terrific assignment and in conjunction with the RCAF aircrew from Allied Air Forces Central Europe they had their C45 to get their flying time in.

Posted back to Canada in July of 1956 to train on jets for Air Defence Command Refresher Course on Harvards at Centralia for one month and then three months at Portage la Prairie on T33s and one month at I.F. S. Saskatoon on T33 instrument flying. Then to RCAF Station Cold Lake for CF100 O.T.U. He crewed up with F/O Ed Rea and after completing they were posted to 425 (Alouette) A.W.F. Squadron at RCAF Station St. Hubert.

He was training officer for two years with W/C Warren M. Middleton as O.C. It was a pleasure to fly the CF100 and work with the 26 2-man crews they had on the Squadron. When W/C Middleton was appointed Chief Operations

Officer at St. Hubert in 1959, Willis succeeded him as O.C. 425 Squadron was awarded the Steinhardt Trophy in 1960 for the most outstanding AWF Squadron in Air Defence Command.

In July of 1960, he was posted to Bangor NORAD Sector at Topsham Air Force Station Brunswick, Maine and worked in the Exercise Branch as a liaison to FAA, SAC, ADC and USAF. He flew USAF T33s for awhile but then got checked out on a USAF Cessna 310. A lovely aircraft to fly and he flew out of Brunswick Naval Air Station.

STANLEY J. WOODMAN, LIEUTENANT COLONEL, born in Edmonton, Alberta in 1922. He attended Westmount High School and worked for two years in the Imperial Bank before enlisting in the RCAF in 1941. After completing aircrew training in Edmonton, Lethbridge and Rivers, Manitoba, he served for a year instructing embryo aircrew from New Zealand, Norway and the United Kingdom in the fine art of air navigation. Then followed operational training and the best part of a tour with RAF Coastal Command operating out of the Azores until the war in Europe ended.

Postwar saw a brief stint as adjutant at Northwest Air Command and completion of the first radio navigator radar and communications course at Clinton, Ontario. Then, in April 1947, he was transferred to 412 (K) Squadron for the first time. He stayed only briefly, however, as, a few months later, he returned to Clinton to instruct and there to command the Air Training Section at that unit

During this period he married the former Bernice MacRae of Vancouver and Edmonton. In 1950 he rejoined 412 and this time managed to serve for nearly a year before being promoted and moved across town to a four-year stint with the ground and air training staffs at AFHQ. He then completed the course at the RCAF Staff College and upon graduation, filled the newly established position of Staff Officer Electronic Warfare at ADCHQ, St. Hubert. Six years later he left this position to join the faculty of the Staff College.

Early in 1965 he and his wife began intensive training in the Russian language to prepare them for two years in the Soviet Union where Stan served as Canadian Air Attache. Here the couple took full advantage of all opportunities to travel, visiting most of the Soviet Republic and fitting in several trips to the UK, Finland, Europe and Iran.

Returning to Canada, Stan spent five-and-a-half years in the Chief of Programs division at CFHQ, retiring as Director of Program Analysis and Control in 1973.

Then followed nearly 14 years with the Provincial Department responsible for tourism and parks in Prince Edward Island, culminating in a second retirement. Stan now keeps fully occupied as an occasional tourism consultant and with a variety of volunteer work.

Stan and Bernice Woodman have one son who is an architect in Ottawa, and three grandchildren, one now married to a recent RMC graduate, the other two attending university in Charlottetown and Peterborough.

RUSS WREGGITT, WARRANT OFFICER,

born in Winnipeg in 1932. Joined RCAF in 1949. Following ETECH (A) training, he was transferred to 442 Squadron Vancouver in 1950. In 1953, Russ went to Uplands to help form 422 (F) Squadron, continuing to #4 Wing in 1954.

After a few months in Langar, England, he returned to Winnipeg and following promotion to Sergeant in 1959 was transferred to 412 (T) Squadron. While there Russ helped maintain various aircraft, ensuring timely, serviceable, VIP departures. Many hours were spent in long range fault diagnosis and despatching the right tools, parts, and technicians to effect repairs in many exotic areas of the world.

Major duties included fending off agitated senior officers from technicians who were frantically repairing unexpected faults while on the VIP ramp. While Russ doesn't like to brag, his crew did repairs at a gallop!. He was transferred to #4 FTTU Trenton in 1964 for instructional and technical writing duties. While there, Russ enrolled in Queen's V and helped to successfully restore Comet 5301 from scrap to flight status. The Comet was then exported to the USA where it was registered as a DH125.

Seconded to External Affairs in 1969, he saw service in Tanzania, E. Africa where he helped close that aid programme. Following an integrated year with VV-33 at Pat Bay BC in 1970, Russ took early release in 1971 and returned to Queens to graduate with a BA.

Hired by Employment and Immigration in 1972, he served in Terrace and Victoria before taking the Managers position in the Courtenay-Comox office from 1976-1987, when he took early retirement.

Currently living contentedly in a waterfront home near Courtenay with Margaret, his wife of 35 years, Russ maintains an active interest in golf, skiing, and community affairs. One daughter, Karen, is banking in Victoria while Linda is a Flight Nurse in Yellowknife N.W.T.

GEORGE HARRY WYNNYK, CAPTAIN,

born on 22 April 1928 in Holden, Alberta. He completed high school at St. Joseph's College, Yorkton, Sask. in June 1947 and 12 July 1948 joined the RCAF in the Radar trade. After going through Boot Camp at RCAF Station, Trenton, he graduated from the Radar & Communication School, RCAF Clinton, Ontario, in December 1948. He served in the Radio/Radar division at RCAF Stations - Centralia, Rockcliffe, Goose Bay (as radio jockey at CFGB Goose Bay) and Trenton. In September 1952 he re-mustered to aircrew and was selected for pilot training. Due to a slight problem in depth perception while at No. 1 FTS Centralia, he was mustered into the Air Navigation Trade and graduated from Air Navigation School, Winnipeg on 27 November 1953.

Captain Wynnyk flew with 436 and 426 Squadrons at Dorval (RCAF Lachine) on C119 and North Star Aircraft. After a year's tour of duty with 115 Com. Flt. U.N.E.F. El Arish, Egypt, he joined 412 (T) Squadron on 15 September 1958. In the two years with 412 Squadron, he flew as Air/Nav to qualifly on the support flight for the Queen's tour in 1959 and on the six week National Defence College Tour to the Middle and Far East and also as the Navigator on the USAF C54.

On 1 October 1960 he was transferred to Air Transport Command Headquarters SOPC Branch. Four years later he was transferred to 435 (T) Squadron, CFB Edmonton (Namao). While on a Transport Air Support Aircrew Course for the C119 Aircraft, he was the first RCAF Air/Nav to qualify in the Air Support Role of Para Troop dropping from the C130 Aircraft. In March, 1969 he was assigned to the Tactical Airlift School at Namao as Chief Navigation Instructor.

Captain George Wynnyk retired from the Canadian Armed Forces on 1 May 1972, having flown as Air/Nav in eight types of Transport Aircraft and logging a total of 9,074 nav. hours and 30 hours in pilot training.

M.M ZRYMIAK, COLONEL, OMM CD,

born in Glenavon, Saskatchewan. He enrolled in the RCAF Pilot Training Program in August 1954 and received his wings in October 1955. He served his first tour in Moose Jaw, Saskatchewan, as a Harvard instructor.

In 1959 he was posted to 412 Squadron, Ottawa, then in 1963, to Northern Region Headquarters in North Bay, Ontario. In 1965 he moved to Portage La Prairie as the Chief Flying Instructor at No. 3 Flying Training School, having been promoted to the rank of Squadron Leader.  In 1968 he attended Staff College in Toronto and, on completion, was transferred to National Defence Headquarters. In 1972 he was posted to Lahr, Germany as the Commanding Officer of No. 5 Air Movements Unit and as the Lahr Airfield Commander. In 1973 he was promoted to the rank of Lieutenant Colonel and transferred to Canadian Forces Base Ottawa as the Base Operations Officer.

In January 1974, he was appointed Commanding Officer of 412 Squadron. He was the pilot for the Queen Mother during her visit in 1975 and also for Her Majesty Queen Elizabeth, and other members of the Royal Family, during her official attendance at the Montreal Olympics. As well, he was the base organizer of the 1975 Ottawa International Air Show.

He was posted to National Defence Headquarters in 1978 as the Executive Assistant to the Deputy Chief of the Defence Staff. Also promoted to the rank of Colonel in 1978 and posted to the National Defence College. In 1980 he began a tour in Prague, Czechoslovakia, as the Canadian Forces Attache. On completion of this most interesting tour he was posted to Air Command in Winnipeg as the Deputy Chief of Staff Reserves and as the Commander of Air Reserve Group.

In April 1985, he was appointed Base Commander, Canadian Forces Base Edmonton. He served in Edmonton until his decision, in September 1986, to leave the regular force and transfer to the primary reserve list.

Colonel Zrymiak then located to Langley, BC and entered into private business. His interests include real estate, and nursery and aviation consulting. In October 1989 he took up a new position as the Langley Airport Manager. He and his wife Terry have four children.

Colonel Zrymiak was awarded the Order of Military Merit in 1982.

Bill Roberts and four other men are photographed before slated to go overseas. (Courtesy of Bill Roberts.)

The last flight with 412 Squadron for Gen. F. R. Sharp was marked by the presentation of a plaque by 412 CO Lt. Col. Glen Parslow. Looking on are acting Base Commander Lt. Col. G. A. Thomas-Peter and the aircraft commander Capt. W. McMurray.

RCAF CC-106 Yukon

Princess Margaret's Canadian Tour 1968. Left foreground: W/C Carr, Princess Margaret shaking hands with Sgt. Jerry Mignon. Photo also includes Sgt. Bob Cameron and Flt. Sgt. Al Cooper.

CC-109 Cosmopolitan and CC-117 Falcon in formation over the Ottawa Valley.

Departure of 412 Squadron Cessna Fleet July 1969. (Courtesy of 412 (T) Squadron.

www.ingramcontent.com/pod-product-compliance
Lightning Source LLC
Chambersburg PA
CBHW081827170426
43202CB00019B/2975